BLACK MALES
LEFT BEHIND

Also of interest from the Urban Institute Press:

Low-Wage Workers in the New Economy, edited by Richard Kazis and Marc S. Miller

Health Policy and the Uninsured, edited by Catherine G. McLaughlin

BLACK MALES LEFT BEHIND

Edited by Ronald B. Mincy

THE URBAN INSTITUTE PRESS
WASHINGTON, DC

THE URBAN INSTITUTE PRESS
2100 M Street, N.W.
Washington, D.C. 20037

Library of Congress Cataloging-in-Publication Data

Black males left behind / edited by Ronald B. Mincy.
    p. cm.
  Includes bibliographical references and index.
  ISBN 0-87766-727-6 (alk. paper)
  1. African Americans—Employment. 2. Men—Employment—United States. 3. Blue collar workers—United States. I. Mincy, Ronald B.
  HD8081.A65B53 2006
  331.3'40810973—dc22

                                                                    2005035457

Printed in the United States of America

10 09 08 07 06   1 2 3 4 5

THE URBAN INSTITUTE is a nonprofit, nonpartisan policy research and educational organization established in Washington, D.C., in 1968. Its staff investigates the social, economic, and governance problems confronting the nation and evaluates the public and private means to alleviate them. The Institute disseminates its research findings through publications, its web site, the media, seminars, and forums.

Through work that ranges from broad conceptual studies to administrative and technical assistance, Institute researchers contribute to the stock of knowledge available to guide decisionmaking in the public interest.

Conclusions or opinions expressed in Institute publications are those of the authors and do not necessarily reflect the views of officers or trustees of the Institute, advisory groups, or any organizations that provide financial support to the Institute.

To the memory of Paul Offner,
our dear friend and colleague,
and his "true dedication to the public
and to making public programs work."
(Mark Schmitt, *The Decembrist*, April 23, 2004)

Contents

Preface

This volume is the result of the Extending Opportunities Project (EOP), which was hosted at the National Partnership for Community Leadership in May 2001 and March 2002. The purpose of the project was to examine how young, less-educated men fared in the economic boom of the 1990s. We thank the Charles Stewart Mott Foundation and the U.S. Department of Labor for financial support for the Extended Opportunities Project, including the conferences, dissemination of the conference proceedings, and production of the volume. Several researchers and policy experts offered valuable comments on the drafts of papers included in this volume and gave valuable feedback at the Extended Opportunities Project. We thank Robert Lerman, Gary Burtless, Keith Islanfedt, Luis Falcon, Mark Elliott, Irwin Garfinkel, Stephanie Robinson, and Hugh Heclo. The authors remain responsible for any errors.

Beginning with Harry Holzer and Paul Offner, several authors in this volume examine how poorly young, less-educated black men performed relative to other less-educated young people during the economic expansion of the 1990s, and why. They explore the roles of the macroeconomy, the deconcentration of blue-collar employment, criminal justice policy, and the employment aspirations of young, less-educated black men, and consider their implications for the design of employment services, welfare-to-work policies, workforce development policy, and child support enforcement policy. Two subsequent chapters comprehensively review policy opportunities to assist less-educated young black fathers and discuss how to overcome political resistance to initiatives serving less-educated black men.

In chapter 2, "Trends in the Employment Outcomes of Young Black Men, 1979–2000," Holzer and Offner paint a troubling picture of the decline in employment and labor market participation rates among less-educated young black men in the 1980s and 1990s despite the robust economic conditions that defined both periods. Using data from the Current Population Survey's Outgoing Rotation Groups, Holzer and Offner compare the labor market outcomes of less-educated young black men with other groups of young men and women between 16 and 24 years old who are not enrolled in school or enlisted in the military. They consider three outcomes: employment–population ratios, labor force participation rates, and real wages. For each outcome, young white and Hispanic men improve slightly, compared with women, but black men decline. Holzer and Offner also statistically test various hypotheses that could explain the deterioration in labor market outcomes for less-educated young black men.

In chapter 3, "Forecasting the Labor Market Prospects of Less-Educated Americans," William M. Rodgers III contemplates how "looser" labor markets will affect less-educated young workers and the implications for social policy. Before addressing these issues, Rodgers puts recent labor market conditions into historical perspective. Although unemployment has risen since 1990, by historical standards the national unemployment rate remains low, as is the unemployment rate of our target population.

Next, Rodgers decomposes the effects of national labor market conditions on the labor market outcomes of specific groups in our target population. He finds that less-educated young black workers are the most sensitive to macroeconomic conditions. He then uses the decomposition methods and the Bush administration 2004 and 2005 forecasts of the national unemployment rate to predict labor market outcomes for less-educated young black men over the next decade. He suggests that employment–population ratios of less-educated young workers will improve over the next decade. However, for most demographic groups, ratios will not return to the values evident at the peak of the 1990s boom. Policymakers must therefore find other ways to reduce barriers to labor market search, entry, and retention, and cushion the effects that skill-based technological change and globalization will have on less-educated workers.

Holzer, Steven Raphael, and Michael A. Stoll explore the effects of ties to the criminal justice system in chapter 4, "How Do Employer Perceptions of Crime and Incarceration Affect the Employment Prospects of Less-Educated Young Black Men?" The authors use data from a unique survey of employers to study if high rates of crime and incarceration have had a chilling effect on the labor market prospects of less-educated young black males—both those who have participated in illegal activity and those who have not. Because black men have higher rates of crime and incarceration than young men of other racial and ethnic groups, the flow of young black men out of prison and back into the community is likely to be large each year, as is the total number of ex-prisoners or ex-felons. The reentry phenomenon, along with at least moderate effects of arrest rates on black men's earnings and employment, suggests negative effects of crime on young black men working or looking for work, and on their observed earnings.

Holzer, Raphael, and Stoll show that employers are much more reluctant to hire ex-offenders than welfare recipients, workers with long-term unemployment, or any other group. However, most employers in the survey do not regularly check the criminal background of their employees. Employers who are unwilling to hire ex-offenders but do not check for criminal backgrounds might be engaging in a form of "statistical discrimination" or racial profiling against black men, based on their aversion to hiring offenders as well as their scant information about which job applicants actually have criminal backgrounds. Thus, the growing presence of ex-offenders among low-income black men will have serious negative consequences for their employment rates.

In chapter 5, "Are Less-Educated Women Crowding Less-Educated Men Out of the Labor Market?," Rebecca M. Blank and Jonah Gelbach explore whether there is a causal relationship between increases in female labor market participation and declines in labor market participation among less-educated men. Expansion in female labor supply spurred during the 1990s could have reduced male labor supply in two ways. First, rising income among mothers, sisters, and girlfriends could have reduced the incentives for men to work. Second, female workers could have more than compensated for the increase in demand for low-skilled workers, perhaps reducing the number of jobs available for men. While the first argument, called an income effect, remains plausible,

Blank and Gelbach gather several kinds of evidence and arguments that cast doubt on the second argument, called a displacement effect.

First, Blank and Gelbach explain that displacement of less-educated men by women would result in falling wages and rising unemployment among less-educated men, neither of which occurred. Second, they argue that occupational segregation by gender makes displacement unlikely. Third, they show that there is a relatively strong and positive correlation between the labor supply of male and female less-educated workers, and that the simple correlations between changes in hours of work among male workers and female labor force participation are negative, but essentially zero. Fourth, they examine labor supply changes among less-educated men and women in metropolitan areas where female labor force participation grew very rapidly and those where it grew very slowly. They also find little evidence of substitution. Finally, Blank and Gelbach find no evidence of adverse effects of Temporary Assistance for Needy Families (TANF) implementation on male labor force participation among less- or more-educated men or of adverse associations between female and male transitions to employment.

In chapter 6, "Did Spatial Mismatch Affect Male Labor Force Participation during the 1990s Expansion?" John A. Foster-Bey Jr. explores how the employment prospects of less-educated young men were affected by the decentralization of jobs that occurred in most metropolitan areas during the 1970s and 1980s. He examines this phenomenon in eight metropolitan areas selected for their geographic and racial diversity and range of metropolitan types. Foster-Bey finds that blue-collar jobs have disproportionately left the central cities and urban core for the suburbs and that wages of blue-collar workers in the urban core declined relative to wages of blue-collar suburban workers in five of the metropolitan areas. Finally, Foster-Bey examines whether urban–suburban differences in male labor force participation trends during the 1990s were related to whether metropolitan areas experienced job deconcentration. He finds that (with one exception) all metropolitan areas where male labor force participation grew slower in the urban core than in the suburbs also experienced high levels of job deconcentration in the blue-collar sector, as expected.

Solutions to the deteriorating labor market outcomes of less-educated young black men (and other less-educated young workers) are most likely to be crafted in education, workforce development, and income security policies. For this reason, the next two chapters of the volume examine how less-educated young black men see the labor market, including their views about good jobs, how they use employment programs to secure those jobs, and what changes in workforce development policy have affected the availability of employment services. The chapters also address changes in public assistance policies, which are likely to affect less-educated young black men because many are (or will be) fathers of children who receive public benefits.

Alford A. Young Jr. looks closely into the world of less-educated young black males in chapter 7, "Low-Income Black Men on Work Opportunity, Work Resources, and Job Training Programs." Relying on qualitative data from a convenience sample of young black men living in Detroit, Young explores how these men interpret the available and desirable work opportunities, including what jobs they believe are available for men like them, how these jobs might be acquired, and how the available jobs compare with the kinds of work they most desire. Then Young explores how these men view employment programs and support agencies.

Young finds no lack of commitment to work among these young black men, who believe that job training and placement programs should provide entry into "good" jobs, such as factory jobs with good pay and benefits that compensate for the undesirable working conditions. They often seek work at temporary employment agencies, which link them to jobs where one worker can easily substitute for another. This makes temporary agencies more tolerant of absences due to family or other emergencies. Moreover, with adequate private funds, temporary agencies can afford to hire staff and buy furnishing that create a pleasant environment.

By contrast, publicly funded employment programs have limited staff and their facilities are furnished with the bare essentials. They are also overcrowded with people who often use these agencies to maintain eligibility for unemployment benefits and who are distressed by their inability to find work. Clients see a different employment counselor each time they visit the program, and therefore counselors do not have the opportunity to become familiar with the employment aspirations and barriers of particular clients. Finally, publicly supported employment programs do not offer the supportive services needed to help clients overcome the legal, educational, transportation, and other barriers that keep them from obtaining good jobs, or the stress associated with being unable to obtain such jobs. To serve young black men effectively, employment services might have to be treated as one component of a more comprehensive array of services, available in programs that serve long-term welfare recipients and other hard-to-serve populations.

Demetra Smith Nightingale and Elaine Sorensen explore the role of changing workforce development policy in chapter 8, "The Availability and Use of Workforce Development Programs among Less-Educated Youth." Funding for workforce development programs for young less-educated workers declined during the 1990s as available funding was heavily targeted to welfare reform efforts. As a result of these changes, Nightingale and Sorensen find less-educated young black men with low earnings were significantly less likely to receive job services than other less-educated young workers with low earnings.

Besides differences in the amount of job services, Nightingale and Sorensen also find that young, less-educated black men were less likely than other groups of less-educated workers to receive job services leading to higher-paying jobs. Less-educated young black men were just as likely to receive job search assistance as less-educated young black women and nearly twice as likely to receive this service as less-educated young nonblack men. The authors also find that young minority men in the Job Training Partnership Act (JTPA) program were more likely to receive basic education and less likely to receive skills training than other groups. Black men were also less likely than other young people to participate in on-the-job training, the most promising job training component in terms of increased employment and earnings.

Nightingale and Sorensen conclude that these participation imbalances need to be corrected and that more young black men should participate in occupation-specific training to simultaneously improve their basic education ability and occupational skills. Finally, the authors show that jobs with features accommodating the preferences of less-educated men should be available if they participate in short-term occupational skills training and slightly modify their views about what constitutes "masculine" work.

Cyclical sensitivity of employment, declining labor force participation, and stagnant real wages of young, less-educated men are undoubtedly contributing to delays in marriage and increases in nonmarital fertility among youth and young adults. Increased risks of child poverty are also likely to result, especially among black children, because the employment rates of less-educated black adults are most sensitive to the business cycle, and black men have the lowest employment and labor force participation rates of all racial and ethnic groups. For these reasons, income security is another policy arena where we might look for policy solutions.

Over the past two decades, Wendell Primus and Ron Haskins have observed and shaped income security policy, as key staff to House and Senate committees of jurisdiction on both sides of the aisle. Their discussions of policy options in chapters 9 and 10 build upon federal and state policymakers' increasing interest in the role of both parents in reducing child poverty.

In chapter 9, "Improving Public Policies to Increase the Income and Employment of Low-Income Nonresident Fathers," Primus culls lessons from welfare reform to propose incentives (operating principally through the child support enforcement system) that might help increase the employment of less-educated young men. First, he describes how onerous child support enforcement has become for low-income noncustodial parents, most of whom are fathers. Child support orders can push low-earning noncustodial parents far below the poverty level, especially if they have unstable employment. Many low-income fathers do not pay child support regularly because they are poor. Many accumulate large arrearages, which deter them from seeking stable employment, encourage them to move into underground economies, or limit their employment to jobs that pay cash. They may also be subject to license suspension and incarceration, which sever ties with their families.

Primus proposes a new vision for child support enforcement that corresponds with the transition of child support from a mechanism for cost recovery to a potential source of income for poor families. He argues for supplementing standard enforcement activities with services for low-income noncustodial parents who cannot pay child support regularly. All child support payments would be passed through to children in custodial families, and the government would supplement the child support payments of low-income noncustodial parents.

In chapter 10, "Poor Fathers and Public Policy: What Is to Be Done?," Ron Haskins argues that low marriage rates and higher child poverty rates are among the most important consequences of the poor labor market outcomes of less-educated men. He suggests that the adverse effects of paternal absence on child development and the dismal performance of less-educated black men require "substantial and long-term solutions." Haskins comments that congressional interest in disadvantaged men is no longer confined to the difficulty with collection of child support payments from them. Instead, consistent with congressional interest in rebuilding the traditional family in America, there is now more legislative support for helping disadvantaged men marry and become responsible fathers.

Haskins lists many policies that could be reformed to ameliorate some of these problems, especially policies intended to increase marriage and fathers' financial and emotional contributions to children. His discussions of each policy area include recent congressional activity and recent evidence about the effects of programs on the relevant outcomes. Haskins recommends demonstration projects to examine if block granting Head Start funding improves states' abilities to coordinate and evaluate preschool programs and increases the educational attainment of low-income minority children. He also recommends gradually increasing funds for the Job Corps, the only federally funded workforce development program that has been proved effective, by rigorous evaluation, for less-educated young men. He also discusses expansion of demonstration projects designed to help ex-offenders find jobs.

Perhaps Haskins' most extensive recommendations arise in relation to welfare and child support. First, he suggests that state and federal income security programs should be reviewed to identify barriers to serving fathers and married couples, especially in welfare-to-work programs. Second, while not mentioning subsidies for child support payments, he echoes Primus' recommendations about passing all child support through to custodial mothers and offering job services to fathers who are unable to meet their child support obligations. Third, he endorses the Bush administration's proposal for healthy marriage demonstration programs, through marriage education and relationship skills as well as programs that attempt to reduce barriers to marriage.

In "Toward a Fruitful Policy Discourse about Less-Educated Young Men," Hillard Pouncy points out the current obstacles to initiatives that would assist less-educated young black men. Opposition comes from advocates for low-income women, who believe that limited discretionary spending should be reserved to move former welfare recipients out of working poverty. Opposition also comes from some conservatives who use the results of previous employment programs to argue that less-educated young black men face so many barriers that further investments in their education and training would be unwise.

However, Pouncy suggests that some of this resistance could be overcome by pointing out that young black men are not the only ones threatened by inadequate job preparation. While incarceration rates have reached epidemic levels among blacks, they have grown among all less-educated young men, despite declines in actual crimes rates. Moreover, the declining labor force participation and employment rates of young less-educated black men may be partly attributable to antiquated, though not antisocial, attitudes and information about available job opportunities. Thus, Pouncy suggests new demonstration research that would alter the employment preferences of less-educated young black men, provide information about mechanical and technical jobs in the sectors identified by Sorenson and Nightingale, provide relatively short-term occupational training, and, building on recent sectoral employment initiatives, place these men in higher-earning jobs than they currently occupy.

1

Left Behind

Less-Educated Young Black Men in the Economic Boom of the 1990s

Ronald B. Mincy, Charles E. Lewis Jr., and Wen-Jui Han

For more than 15 years, social scientists and policy advocates have been warning Americans that half of our youth and young adults are having great difficulty transitioning into adulthood (Edelman and Ladner 1991; William T. Grant Foundation 1988). These young people are distinguished by the absence of postsecondary schooling. Dropouts, 16 to 18 years old and older, have the most difficulty. However, many 18- to 24-year-olds who graduated from high school but are not enrolled in any form of postsecondary schooling (the "non-enrolled") remain out of work or have jobs paying too little to sustain themselves and their families. Joblessness and low earnings among these less-educated youth and young adults are contributing to reductions in marriage and increases in nonmarital childbearing (Lichter, LeClere, and McLaughlin 1991; Oppenheimer 1988; South and Lloyd 1992; Xie et al. 2003). Since poverty rates are higher among unmarried mothers and family income is positively associated with postsecondary schooling, these children are unlikely to escape the fate of their young parents (McLanahan and Casper 1995).

In response, policy analysts and advocates for youth and young adults have been calling for a wide range of special initiatives targeting all 16- to 24-year-old less-educated youth—*the forgotten half,* or, for those who are both out of school and out of work, *disconnected youth* (Besharov 2000). The School-to-Work Opportunities Act of 1994 and the Youth

1

Opportunity grant program were modestly funded and short-lived responses. However, the sustained economic growth of the 1990s was sufficient to increase employment and earnings among most of this population (Sum et al. 2002). Because many less-educated women also benefited from welfare reform efforts, the employment and earnings gains for women were much stronger than the corresponding gains for men. In fact, unmarried young black mothers, one subgroup singled out for special attention by youth advocates, recorded the strongest employment and earnings gains, resulting in declines in poverty and welfare receipt among black children (Blank and Schmidt 2001; Haskins 2001).

Despite some erosion since the 2001 recession, the urgent need for special youth-targeted programs has been undermined by reports of the gains during the 1990s, including a widely cited study suggesting that the economic recovery would absorb less-educated young black men— historically, the hardest-to reach-population—into the labor market (Freeman and Rodgers 2000). After all, business cycles affect the fortunes of most Americans, so many observers assume that economic recovery will once again lift the fortunes of young, less-educated men.

But such optimism is unwarranted. Less-educated young black men were left behind in the economic boom of the 1990s. During the 1990s, the employment rate of 16- to 24-year-old, less-educated black men actually fell from its peak during the 1980s economic expansion. What's more, their labor force participation rate continued the decline that occurred throughout the 1980s. These findings question the wisdom of a broad strategy for all less-educated youth and young adults, and suggest that targeted approaches are needed to recover a subpopulation for which sustained economic growth is apparently not enough.

Given the recent attacks on affirmative action, new policies targeting young black men exclusively are unlikely. Their needs will be weighed against those of similarly situated people. Therefore, most chapters in this volume compare the labor market outcomes for less-educated young black men with those of other young, less-educated men (and women). To provide some background for these analyses, this chapter uses decennial census data to describe the demographic characteristics of less-educated, non-enrolled young men and connect these men to employers, families, and children, the poor, and geographical areas (regions and metropolitan/nonmetropolitan areas).[1] The chapter views these connections between 1979 and 2001, a period that includes the two longest economic expansions in our nation's history.

Black and Other Less-Educated Young Men

The racial and ethnic distribution of our target population exhibits the results of dramatic demographic changes over the past few decades. In 2001, more than half of less-educated non-enrolled young men (57.6 percent) were white, 15.7 percent were black, and 23.5 percent were Hispanic.[2] The proportion of whites in this group has declined over time from 78 percent in 1979. In fact, the number of less-educated white men declined by nearly 50 percent, from 6.16 million in 1979 to 3.3 million in 2001.

At the same time, the number of less-educated Hispanic men in the labor force more than doubled, from 593,000 in 1979 to 1.34 million in 2001. As a proportion of less-educated non-enrolled young men, Hispanics grew from 7.5 percent in 1979 to 15.8 percent in 1989 and 23.5 percent in 1999.

While the proportion of less-educated non-enrolled young men that is black has remained fairly stable (13.1 percent in 1979, 15.8 percent in 1989, and 15.0 percent in 1999), the actual number of these men in the labor force declined from 1.03 million in 1979 to 898,000 in 2001. This drop coincided with a rapid growth in the number of young black men who were incarcerated or otherwise involved in the criminal justice system.

What Do They Mean to the Labor Force?

Men between the ages of 16 and 24 are an important subgroup of the U.S. population, despite making up only 14.8 percent of the total male labor force. Men at these ages make critical decisions about work, schooling, vocational training, fertility, and family formation that will have implications for themselves and others. In 2001, the most recent year for which complete data are available, our target population—non-enrolled men with a high school education or less—represented 49.5 percent of all male workers 16 to 24 years old. This group of just less than 6 million young men made up about 7.5 percent of the male American labor force in 2001.

Wages for less-educated non-enrolled young men have fluctuated over the past three decades. Their median hourly wage was $7.72 in 2001, a slight increase from $7.22 in 1989, which represented a substantial decline from $8.73 in 1979.[3] Those who completed high school saw their median hourly wage fall from $10.96 in 1979 to $8.77 in 2001. The median hourly wage for men who did not complete high school was $6.75 in 2001, down from $7.29 in 1979.

Wages for the less educated were substantially lower than wages for their more-educated counterparts. More than two-thirds of young less-educated male workers (68.5 percent) had median hourly wages below the median hourly wages of workers age 16 to 24. Slightly fewer of those who completed high school fell below this level (62.6 percent). The bulk of less-educated non-enrolled young men who did not complete high school (80.5 percent) had median hourly earnings below the midpoint mark for workers age 16 to 24.

However, little education meant joblessness for substantial number of young men. More than a quarter (27.7 percent) of less-educated non-enrolled young men reported no earnings in 2001. Though substantial, this proportion was an improvement over 1979, when 32.5 percent reported no earnings. Of those who completed high school, 22.3 percent reported no earnings in 2001, down from 29.0 percent in 1979. The share of less-educated non-enrolled young men with no high school diploma or earnings was 38.8 percent in 2001 and 37.7 percent in 1979.

The substantial racial and ethnic differences in labor market outcomes among young men are well known. Less-educated non-enrolled young black men experience the poorest outcomes, with 82.9 percent earning no more than the median hourly wage for all male workers between 16 and 24 years old. Nearly half (46.2 percent) of less-educated non-enrolled young black men reported no earnings in 2001. Hispanics fared better, with 73.3 percent earning wages below the midpoint for all workers. Among less-educated white male workers, 62.6 percent had hourly earnings at the median or below.

Among less-educated non-enrolled young men, 76.1 percent of whites had completed high school in 2001, compared with 62.2 percent of blacks and less than 50 percent of Hispanics. For less-educated non-enrolled young white men, high school completion rates improved steadily from 64.5 percent in 1979 to 70.0 percent in 1989 and 75.1 percent in 1999. Completion rates for less-educated non-enrolled young black men jumped from 48.5 percent in 1979 to 63.3 percent in 1989, a 30.5 percent increase. The rate improved slightly in 1999 to 64.1 percent, but fell slightly in 2001 to 62.2 percent.

Less-educated non-enrolled young Hispanic men lagged behind whites and blacks in high school completion rates over time. Just 39.6 percent finished high school in 1979. Hispanic completion rates declined to 35.3 percent in 1989, but increased to 48.9 percent in 1999 before falling slightly to 48.3 in 2001. Given their strong commitment to employment, these workers are destined to remain at the lower end of the wage distribution unless additional investment in education and training occurs.

What Do They Mean to Families and Children?

Parents of less-educated non-enrolled young men may be concerned for their sons, who are coming of age without the necessary credentials for high earnings in a modern economy. However, these men raise other concerns for families as well. Marriage rates among less-educated non-enrolled young men have declined significantly since 1979, when more than a quarter (25.9 percent) were married. By 2001, the proportion of these young men that was married fell to just 13.3 percent.

This decline is a manifestation of the retreat from marriage, which has been especially important among the less educated. The decline in marriage does not indicate a decline in the number of less-educated non-enrolled young men responsible for children; increases in cohabitation have almost completely offset declines in marriage, and unwed births to cohabiting women account for nearly all the growth in unwed births since 1975 (Bumpass and Lu 2000; Bumpass, Sweet, and Cherlin 1991). Both the decline in marriage and the increase in unwed births have been greater among less-educated women (Elwood and Jencks 2004). Unfortunately, the Current Population Survey (CPS) does not provide separate estimates of unmarried fatherhood. However, Sorenson and Nightingale (chapter 8, this volume) suggest that as many as 25 percent of 18- to 24-year-old, less-educated black males are fathers.

Although racial differences in family structure are also well known, the proportions of less-educated men who are married or living with children has declined substantially among all racial and ethnic groups. The proportion of less-educated non-enrolled young white men who were married fell from 27.4 percent in 1979 to 14.2 percent in 2001, a 48.2 percent drop. Similarly, the proportion of these men who lived with their children fell from 14.2 percent in 1979 to 11.6 percent in 2001. Likewise, the proportion of less-educated non-enrolled young Hispanic men who were married fell from 28.8 percent in 1979 to 16.3 percent in 2001, a 43.4 percent drop. The proportion of these men who lived with their children fell from 22.1 percent in 1979 to 15.1 percent in 2001, a 31.7 percent decrease.

Nevertheless, marriage and living with children is least likely for less-educated black men. Just 38.5 percent of black children under 18 years old live with both parents, compared with 76.9 percent of white children and 65.1 percent of Hispanic children. In 2001, only 7.4 percent of less-educated non-enrolled young black men were married, down from 15.7 percent in 1979, a 52.9 percent drop. However, the decrease in the proportion of less-educated black men who lived with their children was much less, from 12.4 percent in 1979 to 10.1 percent in 2001, an 18.5 percent decline.

A surprising development was that by 2001, the proportion of married less-educated young white men (16.5 percent) and Hispanic men (16.4 percent) who had not completed high school slightly exceeded those who had graduated (14.2 and 16.3 percent, respectively). Less than 2 percent of less-educated young black men without a high school diploma were married in 2001, a staggering 82.5 percent drop from 1979, when 11.4 percent of these men were married.

Almost a quarter of these less-educated non-enrolled young men reported that they were living independently in 2001. This was a substantial increase from the 11.6 percent who lived independently in 1979. A greater proportion of white (24.3 percent) and Hispanic less-educated non-enrolled young men (24.7 percent) lived independently than black less-educated non-enrolled young men (16.3 percent).

What Do They Mean to the Poor?

The correlation between living in a poor family and having no more than a high school diploma has apparently weakened over time. Between 1979 and 1989, the proportion of less-educated non-enrolled young men living in households with incomes below the poverty threshold declined significantly. In 1979, 34.1 percent lived in such households and 43.1 percent lived in poor or near-poor households, (i.e., households with incomes up to 150 percent of the poverty level). By 1989, the proportion living in households below the poverty level fell to 16.0 percent and the proportion living in poor or near-poor households dropped to 27.3 percent. These rates fell again in 2001 to 14.3 and 26.5 percent, respectively.

As expected, less-educated non-enrolled young men without a high school diploma had higher rates of poverty (22.1 percent) and near-poverty (39.7 percent) in 2001 than those who completed their high school education (10.5 and 20.1 percent, respectively). Again, these figures were significantly lower than their poverty (38.4 percent) and near-poverty (49.0 percent) rates in 1979.

The decline in poverty rates was greatest among white less-educated non-enrolled young men, falling from 30.9 percent in 1979 to 10.4 percent in 1989 and 8.6 percent in 2001. The decline in poverty rates for black less-educated non-enrolled young men was less dramatic; these rates fell from 44.5 percent in 1979 to 29.2 percent in 1989 and 26.1 percent in 2001. Less-educated Hispanic young men had their poverty rates cut almost in half from 1979 (48.4 percent) to 1989 (25.0 percent). By 2001, their poverty rate was well below the rate for blacks, at 20.1 percent.

The proportion of white less-educated non-enrolled young men in poor or near-poor families fell from 40.0 percent in 1979 to 19.0 percent in 1989 and 21.2 percent in 2001. Poor and near-poor rates for black less-educated non-enrolled young men fell from 55.8 percent in 1979 to 45.8 percent in 1989 and 37.9 in 2001. Less-educated Hispanic young men experienced similar dramatic declines, from 58.2 percent in 1979 to 42.6 percent in 1989 to 37.4 percent in 2001.

Where Do They Live?

Less-educated non-enrolled young men are voters, parents, consumers, workers, and neighbors. If they are more highly concentrated in some parts of the country than others or in metropolitan areas than in non-metropolitan areas, they can affect voter participation, child poverty rates, the composition of the student population, the mix of goods and services, and the quality of the labor force. For example, teachers in areas with high concentrations of less-educated young men are more likely to work in schools with large numbers of children from homes headed by poor, single mothers. Because welfare reform now requires these mothers to work, many of these children will be "latchkey" children with no one to supervise them or help with their homework when they return from school. Crime rates are also higher among less-educated men, so residents of communities in which these men are concentrated will be at greater risk of victimization and disproportionately affected by the flow of ex-offenders now reentering society. Again, one of the most apparent manifestations of high concentrations of less-educated young men is homelessness, because public housing assistance is usually unavailable to childless adults.

Less-educated non-enrolled young men are unevenly distributed across the country. They are concentrated in the South, which has 40 percent of our target population. Nearly a quarter (24.2 percent) of these young men live in the West, 21 percent reside in the Midwest, and 15.3 percent live in the Northeast. The proportion of less-educated non-enrolled young men in the South increased 7 percent from 1979 to 2001 and the proportion in the West increased 6.4 percent.

The proportion of all racial groups living in the South has increased since 1979. Less-educated non-enrolled young black men remained heavily concentrated in the South, with 61.6 percent residing there in 2001, up from 54.9 percent in 1979. The proportion of less-educated white men living in the South increased from 30 percent in 1979 to 35.6 percent in 2001, and the proportion of Hispanics increased from 30.3 percent in 1979 to 37.6 percent in 2001. Thus, the present concentration of less-educated non-enrolled young men in the South may be a consequence of migration, immigration, and technological or other changes, which increased demand for educated workers in some regions (such as the Northeast) more than in others.

Despite a significant growth in the numbers of Hispanic less-educated non-enrolled young men in the South, the greatest concentration of these men is in the West. In 2001, 41.9 percent of less-educated Hispanic men lived in the West. These proportions have fluctuated over the years, with 44 percent of less-educated Hispanic young men living in the West in 1979, 49 percent in 1989, and 46 percent in 2001. The proportions of Hispanic less-educated, non-enrolled young men living in the Midwest and the Northeast declined slightly.

The overwhelming majority of these less-educated non-enrolled young men are concentrated in urban areas, with more than three-quarters living in designated metropolitan statistical areas (MSAs). Between 1979 and 1989, the proportion of less-educated non-enrolled young men living in MSAs jumped from 39 to 72.5 percent, an 85.9 percent increase. By 2001, more than three-quarters of less-educated non-enrolled young men (75.9 percent) lived in MSAs.

Blacks (82.4 percent) and Hispanics (91 percent) were most heavily concentrated in urban areas, while slightly more than two-thirds of whites (68.3 percent) were living in urban areas. The proportions of all racial and ethnic groups living in MSAs increased substantially between 1979 and 1989. White less-educated non-enrolled young men increased from 35.7 to 67.9 percent, Hispanics jumped from 48.5 to 74.7 percent, and blacks grew from 55.4 to 90 percent. This increased concentration of less-educated men in urban areas has gone virtually unnoticed in the literature, and raises special concerns for how education and workforce policies operate in urban areas.

NOTES

1. Less-educated young women have been the subject of similar decompositions in volumes that study the effects of welfare reform. See, for example, Blank and Schmidt (2001).

2. For brevity we abbreviate our racial and ethnic categories. By black, we mean non-Hispanic black; by white, we mean non-Hispanic white. Hispanics may be of any race.

3. All median hourly wages are measured in 2001 dollars.

REFERENCES

Besharov, Douglas J. 2000. *America's Disconnected Youth: Toward a Preventive Strategy.* Washington, DC: Child Welfare League of America Press and AEI Press.

Blank, Rebecca M., and L. Schmidt. 2001. "Work, Wages, and Welfare." In *The New World of Welfare,* edited by Rebecca M. Blank and Ron Haskins (70–102). Washington, DC: Brookings Institution Press.

Bumpass, Larry, and Hsien-Hen Lu. 2000. "Trends in Cohabitation and Implications for Children's Family Contexts in the United States." *Population Studies* 54(1): 29–41.

Bumpass, Larry, James A. Sweet, and Andrew Cherlin. 1991. "The Role of Cohabitation in Declining Rates of Marriage." *Journal of Marriage and the Family* 53(4): 913–27.

Edelman, Peter B., and Joyce A. Ladner, eds. 1991. *Adolescence and Poverty: Challenges for the 1990s.* Washington, DC: Center for National Policy Press.

Ellwood, David T., and Christopher Jencks. 2004. "The Spread of Single Parent Families in the United States Since 1960." Working Paper No. RWP04-008. Cambridge, MA: John F. Kennedy School of Government, Harvard University.

Freeman, Richard B., and William M. Rodgers III. 2000. "Area Economic Conditions and the Labor Market Outcomes of Young Men in the 1990s Expansion." In *Prosperity for All? The Economic Boom and African Americans,* edited by Robert Cherry and William M. Rodgers III (50–87). New York: Russell Sage Foundation.

Haskins, Ron. 2001. "Effects of Welfare Reform on Family Income and Poverty." In *The New World of Welfare,* edited by Rebecca M. Blank and Ron Haskins (103–36). Washington, DC: Brookings Institution Press.

Lichter, Daniel T., Felicia B. LeClere, and Diane K. McLaughlin. 1991. "Local Marriage Markets and the Marital Behavior of Black and White Women." *American Journal of Sociology* 96(4): 843–67.

McLanahan, Sara, and Lynne Casper. 1995. "Growing Diversity and Inequality in the American Family." In *State of the Union: America in the 1990s. Vol. 2: Social Trends,* edited by Reynolds Farley (1–46). New York: Russell Sage Foundation.

Oppenheimer, Valerie Kincade. 1988. "A Theory of Marriage Timing." *American Journal of Sociology* 94(3): 563–92.

South, Scott J., and Kim M. Lloyd. 1992. "Marriage Markets and Nonmarital Fertility in the United States." *Demography* 29(2): 247–64.

Sum, Andrew, Ishwar Khatiwada, Nathan Pond, and Mykhaylo Trub'skyy. 2002. "Left Behind in the Labor Market: Labor Market Problems of the Nation's Out-of-School, Young Adult Populations." Boston: Northeastern University Center for Labor Market Studies.

The William T. Grant Foundation Commission on Work, Family, and Citizenship. 1988. *The Forgotten Half: Pathways to Success for America's Youth and Young Families.* Washington, DC: The William T. Grant Foundation Commission on Work, Family, and Citizenship.

Xie, Yu, James M. Raymo, Kimberly Goyette, and Arland Thornton. 2003. "Economic Potential and Entry into Marriage and Cohabitation." *Demography* 40(2): 351–67.

2

Trends in the Employment Outcomes of Young Black Men, 1979–2000

Harry J. Holzer and Paul Offner

The employment rates of young and less-educated women, especially single mothers, have increased dramatically in recent years (Blank and Schmidt 2001; Burtless 2000). These increases have been attributed largely to a booming economy, welfare reform, and increases in the Earned Income Tax Credit (EITC) and other supports for low-wage workers in families with children.[1]

In contrast, the trends among young and less-educated men, especially blacks, have been much less clear. In a widely cited paper, Freeman and Rodgers (2000) claim that employment rates of less-educated young black men improved substantially between 1992 and 1999, an increase they attribute largely to the economic boom of those years. However, various tabulations of household survey data from the Bureau of Labor Statistics and other sources suggest somewhat less positive, or even negative, employment trends for young black men in the 1990s (Lerman, Aron, and Riegg 2000). Further, while researchers expect young black men to have benefited relatively little from welfare reform or expansions of supports for custodial parents (such as the EITC), researchers do not know how young black men's employment may have been affected by other social or economic developments, such as the rising enforcement of child support orders or growing incarceration rates.

This chapter presents data on the trends in employment rates of young black men and other groups of young men and women from 1979 to

2000. It uses data from the Current Population Survey's Outgoing Rotation Groups (CPS-ORG) to estimate these trends as well as some of their determinants. It pools the CPS data from these years and analyzes differences between individuals and metropolitan areas as well as trends over time.

Like Freeman and Rodgers, this chapter is focused primarily on less-educated young black men—that is, those age 16 to 24 with a high school education or less. But our work also builds on theirs in several ways. By considering a longer time period than Freeman and Rodgers did, this chapter hopes to disentangle cyclical trends from secular trends in employment rates. The analysis compares outcomes across different racial and gender groups, and across subgroups (by age, education, or area of residence) within the population of young black men. It also considers a wider range of outcomes, including labor force participation and real wages, as well as employment rates. Finally, the analysis hopes to explain some discrepancies between their results and those of others, including ourselves.

The first section of this chapter reviews earlier literature on employment trends among young black men and describes the data used for this chapter in greater detail. The next section presents empirical estimates of trends over time, with regression analysis of their potential determinants. The chapter concludes with a discussion of results and suggestions for further work.

Existing Literature

The declining employment rates among young black men over several decades have been well documented in earlier work, including that of John Cogan (1982) for the period through 1970 and Freeman and Holzer (1986) for the years up to 1980.[2] Bound and Freeman (1992) document declines not only in the relative employment rates of young black men during the 1980s but also in their relative wages. The work of William J. Wilson (1987) and John Kasarda (1995) suggests that the industrial and geographic shifts in employment during the 1970s and 1980s, such as declining shares of employment in manufacturing and in the central cities, seriously impaired the employment prospects of young black men. These effects were documented in a series of papers (Bound and Holzer 1993, 2000; Ihlanfeldt and Sjoquist 1990), along with the additional negative effects of declining wage opportunities and rising opportunities for illegal income (Freeman 1992; Juhn 1992).[3]

Little of this work goes beyond the 1980s in considering employment trends of young black men and their determinants. Thus, it has often been unclear whether these forces and their effects grew more serious during the 1980s and 1990s. While various studies in the 1990s shed more light on the labor market disadvantages associated with weak education and cognitive skills, segregated neighborhoods, or discrimination, most of this work was cross-sectional and shed little light on the trends over time in relative employment or earnings among young minority men.[4]

Other literature has focused on cyclical rather than secular changes in employment for various disadvantaged groups, such as minorities and less-educated workers (Clark and Summers 1981; Hines, Hoynes, and Krueger 2001; Hoynes 2000). Almost invariably, this literature finds that employment and earnings for disadvantaged groups are more heavily affected by the business cycle than employment and earnings for other groups. Freeman (1991) and various studies in Cherry and Rodgers (2000) document the strong effects of the booms in the late 1980s and the mid- to late 1990s on employment rates of young blacks, but those analyses made little effort to disentangle cyclical from secular trends in the employment rates.[5]

In sum, while researchers know a great deal about the various barriers that young black men face in gaining employment and about how their employment rates changed through the 1980s, relatively little research has analyzed secular trends in these rates during the 1990s.

Data and Estimation Issues

Data from the CPS-ORG can be used to analyze employment trends of young black men and other groups since 1979.[6] The samples of young black men and of less-educated men and women from other race and gender groups were limited to those age 16 to 24 with a high school education or less and who were not enrolled in school (or enlisted in the military) at the time of the survey. All estimates of means are sample-weighted.

The chapter considers trends over time in three labor market outcomes: employment–population ratios, labor force participation rates, and real wages. It focuses separately on employment and labor force participation, rather than on unemployment, because of the ambiguity inherent in the labor force definition (Clark and Summers 1982; Flinn and Heckman 1983). Trends in unemployment, however, can easily be inferred by comparing trends in the other two variables.[7] Real wages are defined for the sample of all wage and salary workers, using the Consumer Price Index for Urban Consumers to deflate nominal wages over time.[8]

After considering summary data on these trends over time, the chapter presents estimated regression models for employment and labor force participation. These regressions are based on pooled samples of individuals over time. The regressions are of the following form:

$$Y_{ijkt} = f\left(X_{ijkt}, UNEMP_{kt}, MSA_k, TIME_t; X_{kt}\right) + u_{ijkt}$$

where i, j, k, and t denote the individual, his race/gender group, his/her metropolitan statistical area, and the year, respectively; Y is the outcome being considered (either employment or labor force participation); $UNEMP$ reflects the unemployment rate in an individual's metropolitan area in a particular year; $TIME$ reflects a time trend; MSA reflects a set of metropolitan statistical area (MSA) dummies; and X_{ijkt} reflects characteristics of the individual (such as age or attainment of a high school diploma). All equations are estimated as linear probability models.[9]

Some regressions also include characteristics of metropolitan areas in particular years (X_{kt}), in an attempt to explain any estimated trends over time observed in earlier regressions. These characteristics include the following:

- the enrollment rates of young black men, designed to measure the possible changes over time in the quality of non-enrolled young black men;
- the shares of jobs that are blue collar or in the manufacturing sector, to capture structural changes in the economy that may have disadvantaged less-educated young men; and
- the shares of employment accounted for by all women or black women, or the employment rates of these groups, to capture possible increases in competition for jobs between young black men and various groups of women.[10]

One issue that arises in pooling CPS data across time involves changes to the survey over time. For instance, the set of MSAs specified in the CPS increased dramatically in 1985 from 44 to 212.[11] The analysis thus includes dummy variables for being in an unspecified metro area, as well as in specific MSA, in any given year. Then it tests for the effects of that change in our results. Even more important, the analysis uses a definition of employment that remains consistent over time.[12]

Finally, the chapter presents some estimates separately for the periods 1979 to 1989 and 1989 to 2000, to determine how trends over time and their determinants changed in those two decades.[13]

Empirical Results

Let us begin by reviewing summary data on trends in employment outcomes for young and less-educated workers by race and gender. The figures on the next few pages plot employment rates, labor force participation rates, and real wages between 1979 and 2000 for white, black, and Hispanic men and women. In all cases, the samples are limited to those age 16 to 24 who have a high school education or less and are not enrolled in school.

The plots of employment show cyclical patterns for all groups, with declines during the recessions of the early 1980s and early 1990s and recoveries in the later years of each decade (figures 2.1 and 2.2). In general, the patterns for less-skilled men indicate constant or declining employment over time, while those for women show rising employment. The trends in labor force participation show less cyclical variation than those in employment and even sharper contrasts between the declining trends for men and the rising ones for women (figures 2.3 and 2.4).[14] The patterns of declining participation for less-educated men, especially in response to their declining wages in the 1980s (while those for women increased) have all been noted before (e.g., Juhn 1992; Blau and Kahn 1997).

The exact pattern of employment trends in the 1980s versus the 1990s, and how these trends differ by race among men as well as women, is particularly interesting. Among men, employment and labor force participation among blacks consistently lag behind those of whites and Hispanics (figures 2.1 and 2.3). Even more striking, peak-to-peak comparisons across the two decades indicate that employment and labor force participation of young black men declined considerably during the 1980s and 1990s, and much more than the employment and labor force participation of whites and Hispanics. Indeed, employment for young black men declined fairly continuously between 1989 and 1997, despite the economic recovery after

Figure 2.1. *Employment–Population Rates for Less-Educated Young Men by Race, 1979–2000*

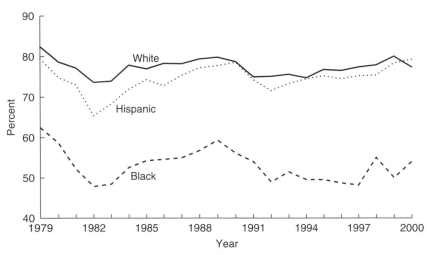

Sources: Current Population Surveys 1979–2000, Outgoing Rotation Groups.

Note: The samples include those age 16 to 24 who are not enrolled in school and have a high school education or less.

Figure 2.2. *Employment–Population Rates for Less-Educated Young Women by Race, 1979–2000*

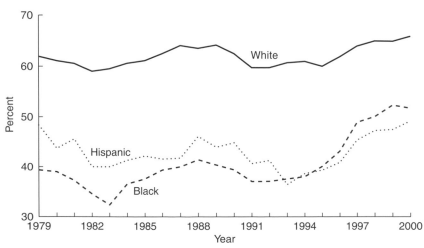

Sources: Current Population Surveys 1979–2000, Outgoing Rotation Groups.

Note: The samples include those age 16 to 24 who are not enrolled in school and have a high school education or less.

Figure 2.3. *Labor Force Participation Rates for Less-Educated Young Men by Race, 1979–2000*

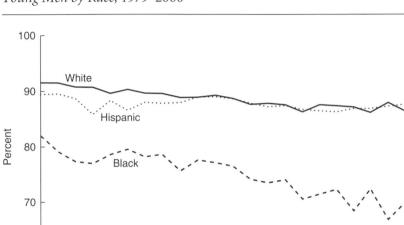
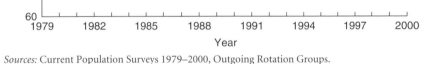

Sources: Current Population Surveys 1979–2000, Outgoing Rotation Groups.

Note: The samples include those age 16 to 24 who are not enrolled in school and have a high school education or less.

1992, while their labor force participation continued its long decline throughout the decade. This contrasts sharply with the experiences of young Hispanic men, who essentially gained parity in employment with young whites over the same period.

The decline in labor force participation for young black men is consistent with the widely noted decrease in their unemployment rates to record lows during the late 1990s, even while their employment rates were also declining relative to the late 1980s. It is also important to remember that the incarceration rates of young black men rose dramatically during the 1990s. The incarcerated do not appear in CPS data; if they did, the trends in the employment of young black men would look even worse than they do now (Western and Pettit 2000).

Striking patterns by decade and by race also appear for young women, and these patterns differ dramatically from those of young men. Among women, the employment rates of young blacks lagged behind those of both whites and Hispanics during the 1980s, but overtook the latter during the 1990s (figure 2.2) as the employment and participation rates of both groups improved dramatically during that decade (figure 2.4).

Figure 2.4. *Labor Force Participation Rates for Less-Educated Young Women by Race, 1979–2000*

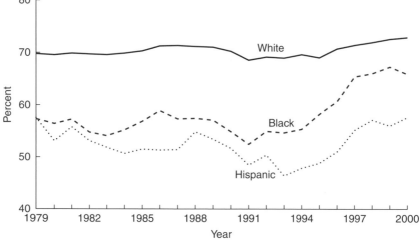

Sources: Current Population Surveys 1979–2000, Outgoing Rotation Groups.

Note: The samples include those age 16 to 24 who are not enrolled in school and have a high school diploma or less.

The strong improvement for young black females in the 1990s no doubt represents increased employment among young single mothers in response to welfare reform efforts and the like. But the continuing decline for young black men is less easily explained. The CPS data for the 1990s show somewhat milder improvements over the business cycle than did the results of Freeman and Rodgers (2000); in particular, their results suggest a 9 percentage-point gain in employment between 1992 and 1999 for young black men where CPS indicates just a 3 percentage-point gain. The divergent results partly reflect differences in the samples used and partly reflect data inconsistencies over time in Freeman and Rodgers' analysis.[15]

The trends in employment for young men of different racial groups can be placed into a wider context by considering similar trends for those 25 to 34 years old with less or more education (those with no more than a high school diploma versus those with some college education).[16] Comparing cyclical peaks to one another over time, these data also show employment declines among less-educated males in this age group (figure 2.5). The declines are milder for whites and Hispanics than for blacks and consider-

Figure 2.5. *Employment–Population Rates for Less-Educated Men
Age 25 to 34 by Race, 1979–2000*

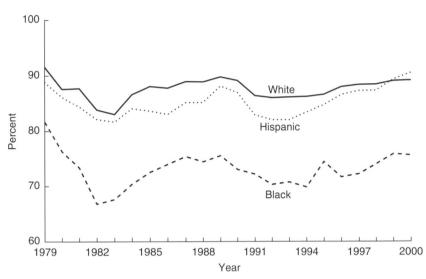

Sources: Current Population Surveys 1979–2000, Outgoing Rotation Groups.

ably milder for this age group than for the youngest cohort.[17] Trends among
more-educated young men of all races were less negative as well (figure 2.6).

Before moving on to consider employment and labor force trends in
greater detail, note the trends in real wages that appear in figures 2.7 and
2.8. The data show generally declining real wages for all less-educated
groups until roughly 1997, when wages begin to recover.[18] These trends
are more negative for less-educated men than for women over much of
the two-decade period, as has been noted elsewhere (Blau and Kahn
1997). The trends changes in the latter half of the 1990s, when real wages
among the less educated began to recover.[19]

These data also reveal little growth in the wage gap between white and
minority less-educated men. This gap has widened more among those
with a college education (Bound and Freeman 1992). It is also possible
that the gap among the less educated would have widened more significantly than it did if the trends in labor force participation and employment among younger black men had not been as negative as they were,
thereby excluding many of the lowest-wage workers from the observable
wage distribution. Either way, the pattern of real-wage increases for these

Figure 2.6. *Employment–Population Rates for More-Educated Men Age 25 to 34 by Race, 1979–2000*

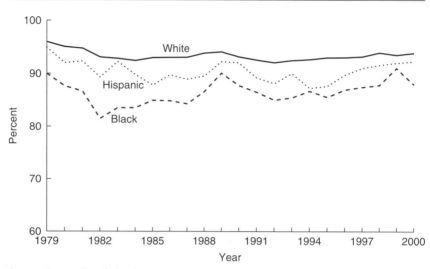

Sources: Current Population Surveys 1979–2000, Outgoing Rotation Groups.

Note: The sample includes those age 25 to 34 who are not enrolled in school and have at least some college education.

young men in the late 1990s will not help explain the relatively larger decline in their work activity compared with the work activity of other ethnic groups over this period.

Were the declines in employment and labor force participation among young and less-educated black men more heavily concentrated among certain subgroups, such as teens or high school dropouts, than others? Table 2.1 presents data on employment for less-educated young black men between three peaks in the business cycle—1979, 1989, and 1999–2000—for subgroups based on age, education, and residence. Similar data are provided for less-educated black men age 25 to 34.

The employment and labor force participation of young black men declined in both periods, but the secular declines in the 1990s were actually sharper than those in the 1980s. Further, the declines occurred among all demographic subgroups within this population—high school graduates and dropouts, teens and those age 20 to 24, and metropolitan and nonmetropolitan residents. The declines, however, were stronger in some subgroups—high school dropouts, teens, and those in nonmetropolitan

text continues on page 24

Figure 2.7. *Real Wages for Less-Educated Young Men by Race, 1979–2000*

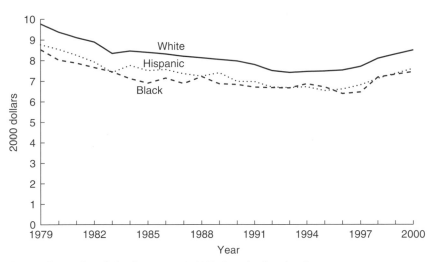

Sources: Current Population Surveys 1979–2000, Outgoing Rotation Groups.

Note: The samples include those age 16 to 24 who are not enrolled in school and have a high school education or less.

Figure 2.8. *Real Wages for Less-Educated Young Women by Race, 1979–2000*

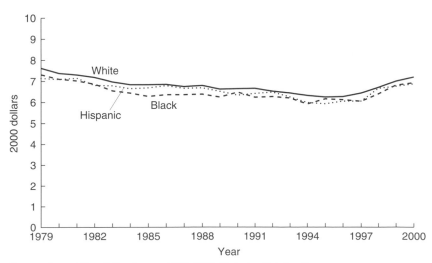

Sources: Current Population Surveys 1979–2000, Outgoing Rotation Groups.

Note: The samples include those age 16 to 24 who are not enrolled in school and have a high school education or less.

Table 2.1. *Employment Outcomes of Less-Educated Young Black Men, 1979–2000*

	Employment–Population Ratio (%)			Labor Force Participation (%)			Real Wages (Yr. 2000 $)		
	1979	1989	1999/2000	1979	1989	1999/2000	1979	1989	1999/2000
Age 16–24									
All 16- to 24-year-olds	62.5	59.3	52.0	82.0	77.1	68.4	8.5	6.9	7.4
Age									
16–19	49.6	47.4	40.0	73.1	64.8	56.3	7.2	5.7	6.5
20–24	70.6	66.0	59.1	87.6	82.3	75.5	9.1	7.3	7.8
Education									
High school dropouts	53.4	45.7	37.0	73.4	66.4	55.7	7.7	6.1	6.5
High school graduates	72.7	68.8	63.8	91.7	84.6	78.3	9.2	7.2	7.8
Area of residence									
Metropolitan areas	59.2	59.2	53.2	80.8	76.8	68.8	8.9	7.0	7.4
Nonmetropolitan areas	71.5	59.8	46.0	85.2	77.9	66.4	7.7	6.4	7.1

Age 25–34

All 25- to 34-year-olds	81.7	75.5	75.8	90.7	86.6	83.8	11.5	9.4	9.9
Age									
25–29	80.7	74.7	72.5	90.4	87.2	82.6	11.2	8.9	9.6
30–34	82.9	76.4	78.8	91.1	85.9	85.0	11.8	10.0	10.2
Education									
High school dropouts	74.0	65.3	59.5	85.3	77.0	70.7	10.2	8.2	8.0
High school graduates	86.7	79.4	79.9	94.2	90.2	87.9	12.2	9.8	10.3
Area of residence									
Metropolitan areas	79.6	74.7	74.9	90.3	86.1	83.5	12.3	9.8	10.1
Nonmetropolitan areas	87.1	79.1	80.5	91.7	88.6	85.5	9.5	7.9	8.8

Sources: Current Population Surveys, 1979–2000, Outgoing Rotation Groups.

Table 2.2. *Characteristics of Young Black Men Over Time (percent)*

	1979	1989	1999/2000
Enrolled in high school or postsecondary education	32.82	38.26	45.39
Teenagers (16–19)	38.72	35.78	36.71
High school graduates	47.00	58.90	56.31
Residing in metropolitan areas	69.21	79.08	83.17

Sources: Current Population Surveys, 1979–2000, Outgoing Rotation Groups.

Note: Enrollment rates are calculated for the sample of all young black men. All other characteristics are calculated for the non-enrolled only.

areas—than in others. Similar but less-pronounced patterns also appeared among those age 25 to 34.

Further evidence appears in table 2.2, which presents data on the trends over time in various demographic characteristics of young black men. These characteristics include the school enrollment rates of all young black men and the proportions who are teens, have high school diplomas, or live in metropolitan areas among those who are non-enrolled. The first category reflects a movement of young men out of the sample of the non-enrolled. This could indirectly change the quality of those left behind if the increases in enrollment occur among the relatively more skilled. The other categories point to changes in the composition of the study sample that should affect employment and participation rates.

Table 2.2 shows increases over time in school enrollment, high school graduation rates, and the tendency to live in metropolitan areas. Age also rose over time, as the proportion of young black men who were teens declined. The overall quality of the non-enrolled sample probably deteriorated as more people enrolled in high school or postsecondary education. The quality of high school dropouts has definitely worsened over time, and perhaps this is also true for high school graduates. But, all else equal, the employment rates of those in the sample should also have improved somewhat based on their greater age and educational attainment.[20] The fact that rates decline despite these changes suggests even more negative secular trends than the summary data imply.

What broader changes in labor markets could be responsible for the continuing employment declines among young black men? While this question will be taken up by other authors in the present volume, at least a few "suspects" come to mind that can be examined using CPS-ORG data. For instance, declining shares of employment in blue-collar occupations or

Table 2.3. *Characteristics of U.S. Employment and Labor Force Over Time (percent)*

Share of employment	1979	1989	1999/2000
Blue-collar sector	34.31	27.17	24.59
Manufacturing	22.72	18.36	14.94
Females	41.76	45.20	46.51
Black females	4.46	5.12	6.03

Sources: Current Population Surveys, 1979–2000, Outgoing Rotation Groups.

manufacturing industries could restrict opportunities for young black men. The ongoing rise in the share of female employment may imply greater competition for young black men in the market (on the demand side), while increases among young black women could also imply a decreased interest in employment among young black men (on the supply side).[21]

Data on the trends in the occupation/industry distributions of jobs and on the shares of employment going to all women or black women appear in table 2.3. The share of jobs accounted for by blue-collar occupations or manufacturing declined consistently in both the 1980s and the 1990s, while the share of employment accounted for by women in general and black women in particular rose. The rise in the share of all female employment decelerated somewhat in the 1990s, whereas employment shares for black women rose more strongly in the 1990s than earlier.

Regression Analysis

Regression equations can be used to analyze trends among young black men in greater detail. As indicated earlier, the estimated regressions for employment and labor force participation use pooled cross sections of individuals in the CPS. Separate equations have been estimated for white, black, and Hispanic males and females. The samples are limited to those age 16 to 24 with a high school education or less who are non-enrolled at the time of the survey. Controls for age, the attainment of a high school diploma, and MSA of residence within this sample are included in the regressions, as are a time trend and the MSA unemployment rate in any year.[22] The last two variables are intended to capture the secular and cyclical trends in employment and participation, respectively, controlling for other characteristics of the sample.

The results for employment appear in the upper half of table 2.4, while those for labor force participation appear in the lower half. Cyclical factors clearly influence the employment rates of young black men, with employment rising by nearly 3 percentage points for every percentage-point

Table 2.4. *Employment and Labor Force Participation Equations, by Race/Ethnicity and Gender*

	MSA unemployment	Time trend	Age	Education	R^2
Employment					
Black men	−2.7921	−0.0077	0.0383	0.0590	.13
	(.1689)	(.0005)	(.0012)	(.0017)	
White men	−2.0392	−0.0038	0.0254	0.0502	.09
	(.0585)	(.0002)	(.0004)	(.0006)	
Hispanic men	−2.2630	−0.0017	0.0479	0.0028	.11
	(.1492)	(.0004)	(.0010)	(.0011)	
Black women	−2.4280	0.0006	0.0183	0.0718	.10
	(.1514)	(.0005)	(.0010)	(.0016)	
White women	−1.4285	0.0010	−0.0050	0.0824	.07
	(.0676)	(.0002)	(.0005)	(.0007)	
Hispanic women	−1.5669	−0.0020	0.0141	0.0512	.08
	(.1707)	(.0005)	(.0012)	(.0013)	
Labor force					
Black men	−0.4994	−0.0071	0.0310	0.0579	.13
	(.1456)	(.0005)	(.0010)	(.0015)	
White men	−0.4128	−0.0030	0.0227	0.0365	.09
	(.0432)	(.0001)	(.0003)	(.0005)	
Hispanic men	−0.2826	−0.0022	0.0355	0.0058	.10
	(.1145)	(.0003)	(.0008)	(.0008)	
Black women	−0.9421	0.0008	0.0098	0.0788	.09
	(.1537)	(.0005)	(.0011)	(.0016)	
White women	−0.5933	0.0014	−0.0115	0.0761	.06
	(.0637)	(.0002)	(.0004)	(.0007)	
Hispanic women	−0.7547	−0.0018	0.0054	0.0543	.08
	(.1720)	(.0005)	(.0012)	(.0013)	

Source: Based on data from the Current Population Survey.

Notes: The equations also include dummies for MSA that are not presented. Samples include high school graduates or less who are not enrolled in school at the time of the survey. Standard errors are in parentheses.

MSA = metropolitan statistical area.

decline in the unemployment rate in the metropolitan area. Somewhat smaller cyclical effects are observed for other men and especially for most less-skilled women.[23] Negative effects of unemployment on the labor force participation rates of these groups are smaller, though still significant.

Most striking in table 2.4 are the strong negative secular trends in both employment and labor force participation for all groups of less-educated young men, especially blacks. The decline in employment and in participation for young black men averages roughly eight-tenths of a percentage point a year over the entire period, or about 17 percentage points over the 21 years considered here. Declines for less-educated young white men are less than half as large, while those for Hispanic men are smaller still. In contrast, the secular trends in employment and labor force participation are positive for young white and black women.

Further, when the full period is split into separate decades, the same estimated equation generates much larger secular declines in the employment of young black men in the 1990s than in the 1980s. In fact, after controlling for the business cycle, the employment rate declines by almost 2 percentage points a year in the 1990s. This explains why the very strong economy of the late 1990s, combined with improvements in educational attainment and growing concentration in metropolitan areas, had such modest effects on the overall employment rate of young blacks.[24]

How do observed changes in school enrollment rates of young men or in the structure of jobs and workforce demographics help account for the negative secular trends in employment and participation of young black men? Some evidence regarding this issue appears in table 2.5, which augments the earlier regressions with measures of characteristics at the MSA level for each year.

For the entire 1979–2000 period and for each decade considered separately, the table presents results from six estimated regression equations. The first equation contains the school enrollment rate of young black men, the share of all jobs in the area in manufacturing, and the share of employment in the area accounted for by women. The second equation adds the share of employment accounted for by black women, while the third replaces the share of employment in manufacturing with that in blue-collar occupations. The fourth through sixth equations replicate the first three, except that they use the female and black female employment/population rates in the metropolitan area rather than their shares of employment to capture the possible substitution of women for young black men in employment.

Table 2.5. *Employment and Labor Force Participation: Additional Regression Estimates for Less-Educated Young Black Men*

	Employed						Labor Force					
	1	2	3	4	5	6	1	2	3	4	5	6
1979–2000												
Enrollment	-0.0478	-0.0477	-0.0490	-0.0477	-0.0422	-0.0417	-0.0112	-0.0109	-0.0132	-0.0061	-0.0002	-0.0012
	(.0292)	(.0292)	(.0292)	(.0292)	(.0299)	(.0299)	(.0252)	(.0252)	(.0252)	(.0252)	(.0258)	(.0258)
Manufacturing	-0.1180	-0.1185	—	-0.0310	0.0157	—	-0.3399	-0.3421	—	-0.2864	-0.2638	—
	(.1579)	(.1583)		(.1555)	(.1578)		(.1361)	(.1365)		(.1340)	(.1360)	
Blue-collar employment	—	—	0.2478	—	—	0.3585	—	—	0.0118	—	—	0.0984
			(.1380)			(.1307)			(.1190)			(.1127)
Female employment share	-0.6317	-0.6288	-0.4376	—	—	—	-0.2639	-0.2490	-0.1696	—	—	—
	(.2151)	(.2279)	(.2438)				(.1855)	(.1965)	(.2103)			
Female employment population ratio	—	—	—	0.0399	-0.0418	-0.0066	—	—	—	0.1862	0.1157	0.1284
				(.0664)	(.0741)	(.0752)				(.0573)	(.0639)	(.0648)
Black female employment share	—	-0.0081	-0.0247	—	—	—	—	-0.0425	-0.0107	—	—	—
		(.2149)	(.2149)					(.1853)	(.1853)			
Black female employment population ratio	—	—	—	—	0.1046	0.1020	—	—	—	—	0.0746	0.0765
					(.0320)	(.0320)					(.0276)	(.0276)
MSA unemployment	-2.7809	-2.7814	-2.7024	-2.7674	-2.6771	-2.5412	-0.5495	-0.5520	-0.4871	-0.3462	-0.2964	-0.1994
	(.1722)	(.1727)	(.1732)	(.1885)	(.1909)	(.1944)	(.1485)	(.1489)	(.1494)	(.1625)	(.1646)	(.1676)
Time trend	-0.0065	-0.0065	-0.0055	-0.0075	-0.0076	-0.0062	-0.0077	-0.0077	-0.0066	-0.0079	-0.0080	-0.0067
	(.0008)	(.0008)	(.0008)	(.0008)	(.0008)	(.0008)	(.0007)	(.0007)	(.0007)	(.0007)	(.0007)	(.0007)
R^2	0.1329	0.1329	0.1330	0.1327	0.1330	0.1332	0.1340	0.1340	0.1338	0.1342	0.1346	0.1346

1979–89

	(1)	(2)	(3)	(4)	(5)	(6)	(7)	(8)	(9)	(10)	(11)	(12)
Enrollment	0.0218	0.0218	0.0273	0.0100	0.0313	0.0421	0.0343	0.0343	0.0347	0.0310	0.0461	0.0512
	(.0510)	(.0510)	(.0510)	(.0512)	(.0521)	(.0521)	(.0423)	(.0423)	(.0423)	(.0425)	(.0432)	(.0432)
Manufacturing	0.2528	0.2623	—	0.4379	0.4969	—	-0.1569	-0.1630	—	0.0113	0.0167	—
	(.2662)	(.2668)		(.2580)	(.2602)		(.2207)	(.2212)		(.2139)	(.2157)	
Blue-collar employment	—	—	0.4543	—	—	0.5953	—	—	0.2285	—	—	0.3642
			(.1984)			(.1853)			(.1644)			(.1537)
Female employment share	-1.1065	-1.1793	-0.9240	—	—	—	-0.9874	-0.9408	-0.7153	—	—	—
	(.3896)	(.4116)	(.4289)				(.3230)	(.3412)	(.3555)			
Female employment population ratio	—	—	—	-0.1305	-0.2070	-0.1633	—	—	—	0.0505	-0.0061	0.0227
				(.1239)	(.1346)	(.1354)				(.1027)	(.1116)	(.1122)
Black female employment share	—	0.2122	0.2224	—	—	—	—	-0.1359	-0.1029	—	—	—
		(.3865)	(.3859)					(.3204)	(.3199)			
Black female employment population ratio	—	—	—	—	.1207	.1157	—	—	—	—	.0715	.0684
					(.0564)	(.0564)					(.0467)	(.0467)
MSA unemployment	-2.9297	-2.9066	-2.8204	-3.1787	-3.0529	-2.8903	-.4292	-.4439	-.3485	-.4960	-.4343	-.2693
	(.2301)	(.2339)	(.2363)	(.2535)	(.2582)	(.2656)	(.1908)	(.1939)	(.1959)	(.2101)	(.2141)	(.2202)
Time trend	-.0016	-.0014	-.0004	-.0037	-.0038	-.0022	-.0010	-.0011	.0005	-.0034	-.0036	-.0013
	(.0020)	(.0020)	(.0019)	(.0018)	(.0018)	(.0018)	(.0016)	(.0016)	(.0016)	(.0015)	(.0015)	(.0015)
R^2	.1368	.1368	.1370	.1365	.1364	.1367	.1327	.1327	.1328	.1323	.1325	.1327

1990–2000

	(1)	(2)	(3)	(4)	(5)	(6)	(7)	(8)	(9)	(10)	(11)	(12)
Enrollment	-.0883	-.0943	-.0967	-.0886	-.0893	-.0921	-.0413	-.0495	-.0535	-.0414	-.0366	-.0398
	(.0388)	(.0391)	(.0391)	(.0388)	(.0398)	(.0398)	(.0354)	(.0356)	(.0357)	(.0354)	(.0363)	(.0363)
Manufacturing	-0.1188	-0.1175	—	-0.0085	-0.0159	—	-0.6388	-0.6370	—	-0.5438	-0.5677	—
	(.2897)	(.2897)		(.2899)	(.2996)		(.2643)	(.2643)		(.2645)	(.2732)	

Table 2.5. (Continued)

	Employed						Labor Force					
	1	2	3	4	5	6	1	2	3	4	5	6
Blue-collar employment	—	—	0.3987 (.2514)	—	—	0.5308 (.2492)	—	—	0.3056 (.2294)	—	—	0.4381 (.2273)
Female employment share	-0.7986 (.3320)	-0.9695 (.3605)	-0.7914 (.3741)	—	—	—	-0.6420 (.3029)	-0.8732 (.3288)	-0.6802 (.3414)	—	—	—
Female employment population ratio	—	—	—	0.1542 (.0935)	0.0580 (.1062)	0.0885 (.1067)	—	—	—	0.1449 (.0853)	0.0227 (.0968)	0.0652 (.0973)
Black female employment share	—	0.3990 (.3281)	0.3135 (.3325)	—	—	—	—	0.5400 (.2993)	0.4768 (.3034)	—	—	—
Black female employment population ratio	—	—	—	—	0.1052 (.0425)	0.1026 (.0425)	—	—	—	—	0.1080 (.0388)	0.1061 (.0388)
MSA unemployment	-2.7330 (.3699)	-2.7398 (.3699)	-2.6966 (.3686)	-2.5569 (.3851)	-2.5161 (.3895)	-2.4457 (.3878)	-0.5578 (.3374)	-0.5669 (.3374)	-0.4663 (.3363)	-0.3923 (.3513)	-0.3500 (.3551)	-0.2038 (.3537)
Time trend	-0.0168 (.0020)	-0.0171 (.0020)	-0.0160 (.0019)	-0.0172 (.0020)	-0.0180 (.0020)	-0.0167 (.0019)	-0.0169 (.0018)	-0.0173 (.0019)	-0.0148 (.0017)	-0.0171 (.0018)	-0.0178 (.0019)	-0.0151 (.0017)
R^2	0.1460	0.1461	0.1462	0.1457	0.1455	0.1459	0.1412	0.1414	0.1411	0.1411	0.1417	0.1416

Source: Based on data from the Current Population Survey.

— Not applicable

Note: The equations also include dummies for MSA that are not presented. Standard errors are in parentheses.

MSA = metropolitan statistical area.

Table 2.5 contains several interesting findings. For the overall 1979–2000 period, it is clear that rising school enrollment rates and declining blue-collar employment both contribute to the declining employment of non-enrolled young black men. The former finding suggests that the quality of those who remain non-enrolled has declined over the period, while the latter indicates that young black men continue to have difficulty finding employment in an economy that continues to shift toward white-collar and service occupations.

In contrast, manufacturing employment does not appear to contribute to declining employment or labor force participation over the period (as it has a negative rather than positive estimated effect in most equations). While the share of employment accounted for by women has the correct negative sign, this is generally not true of the female employment/population rate, which raises questions about the exogeneity of the former measure. The generally positive coefficients on the employment rates of black women also do not suggest any direct substitution of women for men in the black community's labor force. Finally, the coefficients on the time trend (compared with those of table 2.4) indicate that, at best, these factors can account for less than a third of the overall decline in employment of young black men between 1979 and 2000.

When considering the determinants of employment and labor force participation of young black men in each decade separately, results differ between the two periods. For instance, the decline of manufacturing and the rise of female employment seem to have negatively affected the employment of young black men in the 1980s, consistent with earlier results (Borjas 1986; Bound and Holzer 1993). In contrast, rising enrollments appear to have had their most negative effect on employment rates among the non-enrolled in the 1990s.

Only the declining share of blue-collar employment in the economy seems to have negatively affected young black men in both periods. But while the regression equations can account for the secular decline in employment and labor force participation in the 1980s (comparing the coefficients on time trends with those reported in note 24), they appear to explain little of what happened in the 1990s.

Though the results are not presented here, one more hypothesis was investigated: that young black men left the labor force in large numbers because of the long-term decline in their real wages (at least until 1997), as shown in figure 2.7. Lacking direct evidence on the potential wages of the nonemployed, two estimates of their wages were used: (1) predicted wages based on the characteristics of the unemployed as well as regression coefficients (on age, education, etc.) from those who are employed; and (2) average wages earned by all employed less-educated young men across metropolitan areas and over time. But neither measure provided consistent evidence that declining real wages were responsible for the declining employment of young black men in this time period.[25]

If our metropolitan-area characteristics cannot account for the declining employment trends of young black men in the 1990s, what else might contribute to an explain them? Trends in crime and incarceration are one possibility. But the crime rate has declined considerably over the course of the decade, suggesting a rising employment rate. Many more young men are reentering society with criminal records after a period of incarceration, though this is likely to be more of a factor in accounting for declining employment among those age 30 and older.

If crime and incarceration help account for the declining trend in employment of very young black men in the 1990s, perhaps this is because these factors lead to employers' growing reluctance to hire any less-educated young black men (Holzer, Raphael, and Stoll, this volume). It is also possible that falling participation in crime has caused more of the least-skilled young men to appear in CPS data during this decade (since those engage in criminal activity are less likely to respond to surveys).

Likewise, the growth of paternity establishment and court orders for child support over the past decade or two could contribute to declining employment of young black men if these orders deter labor force activity by imposing a large "tax" on the earnings of young men. That issue deserves greater study as well.

Conclusion

Employment and labor force participation rates of less-educated young black men indicate a secular decline in work activity during both the 1980s and the 1990s, despite some mild improvements in employment associated with the booming economy of the latter period. Employment trends among blacks were much more negative than those of less-educated white or Hispanic men, and far more negative than those experienced by young black women, whose employment and labor force activity improved dramatically in the 1990s.

The data suggest that rising enrollment rates of young black men imply some declining quality (from a skills or labor force perspective) among the non-enrolled, especially in the 1990s. The declining availability of blue-collar jobs contributes somewhat to falling employment among young black men as well, while the evidence on manufacturing employment and the rising share of women in the workforce is mixed. Nonetheless, these factors together can account for less than a third of the decline in employment of young black men over the entire two-decade period, and much less than that during the 1990s. These factors can explain even less of black men's decline in labor force participation.

Clearly, other changes must have been occurring that contribute to these developments. These might include changes in the nature and enforcement of child support orders, and growing rates of incarceration of young black men, together with the growing proportion who reenter society with criminal records. These issues are addressed elsewhere in this book, and new data in Holzer, Offner, and Sorensen (2005) provide strong evidence that child support, incarceration, and reentry help account for much of the employment difficulties of young black men in the past two decades.[26] These issues should therefore remain high on the agenda of researchers and policymakers, as should the employment problems of young black men more broadly.

NOTES

The authors thank Susan Iammartino and Karina Olivas for excellent research assistance, Danielle Gao for preparation of the data extracts, and Anne Polivka for her assistance in interpreting changes in the data over time.

1. See, for instance, Meyer and Rosenbaum (2001) for an attempt to disentangle these determinants of higher employment among single mothers. Other supports for working women with families in the past two decades include Medicaid extensions, implementation of the State Children's Health Insurance Program (SCHIP), and increased subsidies for child care.

2. See also Fairlie and Sundstrom (1999) for more evidence covering several decades.

3. Much of this work is reviewed in Holzer (1994).

4. See Neal and Johnson (1996) and Jencks and Phillips (1998) for evidence on the effects of skill gaps by race, Cutler and Glaeser (1997) for new evidence on racial segregation, and Holzer and Ihlanfeldt (1996, 1998) for data on spatial mismatch and discrimination. See also Holzer (1996).

5. Differences in demand levels across areas as well as over time can also significantly affect the employment of blacks and other groups. Studies of demand effects on the disadvantaged are reviewed more broadly in Bartik (2001).

6. In the CPS, individuals are sampled for four consecutive months, after which they drop out of the sample for eight months, and then reenter it for a second spell of

four months. The Outgoing Rotation Groups (ORGs) are made up of individuals in the fourth month of each of these sample stints—that is, individuals who are about to drop out of the CPS sample. As a result, the ORG sample is roughly one-quarter of the regular CPS sample.

7. The unemployment rate for any group is defined as the fraction of the labor force that is not working. Since the proportion that is working (ER) is simply the employment/population rate divided by the labor force participation rate, the unemployment rate would be $1 - ER$.

8. The CPI is known to overstate trends in inflation over time; see, for instance, Boskin et al. (1998) and Abraham, Greenlees, and Moulton (1998). But comparisons of real-wage trends across groups should not be influenced by the relative overstatement of inflation and understatement of real-wage growth for the entire labor force.

9. Estimated logit equations generated very similar results.

10. See, for instance, Borjas (1986). Since the shares of employment accounted for by various demographic groups must sum to one, these coefficients may be negatively biased. But other measures (such as employment rates for various demographic groups) are likely to be biased in the opposite direction by the omission of time-varying characteristics of local areas that generate high employment for all groups.

11. Changes in metropolitan area boundaries at other periods are not addressed here but are unlikely to affect many individuals, since counties newly incorporated into metropolitan areas are generally relatively less populated.

12. It is important to use the labor force code (LFSR) throughout the period, rather than the major activity code (the employment status record, or ESR). Under ESR, a person's major activity could be "with a job not at work," "looking for work," "keeping house," or "other," and the person could still be employed. Under LFSR, an individual is listed as employed if he or she worked in the past week.

13. The year 1989 appears in both subperiods to capture peak-to-peak business cycle periods in both.

14. The patterns of declining participation for less-educated men, especially in response to their declining wages in the 1980s, and the concurrent increases for women have all been noted before. See, for example, Juhn (1992) and Blau and Kahn (1997).

15. In particular, Freeman and Rodgers limit their samples to metropolitan areas, where young black men fared somewhat better than they did in rural areas. Also, the variables they use to define employment (the ESR in the CPS) is not consistent across the sample period because the CPS was heavily revised in 1994 (see note 12).

16. It is difficult to analyze employment among 16- to 24-year-olds with some college education, since so many remain enrolled in school. Most analyses of employment across educational categories therefore begin with those age 25 or older.

17. Although some authors attribute negative employment and labor force trends among those age 25 and above to a shift into disability programs during the past decade, these factors are likely more relevant for older workers. See Ellwood (2001) and Autor and Duggan (2001).

18. The recovery of real wages that began in 1997 reflects general productivity and real-wage growth during that time as well as the minimum wage increases in 1996 and 1997. The benefits in earnings associated with increases in the EITC are not captured by these data.

19. Real-wage growth in that period reflects general real wage and productivity growth in the economy at that time, as well as the positive effects of minimum wage increases on low-wage workers.

20. During this period, there was a substantial movement of young black males from nonmetropolitan areas to metropolitan areas, and employment rates were higher in the nonmetropolitan areas at the start than at the end. This suggests that those who moved had more ability or motivation than those who stayed behind.

21. One version of the supply-side story might be based on a declining need of young black men to contribute financially to families as the earnings of the women in those families rise.

22. The MSA dummies capture fixed area effects, so that changes over time reflect within-MSA changes. The dummies include those for unspecified metropolitan areas, while individuals residing in nonmetropolitan areas constitute the omitted group.

23. The smaller cyclical effects for women might reflect their smaller concentrations in cyclically sensitive industries, such as construction and manufacturing. They could also reflect a tendency of some women to enter the labor market during downturns to offset the lost employment of their spouses (known to labor economists as the "added worker" effect).

24. The coefficients on the time trend in estimated equations for employment were $-.0058$ and $-.0178$ for young black men in the two decades. Comparable coefficients for labor force participation equations were $-.0031$ and $-.0159$.

25. Details of our estimates are available upon request. Many estimates generated the wrong sign and were very sensitive to the inclusion of control variables. Even Juhn's work indicates a much lower ability of declining wages to account for declining labor market activity among less-educated young black men than among young white men, and less in the 1990s than in the 1980s (Juhn 2000).

26. The analysis there is based on lagged incarceration rates of black men by state and year, which proxy for the presence of ex-offenders in the population, and on child support enforcement activities by state and year. Both sets of data were merged into the CPS-ORG data used in this chapter, and both have negative estimated effects on employment and labor force participation of young black men—especially those age 25 to 34.

REFERENCES

Abraham, Katherine, John Greenlees, and Brent Moulton. 1998. "Working to Improve the Consumer Price Index." *Journal of Economic Perspectives* 12(1): 27–36.

Autor, David, and Mark Duggan. 2001. "The Rise in Disability Recipiency and the Decline in Unemployment." Working Paper 8336. Cambridge, MA: National Bureau of Economic Research.

Bartik, Timothy. 2001. *Jobs for the Poor: Can Labor Demand Policies Help?* New York: Russell Sage Foundation.

Blank, Rebecca, and Lucie Schmidt. 2001. "Work, Wages, and Welfare." In *The New World of Welfare,* edited by Rebecca Blank and Ron Haskins (70–102). Washington DC: Brookings Institution Press.

Blau, Francine, and Lawrence Kahn. 1997. "Swimming Upstream: Trends in the Gender Wage Differential in the 1980s." *Journal of Labor Economics* 15(1, pt. 1): 1–42.

Borjas, George. 1986. "The Demographic Determinants of the Demand for Black Labor." In *The Black Youth Employment Crisis,* edited by Richard Freeman and Harry J. Holzer (101–230). Chicago: University of Chicago Press.

Boskin, Michael, Ellen Dulberger, Robert Gordon, Zvi Griliches, and Dale Jorgenson. 1998. "Consumer Prices, the Consumer Price Index, and the Cost of Living." *Journal of Economic Perspectives* 12(1): 3–26.

Bound, John, and Richard Freeman. 1992. "What Went Wrong? The Erosion of Relative Earnings and Employment among Young Black Men in the 1980s." *Quarterly Journal of Economics* 107(1): 201–32.

Bound, John, and Harry J. Holzer. 1993. "Industrial Structure, Skill Levels, and the Labor Market for White and Black Males." *Review of Economics and Statistics* 75(3): 387–96.

———. 2000. "Demand Shifts, Population Adjustments, and Labor Market Outcomes during the 1980s." *Journal of Labor Economics* 18(1): 20–54.

Burtless, Gary. 2000. "Can the Labor Market Absorb Three Million Welfare Recipients?" In *The Low-Wage Labor Market: Challenges and Opportunities for Self-Sufficiency,* edited by Kelleen Kaye and Demetra Smith Nightingale (65–84). Washington DC: Urban Institute Press.

Cherry, Robert, and William Rodgers, eds. 2000. *Prosperity for All? The Economic Boom and African Americans.* New York: Russell Sage Foundation.

Clark, Kim, and Lawrence Summers. 1981. "Demographic Variation in Cyclical Employment Effects." *Journal of Human Resources* 18(1): 61–79.

———. 1982. "The Dynamics of Youth Unemployment." In *The Youth Labor Market Problem: Its Nature, Causes, and Consequences,* edited by Richard Freeman and David Wise (199–234). Chicago: University of Chicago Press.

Cogan, John. 1982. "The Decline in Black Teenage Employment: 1950–70." *American Economic Review* 72(4): 621–38.

Cutler, David, and Edward Glaeser. 1997. "Are Ghettoes Good or Bad?" *Quarterly Journal of Economics* 112(3): 827–72.

Ellwood, David. 2001. "The Sputtering Labor Force of the 21st Century: Can Social Policy Help?" Working Paper 8321. Cambridge, MA: National Bureau of Economic Research.

Fairlie, Robert, and William Sundstrom. 1999. "The Emergence, Persistence, and Recent Widening of the Racial Unemployment Gap." *Industrial and Labor Relations Review* 52(2): 252–70.

Flinn, Christopher, and James Heckman. 1983. "Are Unemployment and Out of the Labor Force Behaviorally Distinct Labor Force States?" *Journal of Labor Economics* 1(1): 28–42.

Freeman, Richard. 1991. "Employment and Earnings of Disadvantaged Young Men in a Labor Shortage Economy." In *The Urban Underclass,* edited by Christopher Jencks and Paul Peterson (103–21). Washington DC: Brookings Institution Press.

———. 1992. "Crime and the Employment of Disadvantaged Youths." In *Urban Labor Markets and Job Opportunity,* edited by George Peterson and Wayne Vroman (201–238). Washington DC: Urban Institute Press.

Freeman, Richard, and Harry J. Holzer, eds. 1986. *The Black Youth Employment Crisis.* Chicago: University of Chicago Press.

Freeman, Richard, and William Rodgers. 2000. "Area Economic Conditions and the Labor-Market Outcomes of Young Men in the 1990s Expansion." In *Prosperity for All? The Economic Boom and African Americans,* edited by Robert Cherry and William M. Rodgers III (50–87). New York: Russell Sage Foundation.

Hines, James, Hilary Hoynes, and Alan Krueger. 2001. "Another Look at Whether a Rising Tide Lifts All Boats." Working Paper 8412. Cambridge, MA: National Bureau of Economic Research.

Holzer, Harry J. 1994. "Black Employment Problems: New Evidence, Old Questions." *Journal of Policy Analysis and Management* 13(3): 699–722.

———. 1996. *What Employers Want: Job Prospects for Less-Educated Workers.* New York: Russell Sage Foundation.

Holzer, Harry J., and Keith Ihlanfeldt. 1996. "Spatial Factors and the Employment of Blacks at the Firm Level." *New England Economic Review* (May/June): 36–46.

———. 1998. "Customer Discrimination and the Employment Outcomes for Minority Workers." *Quarterly Journal of Economics* 113(3): 835–68.

Holzer, Harry J., Paul Offner, and Elaine Sorensen. 2005. "Declining Employment among Less-Skilled Young Black Men: The Role of Incarceration and Child Support." *Journal of Policy Analysis and Management* 24(2): 329–50.

Hoynes, Hilary. 2000. "The Employment, Earnings, and Income of Less-Skilled Workers over the Business Cycle." In *Finding Jobs: Work and Welfare Reform,* edited by David Card and Rebecca Blank (23–71). New York: Russell Sage Foundation.

Ihlanfeldt, Keith, and David Sjoquist. 1990. "Job Accessibility and Racial Differences in Youth Employment Rates." *American Economic Review* 80(2): 267–76.

Jencks, Christopher, and Meredith Phillips, eds. 1998. *The Black-White Test Score Gap.* Washington, DC: Brookings Institution Press.

Juhn, Chinhui. 1992. "Decline of Male Labor Market Participation: The Role of Declining Market Opportunities." *Quarterly Journal of Economics* 107(1): 79–122.

———. 2000. "Black-White Employment Differential in a Tight Labor Market." In *Prosperity for All? The Economic Boom and African Americans,* edited by Robert Cherry and William M. Rodgers III (88–109). New York: Russell Sage Foundation.

Kasarda, John. 1995. "Industrial Restructuring and the Changing Location of Jobs." In *Economic Trends,* vol. 1 of *State of the Union: America in the 1990s,* edited by Reynolds Farley. New York: Russell Sage Foundation.

Lerman, Robert, Laudan Aron, and Stephanie Riegg. 2000. "Youth in 2010." Washington DC: The Urban Institute.

Meyer, Bruce, and Daniel Rosenbaum. 2001. "Welfare, the Earned Income Tax Credit, and the Labor Supply of Single Mothers." *Quarterly Journal of Economics* 116(3): 1063–1114.

Neal, Derek, and William Johnson. 1996. "The Role of Pre-Market Factors in Black-White Wage Differences." *Journal of Political Economy* 104(5): 869–95.

Western, Bruce, and Becky Pettit. 2000. "Incarceration and Racial Inequality in Men's Employment." *Industrial and Labor Relations Review* 54(1): 3–16.

Wilson, William. 1987. *The Truly Disadvantaged.* Chicago: University of Chicago Press.

3

Forecasting the Labor Market Prospects of Less-Educated Americans

William M. Rodgers III

According to recent studies, the economic expansion during the 1990s substantially improved the absolute and relative economic positions of less-skilled and less-educated Americans.[1] The national unemployment rate fell from 6.8 percent in 1991 to 4.3 percent in 2001, setting a new record for the longest economic expansion—120 months. For 34 months, from August 1998 to May 2001, the jobless rate was at or below 4.5 percent. Employment rates for most demographic groups, especially young people and minorities, reached historic highs, eroding some persistent and historical barriers to work.

The economy's ability to reduce barriers to work can be partly attributed to policymakers' willingness to allow growth without fear of inflation. Even as estimates indicated the nonaccelerating inflation rate of unemployment (NAIRU) had fallen, policymakers and economists felt the low unemployment rates were unsustainable. The U.S. Federal Reserve Board of Governors began increasing the federal funds rate on June 30, 1999, when they increased it 25 basis points to 5.0 percent. The board increased the federal funds rate five more times over the next several months until it reached 6.5 percent in May 2000, where it stayed for the rest of the year. Although the board began to see a moderation in economic activity, at the time it felt "the risks continue to be weighted mainly toward conditions that may generate heightened inflation pressures in the foreseeable future." It was not until December 19, 2000, that the economy

39

had slowed enough for the board to shift its bias "toward conditions that may generate economic weakness in the foreseeable future."

In fact, by November 2001, the NBER Business Cycle Dating Committee had concluded that March 2001—three months after the Federal Reserve shifted its bias—marked the beginning of a recession. On July 17, 2003, the Dating Committee determined that a trough in business activity had occurred in the economy in November 2001. This trough signaled the end of the recession that had started in March.

Using November 2001 as the recession's end yields an economic contraction that lasted eight months, making it the second shortest recession since 1969. Over these eight months, the U.S. unemployment rate rose from 4.3 to 5.6 percent, with labor force participation falling from 67.1 to 66.7 percent. Although the recession was mild by historical standards, published Bureau of Labor Statistics data show that it eroded a portion of the gains less-skilled and less-educated Americans achieved during the 1990s boom.

Since November 2001, the economy has shown signs of recovery. Nonfarm payroll employment, one indicator on which the NBER Business Cycle Dating Committee bases its decision, began to trend upward, albeit not until the beginning of 2004. The Bush administration predicts the unemployment rate will end 2004 at 5.5 percent and fall slightly to 5.3 percent in 2005.[2] These unemployment rates are low by historical standards, but they are one full point above the jobless rate at the peak of the 1990s boom. They reflect a growing economy with "looser" labor markets.

If policymakers and the public consider these forecasts the economy's most likely path, what are the implications for the labor market prospects of less-skilled young Americans, especially non-enrolled young minorities? Will these forecasts limit the economy's ability to improve the absolute and relative economic positions of these groups? How sharply will they reduce the number of less-skilled young Americans pulled into the labor market? If these macroeconomic forecasts are realized, how will they affect crime rates? Former welfare recipients trying to obtain employment? The funding of social programs?

This chapter forecasts the post-recession labor market experiences of less-educated men and women (16- to 24-year-olds not enrolled in education or training programs). It first describes recent macroeconomic trends using aggregate published data on gross domestic product (GDP) growth, industrial production, employment, productivity, and real wages.

Based on these measures, the recession from March 2001 to November 2001 was milder than the 1980s recession.

Next the chapter estimates the differential impact of macroeconomic conditions (aggregate demand) on the employment–population ratios, employment rates, and labor force participation rates of non-enrolled 16- to 24-year-olds by race or ethnicity, gender, and educational attainment. The chapter examines the different relationships between macroeconomic policies and various socioeconomic groups, and attempts to explain the constant two-to-one ratio of black–white unemployment rates.[3] The chapter uses these empirical relationships and the Bush administration 2004 and 2005 forecasts of national unemployment rates to predict the employment–population ratios, employment rates, and labor force participation rates of non-enrolled 16- to 24-year-olds. Although the employment–population ratios of less-skilled Americans will improve over the next decade, for most demographic groups, ratios will not return to their 1990s peaks.

U.S. Macroeconomic Trends

The United States has undergone several economic expansions and recessions since 1960. Continuously lower unemployment rates, faster employment growth, accelerated productivity growth, and growth in real hourly earnings distinguish the 1990s boom from previous ones. A smaller rise in unemployment, a smaller drop in employment, and continued growth in productivity and real hourly earnings differentiate the March 2001 recession from past recessions. The recent recession affected less-skilled workers, especially less-skilled black workers, less severely than past recessions have. But compared with prime-age workers, less-skilled workers disproportionately bore the brunt of the slowdown.

The Economic Booms of the 1980s and 1990s

First, let's examine the 1990s economic boom against the 1980s economic boom. As measured by real GDP growth, the economy expanded by 40.0 percent during the 1990s, compared with 36.9 percent during the 1980s.[4] The average annual increase in GDP was also greater during the 1990s expansion. Growth in industrial production during the 1990s was more than four times greater than during the 1980s. Although not back to its growth rates of the 1960s, productivity grew at a faster rate during the 1990s economic expansion than during the 1980s expansion. From 1991 to 2000, productivity grew at an average annual rate of 2.1 percent from 1991 to 2000, compared with 1.8 percent from 1982 to 1990. Poverty among families fell more in the 1990s than in the 1980s, by 2.9 versus 1.9 percent.

Job growth was similar across expansions. Roughly 21 million new jobs were created from November 1982 to July 1990, compared with 24 million new jobs from March 1991 to March 2001. However, the composition of job growth differed across expansions. During the 1980s expansion, 42 percent of the newly created jobs were in service industries, compared with 53 percent in the 1990s expansion.

A very different pattern emerges in real hourly earnings. Inflation was moderate over both periods, with average annual increases of 3.5 and 3.4 percent. Movements in nominal hourly wages therefore explain the stagnation and subsequent growth in real earnings during the 1990s. Before 1996, average real hourly earnings of nonagricultural private-sector workers were approximately $13.28 (2001 dollars). In 1996, real hourly earnings began to rise for the first time in over a decade, jumping to $13.34 and then $13.88. Real hourly earnings finished the boom at $14.33.

Turning to aggregate labor market trends, unemployment declined substantially during the two booms. The employment–population ratio and labor force participation rate increased slightly during the 1990s expansion, presumably because of the higher initial ratios. The employment–population ratio increased by 5.5 percentage points from November 1982 to July 1990 and by 2.5 points from March 1991 to March 2001, while labor force participation increased by 2.3 and 0.8 percent, respectively. Overall, these macroeconomic indicators point to a stronger economy during the 1990s.

Recessions since 1960

The March–November 2001 recession can be placed in context with all recessions from the past four decades. The eight-month 2001 recession is tied for the second shortest recession on record since 1960. The longest recessions over this 44-year period lasted 16 months, from July 1981 to November 1982 and November 1973 to March 1975. Other lengthy recessions lasted from December 1969 to November 1970 (11 months) and April 1960 to February 1961 (10 months). The shortest recessions lasted six months, from January 1980 to July 1980, and eight months, from July 1990 to March 1991.

As measured by real GDP growth, the economy expanded by 0.12 percent a quarter during the 2001 recession, compared with 0.53 and 1.09 percent contractions during the two recessions of the 1980s (figure 3.1). Industrial production fell but was nowhere near its decline in the 1980s. From March to November 2001, industrial production fell at an average monthly rate of 0.42 percent, compared with 0.85 percent during the January to July 1980 recession. Private-sector employment during the 8-month 2001 recession contracted by 2.0 million, 600,000 fewer than during the 16-month recession from July 1981 to November 1982.

Productivity and real-wage growth behaved quite differently during the 2001 recession. Productivity grew more rapidly than it had during previous recessions. Its average annual rate was 3.3 percent from the first quarter of 2001 to the fourth quarter of 2001, compared with 0.2 percent from July 1981 to November 1982. During the recession that ran from the fourth quarter of 1969 to the fourth quarter of 1970, productivity grew by 1.8 percent (figure 3.2). Inflation-adjusted hourly wages continued to rise during the recession, making the 2001 recession the only one in which nominal wage growth has stayed ahead of inflation.

Figure 3.1. *Average Quarterly Change in Real GDP by Recession*

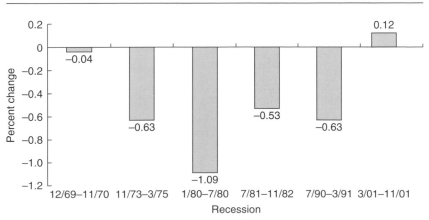

Source: Author's calculations from published Bureau of Economic Analysis data.

Notes: Recession designations come from the National Bureau of Economic Research (NBER). The NBER has not officially designated March 2002 as the end of the 2001 recession.

Figure 3.2. *Average Quarterly Change in Productivity by Recession*

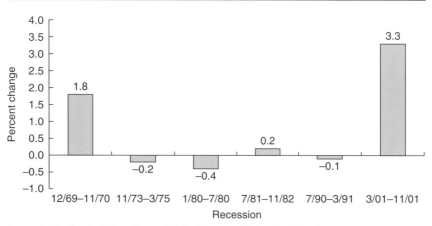

Source: Author's calculations from published Bureau of Labor Statistics data.

Note: Recession designations come from the National Bureau of Economic Research. Figures are the percent change a quarter ago, at annual rate.

Changes in Labor Force Participation from 1970 to 2003

Figures 3.3 and 3.4 compare the labor market outcomes of non-enrolled 16- to 24-year-old whites, blacks, and Hispanics. From 1970 to 2003, non-enrolled whites have consistently higher employment–population ratios than blacks and Hispanics (figure 3.3). The ratio for blacks jumps from 50 to 60 percent during the 1990s boom, but still remains more than 15 percentage points lower than the ratio for whites. The ratio for Hispanics also grew rapidly during the 1990s boom, jumping from around 60 to 70 percent. The labor force participation of blacks and Hispanics both increased, but the key to the large increases in black and Hispanic employment–population ratios was the decline in each group's unemployment rate during the 1990s boom (figure 3.4). Although still high, the black and Hispanic unemployment rates fell to around 20 and 9 percent, both record lows.

Analyzing the labor market experiences of 16- to 24-year-old men and women by educational attainment reveals that high school dropouts have the greatest variation in employment–population ratios from 1970 to 2003 (figure 3.5). After deteriorating during the 1980s recession, the labor market outcomes of high school dropouts recovered, but not to the levels that preceded the recession. High school graduates had higher

Figure 3.3. *Employment–Population Ratios of Non-enrolled 16- to 24-Year-Olds by Race and Ethnicity, 1970–2003*

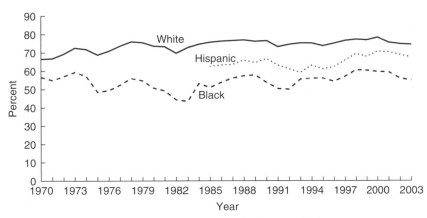

Source: Author's calculations from published Bureau of Labor Statistics data.

Figure 3.4. *Unemployment Rates of Non-enrolled 16- to 24-Year-Olds by Race and Ethnicity, 1970–2003*

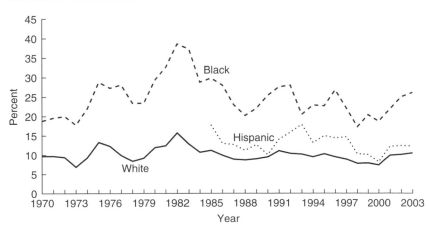

Source: Author's calculations from published Bureau of Labor Statistics October data.

Figure 3.5. *Employment–Population Ratios of Non-enrolled 16- to 24-Year-Olds by Educational Attainment and Gender, 1970–2003*

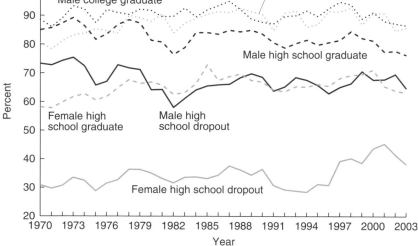

Source: Author's calculations from published Bureau of Labor Statistics October data on 16- to 24-year-olds.

employment–population ratios than dropouts, but these ratios also fell during the 1980s recession and did not return to pre-recession levels. The 1990s boom affected their ratios only modestly (see Holzer and Offner, this volume). The gains were not strong enough to counter the long-term structural decline in participation.[5]

Figure 3.5 presents some startling trends. It clearly demonstrates the collective effects of welfare reform and the tight labor market on the employment–population ratios of non-enrolled women. The employment–population ratios of non-enrolled high school dropout women jumped from 30 percent to almost 50 percent from 1996 to 2000, while the employment–population ratio of high school graduates increased modestly over the same period. Because of the timing, much of this jump is the result of increased labor force participation. The unemployment rate for high school dropout women began to fall before welfare reform, from over 30 percent to around 20 percent. Participation made its biggest increases after 1996. Even at the boom's peak in 2000, however, participation of non-enrolled high school dropout women remained 15 points below the participation of non-enrolled women with high school diplomas.

Having established the differential effects of macroeconomic conditions on employment and labor force participation, this chapter now turns to the relationship between aggregate demand and employment. To place the findings and 10-year forecasts of labor market outcomes for young non-enrolled Americans in their proper context, it is important to understand the econometric models the chapter uses.

Methods

This section uses the simple model used in the widely cited Clark and Summers studies (1981, 1990) to identify the relationships between aggregate demand and the labor market outcomes of non-enrolled young adults. Although simplistic by today's time series methods, Clark and Summers's model provides a clear, straightforward framework for describing the cyclical behavior of employment, unemployment, and labor force participation. These three measures are used to summarize the labor market outcomes of a particular demographic group. For the ith demographic group (e.g., non-enrolled 16- to 24-year-old blacks), the three measures are related by the following identity:

$$(1) \left(\frac{E}{N}\right)_i = \left(\frac{E}{L}\right)_i \left(\frac{L}{N}\right)_i,$$

where E denotes employment, N denotes the civilian population, and L denotes the labor force.

This identity indicates that the employment–population ratio (E/N, share of the civilian population employed) is the product of the employment rate (E/L, 1 minus the unemployment rate) and the participation rate (L/N, share of the civilian population in the labor force). A change in the share of the employed civilian population can be sorted into two components: a change in the unemployment rate and a change in the participation rate. To make it easier to measure the contribution of each component, Clark and Summers take the natural logarithm of equation 1. This transformation of the identity also allows analysts to describe each component's contribution in percentages.

Formally, taking logarithms and differentiating equation 1 yields the decomposition:

$$(2)\, d\ln\left(\frac{E}{N}\right)_i = d\ln\left(\frac{E}{L}\right)_i + d\ln\left(\frac{L}{N}\right)_i.$$

Changes in the employment–population ratio can be decomposed into changes in employment and participation rates. People in the labor force are either employed or unemployed, which implies that

$$(3)\, d\ln\left(\frac{E}{N}\right)_i = d\ln(1-UR)_i + d\ln\left(\frac{L}{N}\right)_i,$$

where UR denotes the unemployment rate. Clark and Summers use this decomposition as the basis for estimating the effects of overall macroeconomic performance on youth employment.

To place this model into an empirical framework, Clark and Summers assume that the employment and participation rates for each group depend on aggregate demand, seasonal factors, and time. The latter captures the average annual change in variables omitted from the equation. Seasonal changes in the data are modeled using monthly dummy variables. The specifications for the participation and employment rates are

$$(4)\, \ln(PR)_{it} = \beta_0 + \sum_{j=0}^{7} \beta_{t-j} URATE_{t-j} + \delta_1 T + \delta_2 T^2 + v_{it}, \text{ and}$$

$$(5)\, \ln(1-UR_{it}) = \alpha_0 + \sum_{j=0}^{7} \alpha_{t-j} URATE_{t-j} + \phi_1 T + \phi_2 T^2 + u_{it},$$

where $URATE$ denotes the unemployment rate, the proxy for aggregate demand. Clark and Summers use the unemployment rate of men age 35 to 44 as their proxy for aggregate demand. The models in this chapter use the national unemployment rate. Both are assumed to describe the variation in job opportunities and the ease of finding a job. Many workers, especially teenagers, may react slowly to changes in the availability of employment. Because of this, lagged values of the unemployment rate are included in the model. The term T denotes a time trend that starts at the beginning of each series, and T^2 denotes the square of the time trend.

How does one interpret the coefficients of the unemployment rate (*URATE*)? The cyclical sensitivity of the *i*th demographic group's participation rate is the sum of the unemployment rate coefficients ($\pi_{PR} = \Sigma\beta_{t-j}$). An estimate of -1.0 implies that a 1 percentage point increase in the *URATE* (e.g., from 0.5 to 0.6) generates a 1 percent decrease in the *i*th group's participation rate (e.g., 0.434 to 0.430).

The earlier identity ensures that the relationship between the employment–population ratio and aggregate demand and time can be written as

$$(6)\ \ln\left(EN\right)_{it} = \beta_0 - \alpha_0 + \sum_{j=0}^{7}\left(\beta_{t-j} - \alpha_{t-j}\right)URATE_{t-j} + \left(\delta_1 - \phi_2\right)T$$
$$+\left(\delta_2 - \phi_2\right)T^2 + e_i.$$

Equations 4, 5, and 6 can be used to decompose cyclical changes in the employment–population ratio into portions due to changes in unemployment and participation, because for the *i*th demographic group,

$$(7)\ \pi_{EN} = \pi_{PR} + \pi_{(1-UR)}.$$

For example, the equation can be used to determine whether an increase in the employment–population ratio is the result of movements from unemployment to employment and/or movements from out of the labor force to employment.

To update Clark and Summers's earlier results on teenagers, the models in this chapter use published monthly data from the Bureau of Labor Statistics that cover the years 1954 to 2004. I estimate the models using an eight-month, first-degree polynomial distributed lag with the restriction that the coefficient on the ninth lag equals zero. I follow Clark and Summers by estimating all the equations with maximum likelihood techniques that correct for the positive serial correlation that exist in the data.

The models for non-enrolled young adults are estimated with shorter time series. The Bureau of Labor Statistics did not begin to publish participation, unemployment rates, and employment–population ratios for non-enrolled blacks and Hispanics until October 1970 and October 1985. Labor market statistics by educational attainment were not published in the October supplement of the CPS until 1970. I estimate the

Figure 3.6. *U.S. Unemployment Rates, 1948–2004*

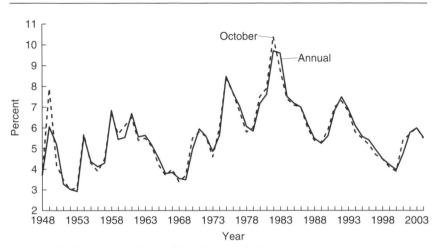

Source: Author's calculations from published Bureau of Labor Statistics data.

models using a four-year, first-degree polynomial distributed lag with the restriction that the coefficient on the fourth lag equals zero.[6]

Figure 3.6 plots the annual and October unemployment rates of men and women age 16 and older. The two series closely track each other, indicating that our estimates of the relationships between the labor market outcomes of non-enrolled young adults and the national unemployment rates will be independent of whether the annual average or October national unemployment rates are used to proxy for aggregate demand.

Results

Table 3.1 presents estimates of the π_{EN}, $\pi_{(1-UR)}$, and π_{PR}, the sum of the coefficients on the unemployment rate in the distributed lag, for white teenagers. They serve as a benchmark to Clark and Summers's estimates, which were based on quarterly data from 1954 to 1976. The first column shows the estimated relationships using the unemployment rate of men age 35 to 44 (or prime-age men) as the proxy for aggregate demand, and the second column shows the estimated relationships with the U.S. unemployment rate. Both measures of aggregate demand exhibit the strong

Table 3.1. *White Teenagers' Cyclical Response of Participation, Unemployment, and Employment, 1954–76 (standard errors in parentheses)*

Variable	35- to 44-year-old male unemployment rate	U.S. unemployment rate
ln(EPOP)	−3.548	−3.099
	(0.216)	(0.177)
ln(EMP)	−2.073	−1.832
	(0.087)	(0.066)
ln(LFP)	−1.475	−1.265
	(0.188)	(0.159)

Source: Author's calculations using published data from the Bureau of Labor Statistics.

Notes: The coefficients are the sum of the coefficients on the unemployment rate obtained from an eight-month polynomial in the first degree with the coefficient on the ninth month set to zero. The estimates have been corrected for first order serial correlation.

ln(EPOP): logarithm of the employment–population ratio

ln(EMP): logarithm of the employment rate (1 minus the unemployment rate)

ln(LFP): logarithm of the labor force participation ratio

relationship between the health of the macroeconomy and youth labor market outcomes that Clark and Summers found. For white teenagers, a 1 point increase in the prime-age male unemployment rate decreases the employment–population ratio of the teen population by 3.5 percent.[7] Over half of the decline comes through a decrease in the employment rate. Constraining the employment–population ratio's effect to equal the sum of the effects of the participation and employment rates yields a coefficient of −3.5.[8] Using the national unemployment rate as the proxy for aggregate demand generates a 3.1 percent decline in the employment–population ratio, with a decline in participation having the same relative importance. The relationship is robust to constraining the employment–population ratio's effect to equal the sum of the effects of the employment and labor force participation rates.

Table 3.2 presents the estimates for white and black teenagers over the length of each group's series (white teenagers from January 1954 to November 2004, black teenagers from January 1972 to November 2004).[9] Extending the series of white teenagers to November 2004 indicates that white teenagers remain sensitive to the macroeconomy. A 1 point increase in the unemployment rate of prime-age men generates a 1.5 percent decline in the employment–population ratio of white teenagers. All the

Table 3.2. *Cyclical Behavior of Unemployment, Participation, and Employment for Teenagers (standard errors in parentheses)*

	White	Black
35- to 44-year-old male unemployment rate		
ln(EPOP)	−1.472	−9.450
	(0.211)	(0.337)
ln(EMP)	−1.608	−5.363
	(0.049)	(0.226)
ln(LFP)	0.133	−4.099
	(0.194)	(0.250)
U.S. unemployment rate		
ln(EPOP)	−1.242	−9.036
	(0.203)	(0.288)
ln(EMP)	−1.652	−5.238
	(0.039)	(0.190)
ln(LFP)	0.408	−3.810
	(0.183)	(0.231)

Source: Author's calculations using published data from the Bureau of Labor Statistics.

Notes: The coefficients for the unemployment rate of men age 35 to 44 are the sum of the coefficients obtained from an eight-month polynomial in the first degree with the coefficient on the ninth month set to zero. The coefficients for the U.S. unemployment rate are the sum of the coefficients obtained from an eight-month polynomial in the first degree with the coefficient on the ninth month set to zero. All models contain month dummy variables and time trends. They have also been corrected for first-order serial correlation. The white teen series runs from January 1954 to November 2004. The black teen series runs from January 1972 to November 2004.

ln(EPOP): logarithm of the employment–population ratio

ln(EMP): logarithm of the employment rate (1 minus the unemployment rate)

ln(LFP): logarithm of the labor force participation ratio

response comes from employment. Using the national unemployment rate as the measure of aggregated demand leads to a smaller decline of 1.2 percent, again with all the relationship attributable to a decline in the employment rate of white teens.

Black teens are more than five times as sensitive to fluctuations in aggregate demand than white teens. Both unemployment rate specifications indicate that a 1 point increase in the unemployment rate is associated with a 9.0 to 9.5 percent decline in black teens' employment rate. Almost 60 percent of the employment–population ratio's decline is because of a decrease in employment.

The next tables shift to describing the sensitivity of the chapter's target population—non-enrolled less-skilled Americans—to macroeconomic fluctuations. Table 3.3 presents estimates of the π_{EN}, $\pi_{(1-UR)}$, and π_{PR}—the sum of the coefficients on the unemployment rate in the distributed lag— for non-enrolled young adults by age, race, gender, and educational attainment. These estimates do not constrain a change in the employment– population ratio to equal the sum of the change in the unemployment and participation rates as shown in equation 7. The estimates are consistent with those of Clark and Summers, as well as others. They exhibit strong relationships between the health of the macroeconomy and labor market outcomes of teenagers and young adults. A 1 point increase in the U.S. unemployment rate lowers the employment–population ratios of non- enrolled 16- to 19-year-olds and 20- to 24-year-olds by 0.72 and 0.76 per- cent, with the decline in each group's employment–population ratio coming from reductions in its employment rate.

Non-enrolled 16- to 24-year-old blacks, male high school dropouts, and Hispanics are the most sensitive to macroeconomic conditions. For non-enrolled whites, a 1 point increase in the unemployment rate lowers their employment–population ratio by 1.0 percent. All the decline comes through a decrease in employment rate. A 1 point increase in the U.S. unemployment rate lowers the employment–population ratios of blacks and Hispanics by 6.4 and 6.0 percent. For blacks, all the reduction is due to weaker job prospects; two-thirds of the reduction in the Hispanic employment–population ratio is due to weaker job prospects.

The employment–population ratios of non-enrolled 16- to 24-year- old men and women have different responses to changes in the U.S. unemployment rate. A 1 point increase in the unemployment rate lowers women's employment–population ratio by 0.50 percent, compared with a 1.85 percent decline for men. All the reductions are due to a decline in each group's employment rate.

Once the data are disaggregated by educational attainment, however, the variation in experience expands. As shown in panel B of table 3.3, non- enrolled high school dropouts, especially men, have the largest sensitivity to changes in the U.S. unemployment rate. A 1 point increase in the U.S. unemployment rate lowers the employment–population ratio of non- enrolled male high school dropouts by 3.7 percent; this figure is 1.9 per- cent for female dropouts. Reductions in the employment rate explain the decline. As one would expect, the sensitivity to macroeconomic fluctua-

text continues on page 56

Table 3.3. Cyclical Behavior of Unemployment, Employment, and Participation of Non-enrolled 16- to 24-Year-Olds (standard errors in parentheses)

Panel A	Age			Race and Ethnicity			Gender	
	16–24	16–19	20–24	White	Black	Hispanic	Men	Women
ln(EPOP)	−0.762	−0.717	−0.755	−1.019	−6.403	−5.993	−1.846	−0.459
	(0.357)	(0.455)	(0.324)	(0.576)	(1.293)	(0.789)	(0.368)	(0.502)
ln(EMP)	−1.636	−2.904	−1.537	−1.673	−6.347	−3.968	−1.987	−1.244
	(0.253)	(0.437)	(0.238)	(0.370)	(1.056)	(0.779)	(0.314)	(0.235)
ln(LFP)	0.468	1.411	0.289	0.655	−0.034	−2.025	0.189	0.855
	(0.189)	(0.440)	(0.174)	(0.368)	(0.643)	(0.770)	(0.105)	(0.407)

Panel B	Men				Women			
	High school dropout	High school graduate	Some college	College graduate	High school dropout	High school graduate	Some college	College graduate
ln(EPOP)	−3.692	−2.442	−2.027	−0.210	−1.879	−1.302	−0.341	−0.977
	(0.971)	(0.683)	(0.443)	(0.615)	(2.514)	(0.883)	(0.546)	(0.649)
ln(EMP)	−3.808	−1.732	−1.727	−0.195	−4.414	−2.077	−1.142	−1.136
	(0.832)	(0.474)	(0.383)	(0.504)	(1.006)	(0.360)	(0.346)	(0.392)
ln(LFP)	0.107	−0.542	−0.295	−0.015	2.541	0.796	0.711	0.145
	(0.440)	(0.238)	(0.236)	(0.303)	(2.111)	(0.683)	(0.492)	(0.424)

Source: Author's calculations using published data from the Bureau of Labor Statistics.

Notes: The coefficients are the sum of the coefficients on the U.S. unemployment rate obtained from a four-year polynomial in the first degree with the coefficient on the fifth year set to zero. All models contain a time trend and have been corrected for first-order serial correlation. All data are from October. The series by age run from October 1953 to October 2003. The series for whites and blacks run from 1970 to 2003 and for Hispanic from 1985 to 2003. The series by gender and education run from 1970 to 2003. The series by gender run from 1953 to 2003.

ln(EPOP): logarithm of the employment–population ratio

ln(EMP): logarithm of the employment rate (1 minus the unemployment rate)

ln(LFP): logarithm of the labor force participation ratio

tions falls as educational attainment rises; however, the importance of the employment rate in explaining falling employment–population ratios does not diminish.

As a measure of aggregate demand, the U.S. unemployment rate continually confirms the long-held view that the least skilled are the most likely to be "last hired" and "first fired," with minorities and less-educated men and women the most susceptible to macroeconomic downturns. Education and skills remain one of the best protections against cyclical downturns in the economy.

The next few tables put the estimated coefficients in table 3.3 to use. Using 2003 as the base year, table 3.4 simulates the impact of increases in the national unemployment rate on the labor market outcomes of non-enrolled teenagers and young adults. The simulation can be viewed as a "what if" exercise of the economy stalling and experiencing a mild or severe recession. For comparison, the table also contains the peak values for the 1990s boom. A 2 percentage point increase in the unemployment rate would push the U.S. unemployment rate from 6.0 to 8.0 percent, which would still be well below the peak of the 1980s recession. A 4 percentage point increase in the unemployment rate would be considered a severe recession, moving the unemployment rate to 10.0 percent, the peak of the 1980s' recession.

Panel A of table 3.4 reveals that a 2 point increase in the U.S. unemployment rate would lower the teenage employment–population ratio by 1.2 percentage points, from 56.6 to 55.4 percent; the employment–population ratio for 20- to 24-year-olds would drop 1.7 points. For both age groups, the decline in the employment–population ratio is solely the result of a fall in the employment rate. A severe recession (a 4 point increase in the national unemployment rate) would lower the teenage employment–population ratio to 52.6 percent and the young adult employment–population ratio to 68.7 percent. The reduction in the employment–population ratios is predominately due to larger decreases in the employment rates. These individuals stay in the labor force.

Panel B of table 3.4 presents the results from another "what if" calculation. It uses the estimates in table 3.3 (the October 2003 average employment, participation, and unemployment rates) and the Bush administration forecasts of the U.S. unemployment rate over the next decade to estimate the potential path of employment, participation, and unemployment for non-enrolled young adults.

Panel B suggests that teenage employment will slowly rise as the national unemployment rate falls from 6.0 percent in 2003 to 5.5 percent

Table 3.4. *Simulations of Changes in the U.S. Unemployment Rate on the Cyclical Behavior of Non-enrolled 16- to 24-Year-Olds by Age (percent)*

	Peak of boom (2000)	Base year (2003)	Percentage Point Increase in Unemployment Rate			
			1.0	2.0	3.0	4.0
Panel A: Assuming 1.0 Point Increases in the U.S. Unemployment Rate						
Age 16–19						
EPOP	63.4	56.6	56.2	55.4	54.2	52.6
EMP	83.2	77.8	75.5	71.2	65.0	57.4
LFP	76.3	72.7	73.7	75.8	79.0	83.5
Age 20–24						
EPOP	78.6	74.1	73.5	72.4	70.8	68.7
EMP	92.9	88.9	87.5	84.8	80.9	76.0
LFP	84.6	83.4	83.6	84.1	84.9	85.8

	Peak of boom (2000)	Base year (2003)	Forecast	
			2004	2005
Panel B: Assuming Bush Administration Forecasts of the U.S. Unemployment Rate				
U.S. unemployment rate	3.9	6.0	5.5	5.3
Age 16–19				
EPOP	63.4	56.6	56.8	56.9
EMP	83.2	77.8	78.9	79.4
LFP	76.3	72.7	72.2	72.0
Age 20–24				
EPOP	78.6	74.1	74.4	74.5
EMP	92.9	88.9	89.6	89.9
LFP	84.6	83.4	83.3	83.2

Source: Author's calculations using published data from the October Supplement of the Current Population Survey, Bureau of Labor Statistics.

Note: Base year corresponds to the year in which the impact of an increase in the unemployment rate is based.

EPOP: Employment–population ratio

EMP: 1 minus the unemployment rate

LFP: Labor force participation rate

in 2004 and 5.3 percent in 2005. At the end of the forecast period, the teenage employment–population ratio will be 6.5 points below its peak during the 1990s boom. The employment–population ratio of 20- to 24-year-olds will be 4.1 percentage points below its 1990s peak. Since the erosion in employment is forecast to be slightly larger for teenagers than young adults, a small expansion in the gap will occur. The key result in this table is that the employment–population ratio fails to return to its peak levels because of lower employment rates (higher unemployment rates), which are the result of a higher national unemployment rate.

To illustrate the macroeconomy's recent inability to absorb the least-skilled Americans, consider the following calculation. If the 2004 forecast of a 5.5 percent U.S. unemployment rate occurs, then compared with 3.9 percent, the boom's lowest unemployment rate, 943,000 fewer less-skilled Americans will be employed. To generate these estimates, first multiply the 2004 forecast of the demographic group (e.g., 16- to 24-year-olds) by its civilian population in 2003. This product equals the predicted employment level in 2004, assuming zero population growth. The calculation for non-enrolled 16- to 24-year-olds is $0.709 \times 15,903,000 = 11,275,227$. Then compare this predicted level of 2004 employment to the level of employment in 2000 ($12,218,000 - 11,275,227 = 942,773$). The difference is the reduction in non-enrolled employment that can be attributed to a higher U.S. unemployment rate.

Table 3.5 presents simulations by race and ethnicity. After the employment–population ratios fall to 74.4, 54.9, and 67.5 percent for non-enrolled whites, blacks, and Hispanics, respectively, they are predicted to rise over the next two years. The white employment–population ratio will fall short of its 1990s peak by 3.4 points. The employment–population ratio of blacks will fall short of its 1990s peak by 2.1 percentage points, and the Hispanic employment–population ratio will also fall short of its 1990s peak, by 0.3 points.

Assuming no population growth, the forecasts in table 3.5 imply that since the boom's peak in 2000, the economy has not been able to absorb 773,000 non-enrolled young whites and 213,000 non-enrolled young blacks; however, the number of non-enrolled young Hispanics has risen by 240,000, due in part to the growth in their population.[10]

Table 3.6 shifts to comparing the future experience of non-enrolled men and women. At the higher national jobless rates, not all of those searching for jobs will be able to obtain employment. The men's employment–population ratio is forecast to be 3.6 percentage points below its

Table 3.5. *Simulations of an Increase in the Unemployment Rate on the Cyclical Behavior of Non-enrolled 16- to 24-Year-Olds by Race and Ethnicity*

	Peak of boom (2000)	Base year (2003)	Forecast 2004	Forecast 2005
U.S. unemployment rate	3.9	6.0	5.5	5.3
White				
EPOP	78.3	74.4	74.8	74.9
EMP	92.6	89.5	90.2	90.6
LFP	84.6	83.1	82.8	82.7
Black				
EPOP	59.5	54.9	56.7	57.4
EMP	81.3	73.9	76.2	77.2
LFP	73.2	74.3	74.3	74.3
Hispanic				
EPOP	70.7	67.5	69.5	70.4
EMP	91.8	87.7	89.4	90.1
LFP	77.0	77.0	77.8	78.1

Source: Author's calculations using published data from the October Supplement of the Current Population Survey, Bureau of Labor Statistics.

Note: Assuming Bush administration forecasts of the U.S. employment rate. Base year corresponds to the year in which the impact of an increase in the unemployment rate is based.

EPOP: Employment–population ratio

EMP: 1 minus the unemployment rate

LFP: Labor force participation rate

peak during the 1990s boom. The women's employment–population ratio is predicted to be 4.3 percentage points below its peak.

The final forecasts disaggregate by educational attainment and gender. Table 3.7 indicates that the forecasted national unemployment rates will not be low enough to absorb the least educated of the non-enrolled. Employment–population ratios of both male and female high school dropouts and graduates will be several percentage points below their peak values during the 1990s boom.

Assuming that the civilian population for these subpopulations does not grow from 2003 to 2005, the implied number of non-enrolled men and women that the economy will not pull in is approximately 983,000,

Table 3.6. *Simulations of an Increase in the Unemployment Rate on the Cyclical Behavior of Non-enrolled 16- to 24-Year-Olds by Gender*

	Peak of boom (2000)	Base year (2003)	Forecast 2004	2005
U.S. unemployment rate	3.9	6.0	5.5	5.3
Men				
EPOP	80.5	75.9	76.6	76.9
EMP	90.7	86.9	87.8	88.1
LFP	88.7	87.4	87.3	87.3
Women				
EPOP	69.4	64.9	65.0	65.1
EMP	91.0	87.0	87.5	87.8
LFP	76.3	74.6	74.3	74.2

Source: Author's calculations using published data from the October Supplement of the Current Population Survey, Bureau of Labor Statistics.

Note: Assuming Bush administration forecasts of the U.S. unemployment rate. Base year corresponds to the year in which the impact of an increase in the unemployment rate is based.

EPOP: Employment–population ratio

EMP: 1 minus the unemployment rate

LFP: Labor force participation rate

with 870,000 (or 88 percent) of these young adults possessing no more than a high school diploma.

These results paint a sobering picture of the future for America's non-enrolled youth, especially minorities and those with low levels of education. The administration forecasts an unemployment rate for 2004 of 5.5 percent, which, given the average actual unemployment rate for January to November is 5.53 percent, will most likely occur. The estimates in this section suggest that when the jobless rate fell to 3.9 percent at the boom's peak, 942,000 additional non-enrolled young adults found jobs.

In the absence of the extremely tight labor markets of the late 1990s, policymakers will have to find other ways to reduce barriers to job search, entry, and retention and to cushion the effects that technological change and globalization may have on the labor market opportunities of the less skilled. These strategies become even more important as the Federal Reserve continues to increase the federal funds rate, which will act to slow the economy. Carpenter and Rodgers (2004) show that contractionary monetary

Table 3.7. *Simulations of an Increase in the Unemployment Rate on the Cyclical Behavior of Non-enrolled 16- to 24-Year-Olds by Educational Attainment*

	Peak of boom (2000)	Base year (2003)	Forecast	
			2004	*2005*
U.S. unemployment rate	3.9	6.0	5.5	5.3
Men				
High school dropout				
EPOP	67.7	64.7	65.9	66.4
EMP	83.7	81.7	83.3	83.9
LFP	80.9	79.2	79.2	79.1
High school graduate				
EPOP	81.3	76.3	77.2	77.6
EMP	90.7	86.5	87.2	87.6
LFP	89.6	88.2	88.4	88.5
Some college				
EPOP	90.1	83.9	84.8	85.1
EMP	97.0	90.4	91.2	91.5
LFP	92.9	92.8	92.9	93.0
College graduate				
EPOP	91.1	86.6	86.7	86.7
EMP	94.4	92.8	92.9	92.9
LFP	96.6	93.3	93.3	93.3
Women				
High school dropout				
EPOP	43.7	38.2	38.6	38.7
EMP	79.7	75.2	76.9	77.5
LFP	54.8	50.8	50.2	49.9
High school graduate				
EPOP	71.2	63.2	63.6	63.8
EMP	91.2	85.2	86.1	86.4
LFP	78.0	74.2	73.9	73.8
Some college				
EPOP	78.8	78.5	78.6	78.7
EMP	94.1	91.5	92.0	92.2
LFP	83.7	85.8	85.5	85.4

(continued)

Table 3.7. (*Continued*)

	Peak of boom (2000)	Base year (2003)	Forecast 2004	2005
Women (continued)				
College graduate				
EPOP	90.9	85.8	86.2	86.4
EMP	96.9	93.8	94.3	94.5
LFP	93.9	91.5	91.4	91.4

Source: Author's calculations using published data from the October Supplement of the Current Population Survey, Bureau of Labor Statistics.

Note: Assuming Bush administration forecasts of the U.S. unemployment rate. Base year corresponds to the year in which the impact of an increase in the unemployment rate is based.

EPOP: Employment–population ratio

EMP: 1 minus the unemployment rate

LFP: Labor force participation rate

policy has a disparate negative effect on the employment–population ratio of the least skilled.

Discussion

This chapter presents estimates of the economic opportunities for less-skilled Americans over the next 10 years. The national unemployment rates forecast by the Bush administration will reflect a growing economy, but with a significantly "looser" labor market. If current policies continue, the future macroeconomy will not exhibit the breadth and depth of the 1990s boom.

Non-enrolled young black men and women are the most cyclically sensitive demographic group. A 1 point increase in the U.S. unemployment rate is associated with a 6.4 percent decline in their employment–population ratio because of an increase in their unemployment rate. Surprisingly, the employment–population ratios of non-enrolled less-educated men and women are extremely sensitive to the macroeconomy. Both results have implications for how a "work first" philosophy toward social safety nets, such as welfare, can successfully function. The results also have implications for the ability of ex-offenders to find jobs.

The chapter uses these empirical relationships and economywide Bush administration forecasts to predict employment–population ratios, labor force participation rates, and employment rates of non-enrolled young adults over the next 10 years. The employment–population ratios of young non-enrolled adults will improve over the next decade but will not return to the record lows of the 1990s boom. The lower employment–population ratios will reflect lower employment rates (higher unemployment rates), especially for non-enrolled blacks, as well as non-enrolled men and women with a high school diploma or less.

If the 2004 forecast of the U.S. unemployment rate is realized, then approximately 940,000 fewer less-skilled Americans will be employed than during the peak of the expansion in 2000. The average U.S. unemployment rate over the first 11 months of 2004 was 5.53 percent, and many experts believe that the jobless rate will fall modestly in 2005.

How could a higher national unemployment rate affect social policy? First, if the Bush administration forecasts come to pass, the economy will not provide the breadth and depth of opportunities it did during the 1990s. Second, the macroeconomic policy that underpins these forecasts provides an upper bound on employment–population ratios for the less-skilled. If policymakers seek to raise the employment–population ratios of non-enrolled young adults, they will have to make skill investments and find other vehicles to stimulate aggregate demand. Third, unless these actions are taken, the pool of untapped (unemployed and out of the labor force, but want a job) and partially tapped (working part-time for economic reasons) individuals will continue to grow over the next 10 years, and "work first" employment and welfare policies will not be as successful. Ex-offenders will have greater difficulty finding employment. Communities in the Mississippi Delta, Appalachia, and others throughout the United States that have persistently high unemployment and poverty rates will be left behind.

What policies could strengthen the employment of less-skilled Americans? For one, policies that foster *continuously* tight labor markets. Finding out why the tremendous fiscal stimuli of tax cuts and expenditures on Iraq, Afghanistan, and homeland security have produced less on the jobs front than the administration and independent analysts hoped it would, and seeking ways to recouple economic and employment growth, are extremely important.

Building the skills of adults and youth in a slow-growing economy will be crucial, especially for non-enrolled young adults. Also, raising the value of work via reasonable increases in the minimum wage and creation of living wages and expansions in the Earned Income Tax

Credit will add to the future wage growth and productivity of less-skilled Americans.

A second group of programs includes holistic geographic grant approaches, such as the Youth Opportunity Grants that target funds to and coordinate resources in areas with high unemployment and poverty rates.

Policies that remove barriers to work are a third part of this comprehensive strategy for work. Today, it is the rule rather than the exception that both parents work, and it goes without saying that single parents have to work. Because of this, access to high-quality child care must receive higher priority. Access to transportation must also be a greater priority. Much of the job growth in recent decades has been in suburban areas, placing a greater premium on having an automobile.

Finally—I mention this only in passing, since the topic is addressed elsewhere in this book—policies need to be strengthened that address the adverse impact of incarceration and the dramatic growth in child support arrears on less-skilled men.

During the late 1990s and in the beginning of 2000, the United States was in an excellent fiscal position to make these investments. It was simply a matter of placing the welfare of less-skilled Americans higher on the list of priorities. Since 2001, however, the fiscal position that would make these investments possible has been severely altered. The massive revenue shortfalls that have emerged in most state governments and the federal government's fiscal actions will undoubtedly constrain serious efforts to address the needs of less-skilled Americans. Years from now, when economic historians write about the 1990s boom, many who focus on social policy may label the period as one of missed opportunities.

NOTES

The first draft of this chapter was completed while Rodgers was the Frances L. and Edwin L. Cummings Associate Professor of Economics and director of the Center for the Study of Equality at the College of William and Mary. The author thanks William Spriggs and participants in the Extending Opportunities Project for helpful comments and suggestions. Rebekah Michael and Matthew Milanovich provided outstanding research assistance.

1. See, for example, Reimers (2000); Freeman and Rodgers (2000); Freeman (2001); and Hoynes, Hines, and Krueger (2001). A second round of studies continues to find gains, but less-skilled, less-educated Americans have not made up the ground they lost from the 1970s to 1980s (Milanovich 2002; see also Holzer and Offner, chapter 2 in this volume).

2. Over the next two years, the Congressional Budget Office's forecasts are similar, ending at 5.6 percent during 2004 and falling slightly to 5.2 percent in 2005 (CBO 2002).

3. See, for example, Hoynes (2000); Thorbecke (1999); Moorthy (1988); Korenman and Okun (1989); Spriggs and Williams (2000); Blank and Blinder (1996); Shulman (1991); Wilson, Tienda, and Wu (1991); and Badgett (1994).

4. The NBER Dating Committee designated November 1982 to July 1990 and March 1991 to March 2001 as expansions.

5. The white teenage record was set in August 1978. The black teenage record was set in June 1998.

6. Just as Clark and Summers experimented with different lag structures, I also tried different structures and found that the estimates of the cyclical response were robust to choice of lag structures.

7. Using quarterly data from 1954 to 1976, Clark and Summers (1981, 1990) obtain an estimate for teenage white women and men of 4.25 and 4.4 percent, with 2.78 and 2.38 points of the relationship coming from a decline in participation.

8. I obtain this value by summing −1.938 and −1.004, the estimates for the employment and participation rates in column 1 of table 3.1.

9. Monthly labor force information on Hispanic teenagers is not published.

10. These estimates are constructed as follows: multiply the 2004 forecast of the demographic group (e.g., non-enrolled whites) by its civilian population in 2003. This product equals the predicted employment level in 2004, assuming that population remained constant. The calculation for non-enrolled whites is 0.748 × 12,570,000 = 9,402,360. Compare this predicted level of 2004 employment with the level of employment in 2000 (10,175,000 − 9,402,360 = 772,640). The difference is the decline in employment that we attribute to a higher national unemployment rate. For non-enrolled blacks, the predicted difference is 213,385 [1,543,000 − (0.567 × 2,345,000)]. For non-enrolled Hispanics, the predicted difference is −239,800 [2,151,000 − (0.695 × 3,440,000)].

REFERENCES

Badgett, M. V. 1994. "Rising Black Unemployment: Changes in Job Stability or in Employability?" *Review of Black Political Economy* 22(3): 55–75.

Blank, Rebecca, and Alan Blinder. 1996. "Macroeconomics, Income Distribution, and Poverty." In *Fighting Poverty: What Works and What Doesn't*, edited by Sheldon Danziger and Daniel Weinberg (180–208). Cambridge, MA: Harvard University Press.

Carpenter, Seth B., and William M. Rodgers III. 2004. "The Disparate Labor Market Impacts of Monetary Policy." *Journal of Policy Analysis and Management* 23(4): 813–30.

Clark, Kim B., and Lawrence H. Summers. 1981. "Demographic Differences in Cyclical Employment Variation." *Journal of Human Resources* 16(1): 61–79.

———. 1990. "Demographic Differences in Cyclical Employment Variation." In *Understanding Unemployment*, edited by Lawrence H. Summers (111–20). Cambridge, MA: MIT Press.

Congressional Budget Office. 2002. *The Budget and Economic Outlook: Fiscal Years 2003–2012*. Washington, DC: Congressional Budget Office. Available at www.cbo.gov.

Freeman, Richard B. 2001. "The Rising Tide Lifts. . . ?" Working Paper 8155. Cambridge, MA: National Bureau of Economic Research.

Freeman, Richard B., and William M. Rodgers III. 2000. "Area Economic Conditions and the Labor Market Outcomes of Young Men in the 1990s Expansion." In *Prosperity for All? The Economic Boom and African Americans,* edited by Robert Cherry and William M. Rodgers III (50–87). New York: Russell Sage Foundation.

Hoynes, Hilary W. 2000. "The Employment, Earnings, and Income of Less Skilled Workers over the Business Cycle." In *Finding Jobs: Work and Welfare Reform,* edited by David Card and Rebecca Blank (23–71). New York: Russell Sage Foundation.

Hoynes, Hilary, James Hines Jr., and Alan Krueger. 2001. "Another Look at Whether a Rising Tide Lifts All Boats." In *The Roaring Nineties: Can Full Employment be Sustained?* edited by Alan Krueger and Robert Solow (493–537). New York: Russell Sage Foundation.

Korenman, Sanders, and Barbara Okun. 1989. "Gender Differences in Cyclical Unemployment." In *Structural Changes in U.S. Labor Markets: Causes and Consequences,* edited by Randall W. Eberts and Erica L. Groshen (177–95). Armonk, NY, and London: Sharpe.

Milanovich, Matthew. 2002. "How Great Was the 1990s Boom?" Unpublished manuscript, Center for the Study of Equality, The College of William and Mary.

Moorthy, Vivek. 1988. "On Demographic Adjustments to Estimates of the Natural Rate of Unemployment: A Note." Working Papers in Applied Economic Theory 88–01. San Francisco: Federal Reserve Bank of San Francisco.

Reimers, Cordelia. 2000. "The Effect of Tight Labor Markets on Unemployment of Hispanics and African Americans: The 1990s Experience." In *Prosperity for All? The Economic Boom and African Americans,* edited by Robert Cherry and William M. Rodgers III (3–49). New York: Russell Sage Foundation.

Shulman, Steven. 1991. "Why Is the Black Unemployment Rate Always Twice as High as the White Unemployment Rate?" In *New Approaches to Economics and Social Analyses of Discrimination,* edited by Richard Cornwall and Phanindra Wunnava (5–38). New York: Praeger.

Spriggs, William, and Rhonda Williams. 2000. "What Do We Need to Explain About African American Unemployment?" In *Prosperity for All? The Economic Boom and African Americans,* edited by Robert Cherry and William M. Rodgers III (188–207). New York: Russell Sage Foundation.

Thorbecke, Willem. 1999. "Further Evidence on the Distributional Effects of Disinflationary Monetary Policy." Levy Institute Working Paper 264. Annandale-on-Hudson, NY: Levy Economics Institute of Bard College.

U.S. Federal Reserve Board of Governors. "Increases in the Federal Funds Rates." http://www.federalreserve.gov/fomc/fundsrate.htm.

Wilson, F., Marta Tienda, and L. Wu. 1991. "Racial Equality in the Labor Market: Still an Elusive Goal." Paper presented to the American Sociological Association annual meeting, Cincinnati, August 23.

4

How Do Employer Perceptions of Crime and Incarceration Affect the Employment Prospects of Less-Educated Young Black Men?

Harry J. Holzer, Steven Raphael, and Michael A. Stoll

The very high rates of incarceration and participation in crime among young black men are well known. About a million black men are currently incarcerated, and millions more are either ex-inmates or felons who are or have been on probation.

How does the high rate of criminal activity and incarceration among young black men affect their employment rates? The currently incarcerated are not included in the population of young men on which the estimated employment rates are based; the rates would look far worse if they were. But the employment and earnings of noninstitutional young black men are likely reduced by previous incarceration or participation in crime, in several ways. These reductions are apparently the result of both demand- and supply-side factors in the labor market—employers' reluctance to hire young men with criminal records, and deteriorated skills, employment networks, or interest in legitimate employment among the young men themselves.

What is perhaps less obvious is that the high rates of crime and incarceration among young black men are likely to reduce the employment prospects of those with no criminal background themselves. Employers frequently cannot distinguish accurately between those who do and do not have criminal backgrounds. So, they may tend to avoid hiring those whom they suspect of having criminal records, and they most likely suspect young black men with poor educational attainment and relatively little work experience. If employers avoid hiring young black men, that reluctance would constitute a classic case of statistical discrimination, albeit one that has received little attention in the research literature to date. This avoidance may also help explain why the employment rate of young black men declined in the 1990s as the incarceration rate for this population rose (see chapter 2, this volume).

This chapter considers evidence on how incarceration rates affect the employment and earnings prospects of young black men. It begins by reviewing how criminal records influence the employment prospects of those who have them and estimating how many young black men this affects. It then provides new evidence on employers' reluctance to hire those with criminal records and their limited tendencies to check for criminal backgrounds and thereby gain accurate information on exactly who has such records. This lack of information leads to a reduced tendency to hire black men in general. The data used for this analysis are from a recent survey of employers in several large metropolitan areas and thus give fairly direct evidence on the reduced demand for the labor of young black men that results from incarceration. This chapter discusses the implications of these results for employment among young men and policies to deal with these limitations.

How Crime and Incarceration Affect Employment Outcomes

To understand the relationship between crime and the employment rates of young black men, it is useful to distinguish among three different possibilities for any individual currently or previously engaged in criminal activity: he participates in crime but has not yet been incarcerated; he has been arrested, convicted, or incarcerated; and he has been released from prison.[1]

The decision to participate in crime often entails a decision to engage less fully in legitimate employment. All these effects may not be directly causal, as both decisions can be viewed as the joint products of having relatively weak employment opportunities and more substantial criminal ones.[2] Still, the decision to participate in crime reinforces the decision to forgo regular employment, at least some of the time. Employers may also seek to avoid hiring anyone engaged in criminal activity and who therefore might entail a risk to their customers, their property, and so on (Holzer, Raphael, and Stoll 2004).

Likewise, once people have been incarcerated and released, their incarceration may negatively affect their own decisions to participate in the labor market, their skills and work experience, and their employment networks. Employer willingness to hire them will also be reduced. Legal factors further restrict the ability of employers to hire ex-offenders in certain sectors.[3] Together, these considerations imply that, all else equal, both participation in crime and incarceration should be associated with lower earnings or employment for individual young men, especially those with poor skills and other barriers to labor market success.

Of course, prisoners cannot be employed while incarcerated. But prisoners are also not counted as part of the civilian population. This implies that, while the effects of both crime and incarceration on *actual* employment and earnings are uniformly negative, their effects on *observed* employment may not be. Indeed, by eliminating less-employable individuals from the sample used to measure employment rates, the effects of crime and incarceration on observed employment rates could be positive, even while their actual effects are negative. This phenomenon may also be partly true for the nonincarcerated who participate in crime before or after a spell of incarceration, who are less likely than other young men to appear in a sample of individuals responding to surveys.[4]

Despite these caveats, the effects of crime and incarceration on the observed employment of young black men depend on two factors: the numbers of young men who engage in crime and/or are incarcerated, and the magnitude of the effects of those factors on their legitimate employment and earnings, both before and after incarceration.

Very large numbers of young black men participate in crime and are incarcerated. There are roughly 5 million young black men age 16 to 34 in the noninstitutional population. Of these, perhaps 600,000–700,000 engage in illegal activity each year. A comparable number of young black men is currently incarcerated (but not counted as part of the 5 million). Of those not currently imprisoned, perhaps an additional 500,000 are on felony probation.[5] In addition, the number of young black men released from prison and sent back into their communities each year is likely large, as is the total number of ex-prisoners or ex-felons.[6]

In all, as many as half of all noninstitutional young black men are likely to be engaged in crime or to have been so engaged in the past. The exact breakdown of these categories, however, differs across the various age subgroups in this population. Among those age 16 to 24, crime and arrest rates are quite high, while incarceration rates and especially the presence of ex-offenders are relatively small. The opposite is likely to be true for those age 25 to 34.[7]

The contemporaneous employment and earnings of anyone who participates in crime are somewhat reduced, though (as noted earlier) this effect is not fully causal.[8] The effect of incarceration on subsequent economic activity is less clear. Freeman (1999) estimates that incarceration can reduce subsequent employment by as much as 25 percent, while others find much smaller effects on employment (Grogger 1995; Kling 2000). However, most studies show negative effects on subsequent earnings of 10 to 20 percent or more, even if the employment effects are small (Kling, Weiman, and Western 2000).[9] Thus, the very large numbers of individuals engaging in crime or being incarcerated, combined with at least moderate effects of these factors on their earnings or employment, suggest a negative effect on observed labor market outcomes.

In addition, these estimates could *understate* the negative effects of crime on observed outcomes. Much of the literature on crime and employment deals with the weak, unobserved personal characteristics of those engaging in crime—their skills, motivation, family backgrounds, or employment networks. These characteristics might have led those involved in crime to have negative labor market outcomes regardless of their decisions to participate in crime, in which case the effects of criminal activity might appear more negative than they really are.

Other biases in the estimated statistical relationships between employment outcomes and crime or incarceration could have the opposite effect. As noted above, crime and incarceration eliminate many individuals from the data samples; thus, we are unable to fully observe their negative effects on outcomes and may mistakenly see positive effects on the composition of the remaining individuals in the samples. Further, there is considerable evidence of underreporting in self-reported survey data on crime, especially among young black men (Hindelang, Hirschi, and Weis 1981; Viscusi 1986). Since underreporting constitutes a form of measurement error in the independent variable, it is likely to cause a bias toward zero in estimated effects of crime on outcomes.[10]

An additional source of bias in the estimates comes from the likely effect of crime on those who do *not* participate in it as well as those who do. Since employers cannot distinguish perfectly between those who participate in crime and those who do not, they may well avoid hiring anyone whom they suspect of such activity. Indeed, if individuals choose to conceal their participation in criminal activities, employers have no certain way to infer that behavior in the absence of incarceration. Once an individual has been incarcerated, employers might learn about it from conducting a criminal background check. But, at least until recently, many employers have chosen to forgo such checks, given the costs and difficulties involved. While some evidence says these costs are declining with Internet-based searches, we see little direct evidence that employer behavior has substantially changed in response to these lowered costs.

The next section provides direct empirical evidence of employer reluctance to hire those with criminal records and employer tendencies to conduct background checks. For now, though, we can say that employers likely discriminate statistically against less-skilled young black men, which negatively affects their employment rates. This, in turn, contributes to a bias toward zero in any estimated effects of crime and incarceration on individual employment outcomes for those who engage in crime compared with those who do not.

While the effects of crime and incarceration on outcomes are likely negative, can they also account for the trends over time toward lower employment of young black men observed in the 1980s and 1990s (chapter 2, this volume)? The well-known drop in the nation's crime rate during the 1990s may initially suggest that, all else equal, employment should be rising among young black men. Incarceration rates continued to climb for most of the 1990s, however, even though crime rates declined. More important, the reentry of incarcerated individuals into society has risen dramatically over the past several years (Travis, Solomon, and Waul 2001). This implies that many more individuals are subject to the negative effects of previous incarceration than was true a few years ago.

Of course, given there is relatively more crime but relatively fewer ex-offenders among younger males than among somewhat older groups, the trends described above should contribute more to the declining employment among young black men age 25 to 34 than to declining employment among those age 16 to 24. But employment declined more sharply for the younger group in the 1990s (chapter 2, this volume).

Perhaps these issues contributed more to the declines in employment among very young black men in the 1970s and 1980s, when crime was rising. Alternatively, the drop in crime in the 1990s could be contributing to declining *estimates* of employment rates, rather than declining actual employment, if more young men with poor skills are now being observed in the data samples on which we estimate these rates. Or, given employers' imperfect information about individual tendencies to participate in crime or become incarcerated, perhaps the growing presence of ex-offenders is adversely affecting younger workers through its effect on employer perceptions and behavior.

In sum, participation in crime and incarceration clearly seems to contribute to lower earnings and/or employment among young black men. There are likely to be direct negative effects on those who participate and indirect effects on younger black men in general. The trend over time toward higher incarceration rates and a greater presence of ex-offenders in the population should help explain declining employment trends among some groups of young black men, while the effects of declining crime rates in the 1990s on the youngest group may be somewhat more mixed.

Employer Hiring Activity

While the studies described above focused on the direct effects of crime and/or incarceration on the employment and earnings of young men who engage in crime, the data presented below focus on the indirect effects of criminal activity on the employment of young black men, including those who might not be directly engaged in crime. These effects occur because employers have imperfect information on exactly which job applicants engage in crime, so they may become more reluctant to hire any less-educated young black men.[11] This reluctance is a form of statistical discrimination, in which employers make employment decisions based on characteristics of the groups individuals belong to when it is too costly to gain more information about the individuals themselves.[12] The more information is available to employers about the criminal histories of individuals, the less likely they are to discriminate against young black men in general, even if these employers are reluctant to hire individuals with criminal records.

To analyze the effects of employer attitudes and behaviors regarding criminal background on the hiring of young black men, we use data from a recent survey of employers in four large metropolitan areas. The survey, designed as part of the Multi-City Study of Urban Inequality, is described at length in Holzer (1996). It was administered by telephone to the individual responsible for entry-level hiring at about 3,000 establishments in Atlanta, Boston, Detroit, and Los Angeles between 1992 and 1994. Larger establishments were overweighted to generate a sample that accurately reflected the distribution of workers across establishment size categories in the workforce. Response rates averaged roughly 70 percent, and little evidence of significant response bias was found across observable characteristics of the establishments.[13]

Survey respondents were asked various questions about general characteristics of the establishment and its hiring practices, as well as questions about the last worker hired into a job that did not require a college degree. Of particular interest here is a question about the employer's preferences regarding the hiring of disadvantaged workers. Employers were asked whether they would have been willing to hire members of various disadvantaged or stigmatized groups into the last noncollege job they filled; the categories included welfare recipients, the long-term unemployed, those with only short-term or part-time work experience, and those with criminal records. Possible responses to this question were "definitely," "probably," "probably not," and "definitely not." In addition, employers were asked whether they checked the criminal backgrounds of applicants to this job, with possible responses of "always," "sometimes," and "never."

Table 4.1 presents the stated preferences of employers toward hiring members of various stigmatized groups. According to the data, employers are much more reluctant to hire ex-offenders than welfare recipients, the long-term unemployed, or any other group. Indeed, less than 40 percent of employers would "definitely" or "probably" fill their last noncollege job with an ex-offender.

Table 4.1. *Employer Willingness to Hire Workers from Stigmatized Groups (percent)*

	Employers That . . .			
	Definitely would hire	Probably would hire	Probably would not hire	Definitely would not hire
Applicant				
with a criminal record	13	26	42	20
on welfare	52	40	7	1
with a GED	57	39	2	1
with a spotty work history	19	40	35	6
unemployed for a year	29	54	16	2

Source: Survey data from the Multi-City Study of Urban Inequality.

Note: Rows do not always total 100 because of rounding.

In contrast, over 90 percent of employers would definitely or probably hire a welfare recipient, 96 percent are likely to hire a worker with a GED, and over 80 percent are likely to hire a worker who has been unemployed for more than a year. Interestingly, employers were particularly averse to hiring applicants with spotty work histories, which in themselves may signal previous involvement with the criminal justice system. Nonetheless, even workers with spotty work histories are preferred by a fairly large margin to workers with criminal histories.

Note the question makes no reference to any other characteristics of the groups that might limit their employability, such as skills, substance abuse, or general work readiness. All these characteristics are likely serious barriers to employment for ex-offenders, even when employers are willing to hire from this group (Travis et al. 2001). Limited evidence from a more recent survey of employers suggests that, even during the very tight labor markets of the 1990s, employers were only slightly more willing to hire ex-offenders.[14]

Of course, employers' ability to avoid hiring ex-offenders also depends on their ability to distinguish ex-offenders from other applicants. Table 4.2 presents data on how often employers check criminal backgrounds in filling noncollege jobs. Responses to this question are presented for the overall sample of employers, as well as by their stated willingness to hire ex-offenders.

At the time of the survey, most employers did not regularly check the criminal backgrounds of those they hired. Employers opposed to hiring

Table 4.2. *How Frequently Employers Check the Criminal Backgrounds of Job Applicants (percent)*

	Employers That . . .		
	Always check	Sometimes check	Never check
All firms	32	17	51
Willingness to hire ex-offenders			
Definitely would	19	20	61
Probably would	26	21	53
Probably would not	30	18	53
Definitely would not	56	12	32

Source: Survey data from the Multi-City Study of Urban Inequality.

Note: Rows do not always total 100 because of rounding.

ex-offenders perform background checks somewhat more frequently than employers more open to hiring ex-offenders, though even among opponents the share that always checks is only a slight majority.

One reason employers check backgrounds infrequently may be the time, cost, and inconvenience involved. Anecdotal evidence suggests these costs may be diminishing over time, as both private and public data sources on backgrounds become more available over the Internet (Holzer et al. 2004). Whether employer behavior has responded to these lower costs by increasing the frequency of checks is yet unknown. Evidence from a recent similar survey of employers in Los Angeles suggests employers' use of background checks increased over the 1990s. Survey data for Los Angeles in 2001 indicate that about 63 percent of employers always or sometimes check the criminal backgrounds of those they hire, compared with about 48 percent in the 1992–94 Los Angeles portion of the Multi-City employer data.[15] It is unknown whether the use of background checks increased as substantially in the rest of the nation during the 1990s, when employment rates of young black men were continuing their secular decline of the past several decades.

Some other characteristics of employers are presented in table 4.3, according to whether they are willing to hire ex-offenders and whether they check for criminal backgrounds. Employer characteristics include their industry, size, and location (central city or not) and whether they use affirmative action in recruiting. Also included in this table are some characteristics of the last job filled, such as the daily tasks performed and the required qualifications.

Several interesting findings emerge on the characteristics of employers and jobs open to ex-offenders and whether backgrounds are checked. For instance, larger employers seem more willing to hire ex-offenders than smaller ones; those in manufacturing more willing than those in retail trade, the financial sector, or other service industries; and those using affirmative action more willing than those not using it.

Willingness to hire ex-offenders also seems to be strongly related to the tasks performed on the job and other hiring requirements. For instance, jobs that require daily contact with customers are clearly less available to those with criminal records than those that do not, perhaps reflecting employer concerns about customer safety and potential negligent hiring lawsuits. Similarly, jobs requiring high school diplomas or references are less available than those not requiring them, likely reflecting that jobs requiring greater skills or employer trust of personal qualities tend to be

text continues on page 78

Table 4.3. *Establishment Characteristics by Employer Likelihood of Hiring Applicants with Criminal Backgrounds Crossed with Whether Employer Checks the Criminal Backgrounds of Job Applicants (percent, unless otherwise noted)*

	Willing to hire, doesn't check	Willing to hire, checks	Unwilling to hire, doesn't check	Unwilling to hire, checks
Size, Industry, Location, and Staff Characteristics				
Size				
< 20 employees	33	24	45	29
20–99 employees	33	31	33	32
100–499 employees	29	27	18	27
500–999 employees	3	7	2	6
1,000+ employees	3	11	2	7
Industry				
Mining	0	0	0	0
Construction	3	3	2	2
Manufacturing	38	19	22	11
Transportation, communications, and utilities	4	7	5	7
Wholesale trade	8	8	10	5
Retail trade	16	18	20	17
Finance, insurance, and real estate	4	4	9	16
Services	26	36	30	36
% union	11.99	17.28	8.22	19.59
Central city	0.26	0.32	0.28	0.27
Black hiring agent	0.05	0.08	0.03	0.07
Distance black	18.21	17.22	17.82	17.45
Distance white	22.89	22.26	22.35	22.60
Recruitment Methods				
Help Wanted signs	24	34	21	28
Newspaper ads	43	50	45	53
Walk-ins	72	80	64	70
Referrals from				
Current employees	82	86	80	85
State agency	36	50	24	36
Private agency	20	25	19	20
Community agency	23	35	20	28

Table 4.3. (*Continued*)

	Willing to hire, doesn't check	Willing to hire, checks	Unwilling to hire, doesn't check	Unwilling to hire, checks
School	31	42	29	41
Union	5	10	3	9
Uses affirmative action to recruit	52	64	43	60
Screening Methods				
Drug test/physical exam	11	24	11	21
Aptitude test	7	13	13	15
Knowledge test	15	20	15	17
Personality test	4	6	7	8
Background checks				
Criminal background	0	100	0	100
Education	57	82	55	81
References	91	98	94	98
Daily Job Tasks				
Customer contact	43	59	57	70
Phone conversations	47	50	58	53
Reading	55	55	50	58
Writing	28	28	31	31
Math/computations	65	64	69	63
Computer work	46	48	55	51
Job Qualifications				
High school diploma	60	69	73	77
Recent work experience	67	66	68	71
Specific experience	60	58	61	61
References	62	75	71	78
Vocational education	39	39	38	39
Very Important Requirement of New Employees				
Physical attractiveness	8	12	12	14
Physical neatness	42	49	59	56
Politeness	70	72	82	81
Verbal skills	53	55	65	66
Motivation	59	73	78	74
Ability to speak English	46	47	62	60

(*continued*)

Table 4.3. (*Continued*)

	Willing to hire, doesn't check	Willing to hire, checks	Unwilling to hire, doesn't check	Unwilling to hire, checks
Type of Applicant That Would Probably Not Be Hired				
On welfare	3	4	15	11
With GED	1	2	7	4
Spotty work history	30	32	54	45
Unemployed for a year	12	10	26	19

Source: Survey data from the Multi-City Study of Urban Inequality.

Notes: All figures use the sample weights. Employers who answer that they "definitely will" or "probably will" hire applicants with criminal histories are coded as willing. Employers who check criminal backgrounds "always" or "sometimes" are coded as checking. Numbers do not always total 100 because of rounding.

less open to ex-offenders. Since the percentages of jobs requiring these skills appear to be growing over time and in the sectors less amenable to ex-offenders, the proportion of jobs available to ex-offenders is probably declining, despite their increasing presence in the population.[16]

Even among employers who seem relatively less willing to hire ex-offenders, the tendency to check criminal backgrounds varies considerably. For instance, smaller employers that do not want to hire ex-offenders are considerably less likely to check criminal background than larger employers with similar preferences. Those that have unionized workforces or engage in affirmative action are considerably more likely to check than those who do not, even among those unwilling to hire. All these findings suggest that employers who are relatively less sophisticated about hiring, and perhaps those with fewer resources to invest in it, are less inclined to perform background checks than are those with similar preferences but greater sophistication and resources.[17]

Since some employers gain more information than others about individual applicants' tendencies to engage in crime or be incarcerated, we would expect differences in overall hiring behavior and outcomes associated with such activity. More specifically, those who do not want to hire ex-offenders but who do not engage in criminal background checks should, all else equal, engage in more statistical discrimination and hire fewer black men than those who have similar preferences but check backgrounds.

Table 4.4 presents some data on this issue. It shows the percentages of recently filled noncollege jobs into which black men were hired, according to whether the firm performs background checks ("sometimes" or "always") and whether the firm states a willingness to hire ex-offenders ("definitely" or "probably"). Since the ability or willingness of firms to hire black men should vary according to many other characteristics as well—some observed in the data and some not—a comparison of how hiring black men varies by the use of criminal background checks among those willing to hire ex-offenders versus those unwilling to constitutes a "difference-in-differences" method of controlling for these other determinants of hiring behavior.[18]

Table 4.4 shows a small overall difference in the hiring of black men between employers who are willing to hire ex-offenders and those who are not. Among employers willing to hire, 11 percent of recent hires are black males, compared with 8.9 percent for unwilling employers. This

Table 4.4. *Proportion of Recently Filled Noncollege Jobs into Which Black Men Were Hired, by Firm Preferences and Use of Background Checks (percent)*

	All firms	Firms willing to hire	Firms unwilling to hire	Δ (unwilling − willing)
All firms	9.0 (0.005)	11.0 (0.010)	8.9 (0.007)	−2.1 (0.012)*
Firms that check backgrounds	10.2 (0.008)	11.8 (0.016)	11.7 (0.011)	−0.1 (0.019)
Firms that do not check backgrounds	8.0 (0.007)	10.7 (0.13)	6.1 (0.009)	−4.6 (0.016)***
Δ (check − don't)	2.3 (0.011)**	1.1 (0.021)	5.6 (0.015)**	4.4 (0.025)*

Source: Author calculations based on survey data from the Multi-City Study of Urban Inequality.

Notes: Standard errors are in parentheses. Firms that always or sometimes check criminal backgrounds are coded as checking. Firms that state that they "definitely will" or "probably will" hire a worker with a criminal background are coded as willing to hire, while firms stating "probably not" or "absolutely not" are coded as unwilling.

*Difference significant at the 10 percent level of confidence.

**Difference significant at the 5 percent level of confidence.

***Difference significant at the 1 percent level of confidence.

difference, however, is considerably larger among firms that do not check criminal backgrounds. Among firms that perform checks, there is virtually no difference in the percentage of recent hires that is black. Among firms that do not perform checks, the proportion of recently filled jobs going to black males is 4.6 percentage points lower among firms unwilling to hire. This difference is significant at the 1 percent level of confidence.

The data can be also summarized by comparing establishments that check criminal backgrounds with establishments that do not by their stated hiring preferences. Overall, 10.2 percent of recently filled jobs went to black males at firms that check backgrounds, while the comparable figure for firms that do not check is 8 percent. Among firms willing to hire ex-offenders, there is no statistically discernible effect of checking on the proportion of hires that are black males. Among firms unwilling to hire, however, the percentage of new jobs going to black males is 5.6 percentage points higher than the proportion of jobs filled by black males at firms that do not check (significant at the 5 percent level of confidence).[19]

Subtracting the impact of background checks among firms willing to hire from the comparable effect among firms unwilling to hire provides the "difference-in-difference" estimate of the impact of criminal background checks on the propensity to hire black males.[20] As can be seen, the effect of a background check is larger for firms that are unwilling to hire, yielding a positive difference-in-difference estimate of 4.4 percentage points (significant at the 10 percent level).

Thus, the data suggest that employers who are unwilling to hire ex-offenders but who do not check for criminal backgrounds may engage in statistical discrimination against black men more broadly, based on the employers' aversion to hiring ex-offenders as well as their very limited information about exactly which individuals in their applicant pool have this characteristic.

Conclusion

This chapter reviews existing empirical evidence on the relationship between crime or incarceration and the employment of young black men. While some relationship clearly exists, the true relationship may be stronger than what has been observed in various studies to date, for numerous reasons.

The chapter also presents new evidence from a survey of employers on the relationships between employers' willingness to hire ex-offenders, their tendency to check criminal records, and their tendency to hire black men. The high rates of crime and incarceration among young black men limit the employment opportunities of those directly engaged in such behavior and may also indirectly limit the employment opportunities of those not engaged in crime. This is principally because employers with imperfect information about individual backgrounds are likely to engage in statistical discrimination against black men.

Whether these barriers to employment have increased or decreased over time, and whether they can account for observed employment trends among different ages of young black men, remain somewhat uncertain. Nonetheless, the data strongly imply that the growing presence of ex-offenders among low-income black men has serious negative consequences for employment rates.

Employers may have grown more willing to hire ex-offenders because of the very tight labor markets of the late 1990s, though so far the data have not suggested willingness has increased.[21] The data also suggest employers have grown more willing to perform criminal background checks as the Internet makes such information more accessible. If so, this could improve the employment prospects of less-skilled young men as a group, even while it decreases prospects for those who have been offenders in the recent past. But it is important to ensure the accuracy of these data, and currently there is little government regulation or oversight of background check data often privately provided by for-profit firms on the Internet.

Other policies that might improve employer demand for those with criminal records might include reconsidering federal and state laws that bar offenders from working in many professions and economic sectors; loosening the restrictions on private-sector employers interested in hiring offenders while they are still behind bars (from which offenders might gain useful work experience); updating and extending the federal bonding program (that insures employers for up to $5,000 in losses that might be attributable to ex-offenders whom they hire) and tax credits (like the Work Opportunity Tax Credit) designed to encourage employer hiring of offenders; and creating more financial support for programs designed to aid the transition of newly released offenders into life outside prison.[22] Of course, any efforts that might prevent criminality in the first place, by improving the basic skills and early work experience of at-risk young males, would be welcome as well.

NOTES

1. In this example, those who have been convicted of a crime but put on probation would go straight to the third category, though the disadvantages associated with probation may be fewer than those associated with incarceration.

2. A fuller model of the decision to participate in crime would adjust the relative returns to legal versus illegal work, adjusting the latter for the risks and costs of being caught and punished. The classic treatment of this issue is in Becker (1968).

3. Economic sectors that legally restrict the hiring of ex-offenders include those involving finances, interstate transport of goods, child care, or patient care.

4. The undercount of young black men in almost any survey is greater than that of any other demographic group (Bound 1986).

5. These estimates of the numbers of young men who engage in illegal activity are based on those of Freeman (1996), after adjusting for the declining crime rate of the 1990s and for the fact that roughly two-thirds of those imprisoned for crime are below the age of 35 (Western and Pettit 2000). The estimate of those on felony probation is from Uggen, Manza, and Thompson (2001) and is similarly adjusted for age.

6. Roughly 600,000 men are now released from prison each year (Travis et al. 2001), of which about half are black and about a quarter are young black men. Many of these men will reenter prison within a few years. Uggen et al. (2001) estimate the total stock of ex-prisoners and ex-felons by race, and suggest there may be a half a million or more young black men in the former category and a million or more in the latter.

7. See Freeman (1999) for evidence that crime and arrest rates peak near the age of 20 for most young men. In contrast, Travis et al. (2001) report that the average age of those returning to society after incarceration is about 34.

8. Freeman (1996) shows that, even before incarceration, employment rates among those who admit engaging in illegal activities in surveys are significantly lower than among those who do not. Employment rates among those engaging in such activities are nevertheless substantial. Employment rates of individuals who have been charged with a crime are nearly 20 percent lower than those of other youth; for those who are subsequently jailed, employment rates are over 50 percent lower.

9. Only Grogger's evidence suggests very limited effects on both employment and wages. His data, which link unemployment insurance records on earnings to legal records from California, suggest more negative effects from incarceration than from just arrest or conviction, and significant short-term effects from any involvement with the criminal justice system that tend to fade over time.

10. This statement assumes the measurement error is "classical," or uncorrelated with any other independent variables.

11. While many application forms ask whether the applicant has a criminal record, applicants have little incentive to answer these questions truthfully—especially if they believe that admitting to a criminal record will preclude them from getting hired, while concealing such a background may enable them to get hired. If employers become aware of their backgrounds later, the most serious consequence of providing inaccurate information would be losing a job they might not have gained in the first place had they been more forthcoming.

12. For a comprehensive discussion of statistical discrimination models, see Altonji and Blank (1999). For an earlier discussion of how imperfect information about criminal background might generate such discrimination against young black men, see Bushway (1996).

13. Samples were drawn from lists of employers compiled by Survey Sampling Incorporated. Since these lists include information on the industry, size category, and location of nonrespondents as well as respondents, it was possible to test for differences in response rates across these categories, and relatively little was found (see the appendix to Holzer 1996 for more detail). In addition, the characteristics of the establishments surveyed were broadly similar to those observed in other data sources, such as the County Business Patterns, for the relevant periods and locations.

14. Holzer et al. (2004) compare the earlier survey results to data from a 1998–99 survey that focused primarily on employer willingness to hire welfare recipients (see also Holzer and Stoll 2001). The percentage of employers willing to hire ex-offenders rose by only about 3 points (from 38 to 41 percent) between the two surveys. For additional evidence on the aversion of employers to hiring men with criminal records from a recent tester study of employers, see Pager (2003).

15. The 2001 Los Angeles Employer Survey collected data from 619 firms and used the same sampling framework as the 1992–94 Multi-City Employer Survey.

16. Holzer et al. (2004) compare the numbers of jobs potentially available to ex-offenders with the supply of ex-offenders in the population. The analysis suggests that, while there may be sufficient jobs available to them in the aggregate, the very high concentration of ex-offenders among young black men in low-income neighborhoods makes a mismatch between the number of jobs available and the number of ex-offenders who need them much more likely.

17. For evidence on how employer size and affirmative action are associated with employer hiring behavior, and especially recruiting and screening practices, see Holzer (1998) and Holzer and Neumark (2000).

18. In other words, if the tendency to check criminal backgrounds happens to be correlated with other firm or employer characteristics, these characteristics should be captured by the difference in hiring outcomes between firms willing to hire offenders that check and those that do not. Subtracting this difference from the comparable one among those unwilling to hire should help isolate the true effects of checking backgrounds from effects that reflect other unobserved differences between employers. For a more complete analysis that also uses regression equations to control for observable differences across firms, see Holzer, Raphael, and Stoll (2001).

19. The hiring patterns for white and Hispanic men differ from those for blacks. White men are more likely to be hired by employers who do not check backgrounds than by those who do (24 percent versus 21 percent) among firms unwilling to hire ex-offenders. Similar results hold for Hispanic men (8 percent versus 6 percent). Thus, the relationship observed between background checks and aversion to hiring offenders seems unique to black men.

20. This can also be calculated by the effect of being unwilling to hire ex-offenders among firms that do not check from the comparable effect for firms that do check.

21. The most recent survey evidence on this question is from early 1999. Willingness to hire ex-offenders may have grown sharply over the subsequent two years as the

economic boom proceeded and other potential sources of low-wage labor were more fully exhausted.

22. These options are discussed at greater length in Holzer et al. (2004).

REFERENCES

Altonji, Joseph, and Rebecca Blank. 1999. "Race and Gender in the Labor Market." In *The Handbook of Labor Economics*, vol. 3C, edited by Orley Ashenfelter and David Card. New York: Elsevier.

Becker, Gary. 1968. "Crime and Punishment: An Economic Approach." *Journal of Political Economy* 76(2): 169–217.

Bound, John. 1986. "Appendix: NBER–Mathematica Survey of Inner-City Black Youth: An Analysis of the Undercount of Older Youths." In *The Black Youth Employment Crisis,* edited by Richard Freeman and Harry J. Holzer (443–60). Chicago: University of Chicago Press.

Bushway, Shawn. 1996. "Labor Market Effects of Permitting Employer Access to Criminal History Records." Working paper. College Park: University of Maryland.

Freeman, Richard. 1996. "Why Do So Many Young American Men Commit Crimes and What Might Do About It?" *Journal of Economic Perspectives* 10(1): 25–42.

———. 1999. "The Economics of Crime." In *The Handbook of Labor Economics*, vol. 3C, edited by Orley Ashenfelter and David Card. New York: Elsevier.

Grogger, Jeffrey. 1995. "The Effect of Arrests on the Employment and Earnings of Young Men." *Quarterly Journal of Economics* 110(1): 51–72.

Hindelang, Michael J., Travis Hirschi, and Joseph Weis. 1981. *Measuring Delinquency.* Beverly Hills, CA: SAGE Publications.

Holzer, Harry J. 1996. *What Employers Want: Job Prospects for Less-Educated Workers.* New York: Russell Sage Foundation.

———. 1998. "Why Do Small Establishments Hire Fewer Blacks Than Large Ones?" *Journal of Human Resources* 33(4): 896–914.

Holzer, Harry J., and David Neumark. 2000. "What Does Affirmative Action Do?" *Industrial and Labor Relations Review* 53(2): 240–71.

Holzer, Harry J., and Michael A. Stoll. 2001. *Employers and Welfare Recipients: The Effects of Welfare Reform in the Workplace.* San Francisco: Public Policy Institute of California.

Holzer, Harry J., Steven Raphael, and Michael A. Stoll. 2001. "Perceived Criminality, Background Checks, and the Employment of Black Men." Unpublished manuscript.

———. 2004. "Will Employers Hire Former Offenders? Employer Preferences, Background Checks, and Their Determinants." In *Imprisoning America: The Social Effects of Mass Incarceration,* edited by Mary Pattillo, David Weiman, and Bruce Western (205–46). New York: Russell Sage Foundation.

Kling, Jeffrey. 2000. "The Effects of Prison Sentence Length on the Subsequent Employment and Earnings of Criminal Defendants." Discussion paper. Princeton, NJ: Princeton University.

Kling, Jeffrey, David Weiman, and Bruce Western. 2000. "The Labor Market Consequences of Mass Incarceration." Paper presented at the Urban Institute Reentry Roundtable, Washington, D.C., Oct. 12.

Pager, Devah. 2003. "The Mark of a Criminal Record." *American Journal of Sociology* 108(5): 937–75.

Travis, Jeremy, Amy Solomon, and Michelle Waul. 2001. *From Prison to Home: The Dimensions and Consequences of Prisoner Reentry.* Washington DC: The Urban Institute.

Uggen, Christopher, Jeffrey Manza, and Melissa Thompson. 2001. "Crime, Class, and Reintegration: The Scope and Social Distribution of America's Criminal Class." Unpublished manuscript.

Viscusi, W. Kip. 1986. "Market Incentives for Criminal Behavior." In *The Black Youth Employment Crisis,* edited by Richard Freeman and Harry J. Holzer (301–52). Chicago: University of Chicago Press.

Western, Bruce, and Becky Pettit. 2000. "Incarceration and Racial Inequality in Men's Employment." *Industrial and Labor Relations Review* 54(1): 3–16.

5

Are Less-Educated Women Crowding Less-Educated Men Out of the Labor Market?

Rebecca M. Blank and Jonah Gelbach

T he recent declines in labor supply among less-educated men have been clearly documented in the second chapter of this book. Chapter 2 and other works also clearly document the increase in labor force participation among less-educated women. For instance, Blank and Schmidt (2001) indicate that labor force participation among women without a high school diploma increased by 6 percentage points between 1989 and 1999; single mothers with children increased their labor force participation by over 10 percentage points during this decade. This chapter investigates whether there is any evidence of a causal relationship between increases in female labor supply and declines in male labor supply among less-educated workers (those with a high school education or less).

Changes in Female Labor Supply

The substantial literature on female labor supply changes over the past decade is mostly driven by interest in the work-oriented welfare reforms enacted during the 1990s. A number of papers investigate various measures of female labor supply and attempt to determine how many of these changes are the result of the booming economy of the 1990s and how many are the result of policy changes (Grogger 2003; Moffitt 1999; Schoeni and Blank 2000).

These papers focus on several policy changes. First, they investigate the effects of state waivers, which allowed states to request permission from the federal government to operate welfare programs whose rules varied from the Aid to Families with Dependent Children (AFDC) program, the primary cash assistance program to single mothers. Most of these waivers allowed states to run stronger welfare-to-work programs, often including time limits and strong sanctions for noncompliance with work requirements.

Second, these papers investigate the effect of the 1996 welfare reform legislation. In 1996, the federal government abolished AFDC and gave states much more discretion over the design of cash assistance programs. Federal dollars that had been funding AFDC were converted to the Temporary Assistance for Needy Families (TANF) block grant. Virtually all states took advantage of this change to enact substantially revised TANF-funded welfare programs.[1] While these new welfare programs varied substantially across states, they typically involved strong efforts to move welfare recipients into work, provided both incentives to work and penalties for not cooperating, implemented national and state time limits, and tried to discourage women from ever entering welfare through various diversion efforts. These program changes increased the cost of not working and, in many cases, the economic gains from work.

Several other policy changes further increased less-educated women's incentives to work. Substantial increases in the minimum wage over the 1990s improved wage rates for low-wage workers. In inflation-adjusted dollars, minimum wages were 10.8 percent higher in 2000 than in 1989. These wage increases were supplemented by real-wage growth stimulated by the strong economy; virtually all less-educated workers increased their real wages in the late 1990s (Blank and Schmidt 2001). In the early 1990s, Congress also substantially increased the Earned Income Tax Credit (EITC), a program that supplements wages for low-wage workers in low-income families through the tax system. The combined increases in minimum wage and the EITC helped increase the returns to work and have been clearly linked with increases of single mothers in the labor supply (Eissa and Liebman 1996; Ellwood 2000; Meyer and Rosenbaum 2001).[2]

A final set of policy changes further increased the returns of work for single mothers by reducing work-related expenses through expansions in child care subsidies and access to public health insurance. Federal dollars for child care subsidies to women on welfare rose from $0.6 to $6.6 billion between 1988 and 1999 (Blank and Ellwood 2002, figure 1).[3] Public health insurance (Medicaid) has since also been made more broadly available to women who leave welfare for work, and eligibility for Medicaid is now automatic for all children in very low income families.[4] In the past, families needed to be explicitly eligible for certain assistance programs to receive public health insurance; because so few low-wage jobs offer health insurance coverage, leaving welfare and going to work often meant losing health insurance.

All these programmatic changes should have substantially increased the returns of low-wage work and reduced access to benefits among nonworkers, especially single mothers with children. Of course, the booming economy of the late 1990s also made jobs more available and raised wages. The U.S. unemployment rate remained at or below 5 percent from April 1997 to October 2001. Much of the recent research on female labor supply changes has attempted to measure the impact of these economic and policy changes.

The relative importance of these different factors varies across studies and policies. For instance, both Moffitt (1999) and Schoeni and Blank (2000) conclude that waivers had a significant, positive impact on work behavior among less-skilled women. But Schoeni and Blank find few effects of TANF implementation on labor market participation; once they control for state economic environment, policy changes appear to matter little post-1996. Unfortunately, there are methodological problems with trying to estimate the impact of all these policy changes at the same time, so we have few direct comparisons of the simultaneous role of the economy, the EITC and minimum wage expansions, welfare changes, and other related policies.[5] A good summary of the research, however, is that both the booming economy of the 1990s and a host of related policy changes appear to have increased female labor supply. Blank (2000) argues there were synergies between the various policy changes and the high rate of economic growth, so all these effects reinforced each other.

Possible Links between Male and Female Labor Supply

Of course, the same factors that changed female labor supply may have directly affected male labor supply. Certainly the strong economy and rising real wage rates among less-educated workers should have provided incentives for both low-wage men and women to enter the labor force at a higher rate. For instance, inflation-adjusted wages among male high school dropouts rose 3.5 percent between 1994 and 1999 (Blank and Schmidt 2001). Similarly, the effects of policy changes (such as expanded health insurance or child care subsidies) that reduce the costs of work for parents should also increase male labor supply among less-educated single fathers or married men with children.

Increases in disposable income among low-income working married couples could result in intrafamily labor market substitution, however. Expansions in work opportunities and wage rates for both men and women could increase family income and (through an income effect) provide married men an opportunity to work somewhat less. In most cases, however, we assume the wife has the stronger response to increases in family income by substituting something else for paid work. This substitution makes the most sense for the lower-wage worker in the family, and husbands' wage rates are typically higher than are wives'. Hence, male labor supply would decline only if both parents earn equally low wages and if increased work returns result in income effects on family labor supply. Such a response would be surprising, however, since past evidence suggests married men respond positively to increased returns of work (Blundell and MaCurdy 1999).

In general, the welfare policy changes should have had few direct effects on male labor supply. About 10 percent of welfare recipients in the 1990s were male-headed families—either single male parents or married couples eligible for cash benefits. The AFDC program, like state TANF programs after 1996, established explicit provisions under which married couples could receive welfare. In most cases, however, it was harder for married couples to receive cash assistance, and hence very few of them participated. Among all less-educated women, 9 percent reported receiving welfare income in 1995; among less-educated men, only 1 percent reported receiving welfare. This finding suggests the welfare reforms of 1996 and earlier should have affected only a few men.

Similarly, neither welfare reform nor other policies designed to encourage work or improve the returns to work among low-wage parents (such as the expansions to the EITC and child care subsidies) should have had much direct effect on single men or married men without children. As it turns out, a disproportionately high share of less-educated men are unmarried or in families without minor children. In the March 1996 Current Population Survey (CPS), 44 percent of all less-educated women are in families with no unmarried children age 18 or younger, but 56 percent of men are in such families.

If low-wage men are sharing income with girlfriends or family members, however, all these policies could indirectly affect male labor supply, even among childless and unmarried men, as increases in work effort and wages among the women influence male labor market decisions. This can happen in two ways. First, there may be an indirect income effect on these men. If girlfriends or family members are working more and earning more, the men may feel less need to provide them with income. This could reduce male labor supply.

Second, when female labor supply expands rapidly, the number of available jobs may be limited. Given the booming economy, we expect that labor demand was expanding through most of the 1990s. If an increase in labor demand was the only economic force happening in the 1990s, then the rightward shift in a demand curve would pull up wages and push out employment. One would expect male and female workers to share these benefits. But what if the increase in demand was entirely satisfied by an expanded female labor supply?

The welfare-to-work policies enacted in the 1990s may have pushed up labor supply among female workers. In the language of economics, the expansion in female labor supply may have been because of shifts both in the demand curve (employment increases as one moves up the supply curve to a higher level of demand) and the supply curve (strong enforcement of welfare-to-work efforts pushed more women into the workforce). The outward expansion of the female labor supply curve may have more than accommodated the rise in labor demand, perhaps reducing the number of jobs available for men.

This outcome would be surprising, for two reasons. First, the facts of the late 1990s do not support this simple story. Real wages rose among *both* men and women, and unemployment rates remained low among *both* men and women. A demand substitution story, in which women are hired and men are fired, should result in falling wages and rising unemployment among less-educated men, and these trends did not occur. Indeed, the low overall unemployment rates and constant employer complaints about insufficient labor throughout the late 1990s suggest that jobs were available for less-educated men and women.[6]

Second, most evidence suggests that men and women are in different labor markets. The degree of occupational segregation among less-skilled workers is high, with men more likely to be in manufacturing jobs and women more likely to be in service sector jobs. Under these circumstances, even a rapid expansion in female labor supply should not reduce labor demand one-for-one in traditionally male occupations.[7]

All this suggests that something more than simple displacement had to be occurring in the late 1990s (although displacement could have occurred in some areas with very rapid increases in female labor supply, even if it was not the primary cause of male labor supply changes overall). Perhaps rising income among mothers, sisters, and girlfriends reduced the incentives for men to work, as suggested above. Perhaps *which* men were working changed in the 1990s. Perhaps the economic boom created job opportunities in the underground economy that pulled men away from mainstream employment. Perhaps employers came to prefer women over men as the changing mix of less-educated jobs made the "soft skills" at which women excel more important to employers. Some of these explanations are explored in other chapters of this book.

In the remainder of this chapter, we ask whether there is any evidence that rising female labor supply was associated with declines in male labor supply—through either displacement or income effects. We refer to this phenomenon as the "substitution hypothesis." Certainly the overt evidence that female labor force participation boomed as male labor force participation fell lends at least some credibility to this hypothesis and makes it worth pursuing in the data.

Seeking to identify substitution effects between two closely related groups in the labor market is difficult. In particular, most measures are troubled by simultaneity problems. By this, we mean that underlying economic forces drive the labor force participation of men and women in the same direction. As a result, male and female labor supply will be positively correlated, which implies nothing about the causal effect of changes in female labor supply on male labor supply. One must credibly remove this positive bias to test the substitution hypothesis. Because supply and demand move simultaneously, and because the market for male and female labor overlaps heavily, it is very difficult to separate a potential "substitution" effect from other possible correlations and causes.

While we know of no other literature that focuses on male–female labor market substitution in the booming labor market of the 1990s, others have tried to measure the potential displacement effects of increases in labor force participation among welfare recipients. Bartik (2000) summarizes this literature and contributes a variety of estimates using different theoretical approaches to measuring displacement effects. He concludes there is little evidence that welfare reform alone had large impacts on the overall labor market, but it may have had larger effects among less-educated workers. His estimates suggest the largest effects might occur among other less-educated women rather than among less-educated men.

Our primary way of dealing with simultaneity in the determination of male and female labor supply is to try several different estimation procedures, all with some admitted faults, to see if any produce evidence of substitution. In the next section, we look at the comparative changes in the labor supply of less-educated male and female workers within defined labor markets, trying to control for economic, demographic, and institutional factors. We then investigate the effects of welfare policy changes on male labor supply. If these changes primarily affect work behavior among less-educated women and affect men only indirectly through their impact on female labor supply, then any measured negative effect on male labor supply indicates some sort of substitution effect. (In the language of econometrics, we use these policy changes as an instrument for female labor supply.) In the final empirical section, we focus on transitions into employment and full-time employment, to see if male transition rates are affected by female transition rates. Transitions may be an important margin of adjustment if crowding out occurs during hiring in an expanding economy.

Investigating Changes in Male and Female Labor Supply within Identifiable Markets

In this section we focus on changes in male and female labor supply within defined labor markets. The labor markets used are Metropolitan Statistical Areas (MSAs). MSAs include all cities with more than 50,000 inhabitants along with the county or counties in which they are located and with which they are economically and socially integrated. We use 208 MSAs that were defined in both 1989 and 2000 within the data.[8]

The data come from the Current Population Survey Outgoing Rotation Groups (CPS-ORG). The CPS-ORG data provide wage and employment information on a monthly national sample of respondents.[9] Aggregating the 12 monthly samples collected each year provides enough observations in each of these 208 MSAs to look at skill groups by gender. We primarily focus on men and women with less than a high school diploma or exactly a high school diploma, whom we refer to as less-educated workers. Our unit of observation is the MSA average within a specific gender and education grouping. Sample sizes within these cells range from 2,275 observations of less-educated men in the largest MSA in 2000 to 19 observations in the smallest MSA.

Figure 5.1 shows the changes in male labor supply within our sample between 1989 and 2000. Male labor force participation among those with only a high school diploma declines from 81 percent to 76 percent over this period; among those with less than a high school diploma, labor force participation declines from 56 percent in 1989 to 53 percent in 1994, but then goes back up to 55 percent by 2000.

Since changes in male labor supply can occur along both the intensive and the extensive margin, figure 5.2 shows changes in mean hours among those who work. It is difficult to interpret trends in these data since the hours definitions change between 1993 and 1994. There is little evidence, however, of major changes in hours over time either before or after this breakpoint.

The simple correlation between changes in male labor supply and changes in female labor supply between 1989 and 2000 within these 208 MSAs is shown in Part I of table 5.1, row 1. Column 1 shows the correlations in male–female labor supply changes among all workers, and columns 2 and 3 show the correlations among male–female labor supply changes among those with less than a high school diploma and those with exactly a high school diploma. The first row shows a relatively strong and positive correlation between male and female labor force participation changes for all groups, meaning that areas with larger increases in male

Figure 5.1. *Male Labor Force Participation Rates by Education Level, 1989–2000*

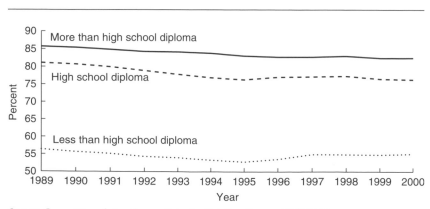

Sources: Current Population Survey Outgoing Rotation Groups, 1989–2000.

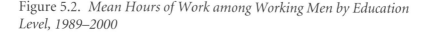

Figure 5.2. *Mean Hours of Work among Working Men by Education Level, 1989–2000*

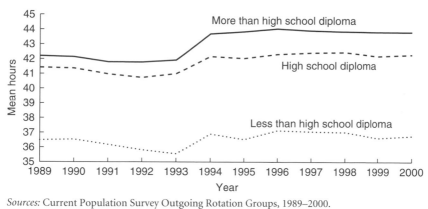

Sources: Current Population Survey Outgoing Rotation Groups, 1989–2000.

Note: Definitional break in the data between 1993 and 1994.

labor supply were also areas with strong increases in female labor supply at all skill levels. This is not surprising, and it almost surely indicates the dominance of economic factors in a labor market that affect both men and women in similar ways.

Row 2 shows correlations between changes in hours of work among male workers and female labor force participation changes. This correlation is negative but very small among all workers. There is a modest negative correlation among high school dropouts between male hours of work and female labor force participation.

Rows 3 and 4 of table 5.1 compare changes in male labor supply in the 20 MSAs where labor force participation among less-educated women (those with a high school diploma or less) increased most quickly in this decade (third row), and changes in male labor supply in the 20 MSAs where changes in less-educated female labor supply increased the least over the decade (fourth row). Row 5 provides a difference-in-difference estimator of the changes in male labor supply over time and between areas with high and low changes in female labor force participation.

A simple displacement story would suggest that male labor supply should fall more (or rise less) in areas of fast-growing female labor supply versus areas of slow-growing female labor supply. The evidence in row 5 suggests just the opposite among all workers (column 1) and among all less-educated workers (column 4). Figure 5.3 reinforces this finding by

Table 5.1. *Simple Relationships between Male and Female Labor Supply, 1989–2000*

		Education Level		
	All	Less than high school	Exactly high school	High school or less (less educated)
Part I: All Adults (Age 16–64)				
Correlations				
1. Change in male LFP rates versus change in female LFP rates within education level	22.6	12.1	19.6	14.3
2. Change in mean hours among male workers versus change in female LFP rates within education level	−0.7	−5.1	−1.1	−4.5
Difference-in-difference calculations				
3. Change in male LFP rates in 20 MSAs with highest rate of LFP growth among less-educated women	−0.032	−0.147	−0.026	−0.063
4. Change in male LFP rates in 20 MSAs with lowest rate of LFP growth among less-educated women	−0.063	−0.113	−0.073	−0.089
5. Difference in differences (row 3 − row 4)	0.031	−0.034	0.047	0.026
Part II: Young Adults (Age 20–35)				
Correlations				
1. Change in male LFP rates versus change in female LFP rates within education level	17.2	−0.7	9.0	12.3
2. Change in mean hours among male workers versus change in female LFP rates within education level	3.8	−7.4	5.9	3.5
Difference-in-difference calculations				
3. Change in male LFP rates in 20 MSAs with highest rate of LFP growth among less-educated women	0.005	−0.082	0.021	0.014
4. Change in male LFP rates in 20 MSAs with lowest rate of LFP growth among less-educated women	−0.028	−0.031	−0.058	−0.045
5. Difference in differences (row 3 − row 4)	0.033	−0.051	0.079	0.059

Sources: Current Population Survey Outgoing Rotation Groups, 1989–2000.

Notes: Correlations based on 208 metropolitan statistical areas (MSAs).

LFP = labor force participation.

Figure 5.3. *Aggregate Labor Force Participation Rates among Less-Educated Men, 1989–2000*

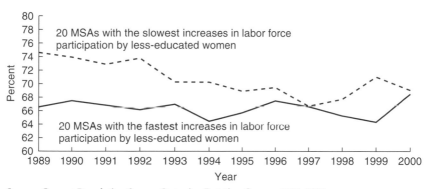

Sources: Current Population Survey Outgoing Rotation Groups, 1989–2000.
MSA = metropolitan statistical area.

plotting labor supply changes among less-educated men in the 20 fastest versus the 20 slowest growth areas in terms of female labor supply. Clearly, male labor supply is falling much faster (by 7 percentage points) in areas with lower increases in less-educated female labor supply, while it increases in the areas with high rates of female labor supply growth.

By itself, this evidence proves little. Without controls for the economy, these correlations are likely driven by common economic effects within metropolitan areas. But these simple estimates establish that there is no prima facie evidence of substitution in these data.

Because other chapters in this book emphasize effects among younger workers, Part II of table 5.1 repeats the same analysis for workers between the ages of 20 and 34. If younger female workers are more affected by the welfare reform effects, then younger male workers may be more affected by displacement effects, and one would expect to see bigger negative correlations among these younger workers. This does not happen among all younger workers or among all less-educated workers. For these groups, the correlations among younger workers are either similar or smaller than the correlations among all workers.

Among those with less than a high school education, however, the evidence in Part II suggests slightly stronger negative correlations between younger male workers' outcomes and increases in labor supply among younger women. In both the correlations and in the difference-in-difference calculations, younger male high school dropouts seem to have slightly worse labor supply outcomes in MSAs with greater female labor force participation growth.[10]

Table 5.2 provides somewhat more controlled regressions using a panel of MSA-specific data for the 12 years from 1989 to 2000. The table indicates what happens to the correlation between changes in male and female labor supply once other variables are controlled for. The dependent variable in Part I is the change in male labor force participation by MSA and year. Columns 1–3 use data on all men, columns 4–6 use data on all less-educated men (those with a high school diploma or less), and columns 7–9 use data on men with less than a high school diploma. Row 1 shows the coefficient on the change in female labor force participation across three increasingly rich specifications for each skill group. With 208 MSAs and 12 years, there are 2,496 observations in each regression.[11]

Columns 1, 4, and 7 show the coefficient on change in female labor supply, with MSA and year fixed effects included. Columns 2, 5, and 8 also control for the unemployment rate (both current and lagged one period), indicating the effect of controlling for differences in economic environment between areas and over time. Columns 3, 6, and 9 add controls for a variety of additional demographic and labor market variables, including percentages of blacks and Hispanics in the MSA labor market, percentage employed in manufacturing, percentage in nonprofessional services, percentage in professional services, percentage in public administration, and an index of gender industry segregation. This industry segregation index is calculated in each MSA in each year among all workers.[12] We might expect that labor markets with greater gender segregation would show smaller substitution effects.

The results in table 5.2 continue to show few indications of substitution in this data set (which should generate a negative relationship between female labor supply changes and changes in male labor force involvement if we have adequately controlled for economic conditions). In all cases, coefficients showing the effect of changes in female labor supply on changes in male labor supply are positive and significant for all specifications and skill levels, even once we control for economic environment, demographic differences, and industry structure. The inclusion of MSA and year fixed effects in all regressions further controls for any common factors within an MSA over time or across all MSAs in a given year.

Columns 3, 6, and 9 offer a relatively rich specification that should control for many of the things that cause a positive bias in the relationship between male and female labor supply.[13] Yet even in these columns the

Table 5.2. *Effects of Changes in Female Labor Force Participation on Male Labor Supply, 1989–2000*

Included variables	All Men			Less-Educated (High School or Less)			Less than High School Only		
	(1)	(2)	(3)	(4)	(5)	(6)	(7)	(8)	(9)
Part I: Dependent Variable = Change in Labor Force Participation Rate among Men									
Change in female LFP[a]	.218	.215	.220	.169	.163	.164	.191	.175	.177
	(.020)	(.020)	(.020)	(.023)	(.023)	(.022)	(.041)	(.041)	(.041)
MSA fixed effects	Yes	Yes	Yes	Yes	Yes	Yes	Yes	Yes	Yes
Year fixed effects	Yes	Yes	Yes	Yes	Yes	Yes	Yes	Yes	Yes
Unemployment rates[b]	No	Yes	Yes	No	Yes	Yes	No	Yes	Yes
Other control variables[c]	No	No	Yes	No	No	Yes	No	No	Yes
Part II: Dependent Variable = Change in Mean Hours of Work among Male Workers									
Change in female LFP[a]	-.537	-.583	-.565	.497	.519	.540	-.516	-.566	-.517
	(.728)	(.730)	(.731)	(.766)	(.769)	(.770)	(1.963)	(1.970)	(1.975)
MSA fixed effects	Yes	Yes	Yes	Yes	Yes	Yes	Yes	Yes	Yes
Year fixed effects	Yes	Yes	Yes	Yes	Yes	Yes	Yes	Yes	Yes
Unemployment rates[b]	No	Yes	Yes	No	Yes	Yes	No	Yes	Yes
Other control variables[c]	No	No	Yes	No	No	Yes	No	No	Yes

Sources: Current Population Survey Outgoing Rotation Groups, 1989–2000.

Notes: Standard errors in parentheses. Number of observations = 2,496 (208 MSAs for 12 years).

LFP = labor force participation; MSA = metropolitan statistical area.

[a] Change in female LFP among all women used in columns 1 through 3. Change in female LFP among all less-educated women (women with less than a high school education) used in columns 4 through 9.

[b] Includes current and lagged unemployment rates by MSA.

[c] Includes MSA-specific variables for each year for percent black, percent Hispanic, percent employed in manufacturing, percent employed in nonprofessional services, percent employed in professional services, percent employed in public administration, and gender industry segregation index.

coefficient on female labor supply is positive and significant for all educa-tion groups. There is little sign that the relationship for the least educated group of men (columns 7 through 9) is significantly different than that among all men.

Part II uses changes in mean hours of work among men who work as the dependent variable, testing whether the degree of male labor market involvement is affected by changes in female labor force participation. The coefficients show the effect of changes in female labor supply on hours worked among men across the same three specifications shown in Part I and for the same skill groups. In this case, the coefficients on change in female labor force participation are small and insignificant in all specifica-tions and for all skill groups.

The results in this section should not be overinterpreted. Because of the simultaneous labor supply responses among men and women in the same labor market, one might expect to find little evidence of substitu-tion. The main message of this section, however, is clear: there is no first-order evidence in these data of substantial substitution between men and women in the labor market during the 1990s. While small effects may be found with more sophisticated estimation techniques, they are likely to be second order. Any large substitution effect should show up in the spec-ifications in columns 3, 6, and 9 of table 5.2, which controls for a relatively rich set of environmental variables.

Using Policy Changes as a Potential Instrument for Female Labor Force Changes

A problem with the above calculations is that both male and female labor supply are simultaneously affected by the economic environment. This simultaneity leads to a strong positive association between the two vari-ables that cannot be interpreted causally and will bias upward any esti-mated coefficient of the effect of female labor force participation on male labor force participation. The classic response in such a situation is to look for an instrument—that is, a variable correlated with female labor supply and not directly correlated with male labor supply. In other words, the variable is correlated with male labor supply only through its correlation with female labor supply. One could then use this variable as a proxy for female labor supply changes and measure only the causal impact of female labor supply on male labor supply, eliminating the positive bias.

In most cases, finding an instrument can be difficult. In this case, the choice is obvious: the policies enacted during the 1990s that were designed to move welfare recipients—predominantly single mothers—into work. For these policies to serve as an effective instrument, they must have had a direct effect only on female labor force participation. Their effect on male labor force participation must come solely through the influence of female labor force changes.

As we noted above, there are some problems with this assumption. A small share of welfare recipients are male-headed families. However, as we also noted, very few less-educated men receive welfare in any given year, while a substantial share of less-educated women are welfare recipients. This difference suggests that policy changes in welfare programs are likely to have few direct effects on male labor supply, and hence may function effectively as instruments correlated with changes in the labor supply of less-educated women.[14]

We use the approach first used in Schoeni and Blank (2000) to estimate the effects of welfare program parameter changes on female labor supply measures, except we use male labor supply measures as our dependent variable. Schoeni and Blank estimate the effects of waivers, enacted in various states between 1992 and 1996, on female labor supply. They also estimate the effects of the implementation of TANF-funded programs in the mid-1990s. Like them, we use data by state, by year, by education level (less than high school, high school, and more than high school) and by age group (16–25, 26–44, and 45–64).[15] We calculate male labor force variables for each age-year-state-education cell and use these as the dependent variables in a panel data set.

Our estimation equation is

$$(1)\ Y_{aest} = Waiver_{st} \times Educ \times \beta_{eWaiver} + TANF_{st} \times Educ \times \beta_{eTANF} + \gamma_{s} + \gamma_{t} + trend \times \gamma_{s} + Z_{aest} \times \beta_{z} + \varepsilon_{aest}$$

The variables are defined for women in age group a and education group e who live in state s in calendar year t as follows:

Y: the outcome variable (either labor force participation or hours among male workers);

Waiver: an indicator variable that takes the value of one if the state in which the man lived had a major waiver in effect; the indicator is turned off when TANF is implemented in the state;

TANF: an indicator variable that takes the value of 1 if TANF was in effect in the state in which the man lived; the TANF implementation date varies across states between 1996 and 1997;

Educ: indicator variables for education groups—less than 12 years; exactly 12 years; and 13 years or more;

γ_s: state fixed effects;

γ_t: time fixed effects;

trend $\times \gamma_s$: linear state-specific time trends; and

Z: a vector of control variables including current and lagged unemployment rate and current and lagged employment growth rate, each interacted with each of the three education groups; log maximum AFDC/TANF benefit levels for a family of three, interacted with each of the three education groups; education dummies for each of the three groups; year effects interacted with each education group indicator; age dummies for each of the four age groups; each age indicator interacted with each education indicator; proportion Hispanic; and proportion non-Hispanic black.

Identifying policy variables occurs in two ways. First, by controlling for a rich set of variables, including state economic measures, state and year fixed effects, and demographic characteristics, the independent effects of the policy variables should be evident. Second, if one believes there are still important omitted variables in this model that bias the coefficients on the policy variables, one can compare the effects of policy among less-educated versus more-educated men (or women) as a test of whether the measured effects make sense. Welfare changes should have few effects on women with more than a high school diploma, since so few women with post–high school training receive welfare, and should have few effects on more-educated men. Schoeni and Blank indicate that most of their measured effects of policy are present among less-educated women but not among more-educated women, lending credibility to their results.

We calculate labor force measures among males and females based on CPS-ORG data within each state-year-age-education cell.[16] We focus on two dependent variables: labor force participation rates and mean hours of work among all workers.

Columns 1 and 2 of table 5.3 essentially show that we can replicate the Schoeni and Blank results for women using our CPS-ORG–based labor market data. Column 1 shows the impact of the implementation of waiver

Table 5.3. *Effects of Welfare Waivers and TANF on Male and Female Labor Supply Variables, 1989–2000*

Policy effects (interacted with skill)	Women		Men	
	Labor force participation	Mean hours (among workers)	Labor force participation	Mean hours (among workers)
Waiver • Educ < 12	.024	.273	.016	.302
	(.006)	(.172)	(.004)	(.172)
Waiver • Educ = 12	.002	.179	−.001	−.064
	(.004)	(.129)	(.003)	(.137)
Waiver • Educ > 12	−.004	−.094	−.002	.242
	(.004)	(.108)	(.003)	(.111)
TANF • Educ < 12	.011	−.649	.001	−.864
	(.014)	(.421)	(.011)	(.422)
TANF • Educ = 12	−.001	.192	.004	.038
	(.011)	(.337)	(.009)	(.356)
TANF • Educ > 12	.006	.104	.002	.618
	(.009)	(.263)	(.007)	(.272)

Sources: Current Population Survey Outgoing Rotation Groups, 1989–2000.

Notes: Standard errors in parentheses. Regressions weighted by population in each cell. Observations are defined by averages within each state-year-education-age group for 51 states across the 12 years indicated. Each column represents a regression that includes current and lagged unemployment rates and employment growth rates interacted with each education group, maximum benefit for a family of three interacted with education groups, age dummies (16–25, 26–44, 45–64), education dummies, age dummies interacted with education dummies, race (Hispanic, non-Hispanic black), year effects, year effects interacted with education dummies, state effects, and state-specific time trends.

policies and of TANF on female labor force participation by education group. Column 2 uses hours of work among all female workers as the dependent variable. Waivers, which were largely designed to increase states' ability to run serious welfare-to-work programs, had a positive and significant effect on female labor force participation among women with less than a high school diploma. But the effect of these waivers is essentially zero on more-educated women. Waivers also have a positive effect on mean hours of work among workers for the least educated.

The implementation of the TANF program also has a positive effect on labor force participation among the least educated women, but the effect is small and not significant. The effect of TANF on hours among the least

educated women is negative (not the expected sign) and marginally significant, certainly suggesting no large hour gains among women due to TANF.
(The negative sign could be the result of the large increase in the number of
less-educated women who entered the labor market after the enactment
of TANF, potentially driving down average hours worked.)

In contrast, columns 3 and 4 show equivalent estimates for men, using
labor force participation among men as the dependent variable in column 3 and mean hours of work among male workers in column 4.[17] If
these policy changes are primarily affecting labor market decisions among
women, then any significant coefficient must reflect the indirect impact
of female labor supply changes on male labor force behavior.

Column 3 shows no evidence of any displacement effect of these policy
changes on male labor supply. Indeed, the implementation of waivers
appears to have had a small but significant positive effect on labor force
participation among the least educated men and no effects on more-
educated men. At best, this suggests there might have been some direct
and positive effects of waivers on male labor supply; it certainly provides
no evidence of displacement or substitution between male and female
workers. The implementation of TANF has no effect on male labor force
participation among less- or more-educated men.

The results on mean hours of work among male workers are a bit harder
to interpret. Consistent with the effect on male labor force participation,
waivers appear to have significantly increased hours of work among less-
educated men, again not consistent with the substitution hypothesis.
TANF implementation appears to have reduced male hours of work
among the least educated. It is hard to interpret this as a substitution effect,
however, since the least educated women also show negative hours effects
from TANF. Even more puzzling, the implementation of TANF appears
to be correlated with a strong and positive increase in labor supply among
more-educated men. While it may be possible to tell a story justifying such
a coefficient (perhaps hiring more less-educated women required an
increase in higher-educated supervisors), it is clear that these coefficients
provide no evidence of displacement or substitution.

In short, these results suggest that the welfare reforms enacted in the
1990s, especially the waivers, had some positive effects on female labor
supply. The effects of TANF on female labor force participation seem relatively minor.[18] Our estimates show no evidence that these policies negatively affected male labor force involvement, however. In fact, the effect of
waivers on the labor force participation of the least educated men is posi-

tive, although displacement might be largest here, given that this policy has the largest positive effects on labor supply among least educated women.

Changes on the Margin in Labor Force Involvement

The analysis conducted so far focuses on levels or changes in overall rates of labor force participation or hours worked. It seems likely that if there are significant substitution effects, however, they will operate largely along the margin of new hires. That is, they should show up more readily in the flows in and out of employment than they do in overall rates of labor force participation. Average measures of labor force participation or hours like the ones discussed above will respond to changes in the hiring process, so they are useful topics of analysis. Changes in the flows into and out of employment, however, may be a step higher in the causal chain. These transitions are the topic of this section.

We use March CPS data to examine the rate at which men are transitioning into, say, full-time jobs. The March CPS is particularly useful because it has information both on individual labor force involvement "last week"—that is, in the week before the CPS interview—and "last year"—that is, in the previous year. We perform two analyses, looking first at prime-age men, age 25 to 54, from 1989 to 2000; and looking second at younger men, age 20 to 34, from 1989 to 2000. In the regression analysis described below (but not the plots), we also restrict our data to men who live in defined MSAs, since the employment transitions among women within the relevant MSA are a key independent variable.

We begin by considering the probability that a man was in full-time employment last week, conditional on whether he was or was not typically employed full-time the previous year on his usual job.[19] Full-time employment is defined as working at least 35 hours last week (or working at least 35 hours a week last year in one's usual job). Figure 5.4 plots the fraction of men who were employed full-time last week conditional on their employment status last year. The figure shows that prime-age men employed full-time faced layoffs during the recession of the early 1990s. By contrast, the probability of working full-time last week among men who did not usually work full-time last year is much lower and does not appear very sensitive to the business cycle.

Figures 5.5 and 5.6 show similar plots among two subpopulations of particular interest, male high school dropouts and black men. These fig-

Figure 5.4. *Fraction of Men Employed Full-Time Last Week Conditional on Status Last Year, 1989–2000*

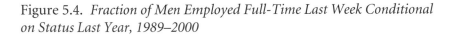

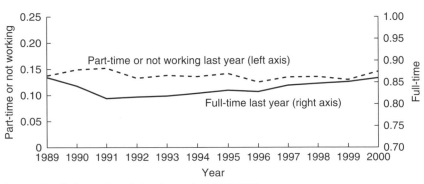

Sources: March Current Population Survey data, 1989–2000.

ures exhibit the same basic pattern as the figure for all men, though the probability of full-time work in the past week is lower for both these sub-groups.

A second outcome of interest is the probability that a man worked at all last week, conditional on his attachment to the labor force last year. We consider men who worked fewer than 13 weeks last year relatively unattached to the labor force, while men who worked at least 13 weeks are considered attached to the labor force. Figures 5.7, 5.8, and 5.9 plot rates of

Figure 5.5. *Fraction of Less-Educated Men Employed Full-Time Last Week Conditional on Status Last Year, 1989–2000*

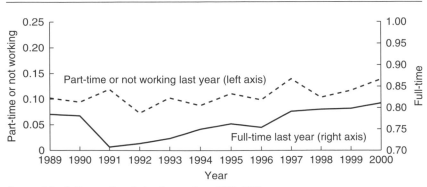

Sources: March Current Population Survey data, 1989–2000.

Figure 5.6. *Fraction of Black Men Employed Full-Time Last Week Conditional on Status Last Year, 1989–2000*

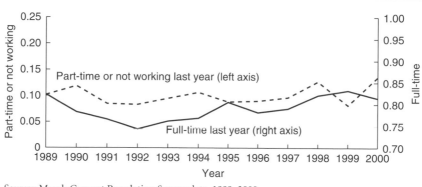

Sources: March Current Population Survey data, 1989–2000.

transition into employment last week conditional on last year's labor force attachment level among all men in the sample (figure 5.7), high school dropouts only (figure 5.8), and black men only (figure 5.9).

These figures are similar to those for the full-time/not-full-time outcomes. They indicate that men who were more attached to the labor force were affected by the business cycle of the early 1990s. Men who were less attached to the labor force in the previous year show fewer cyclical effects but are much less likely to be employed at any level in the previous week.

Figure 5.7. *Fraction of Men Employed Last Week Conditional on Weeks of Work Last Year, 1989–2000*

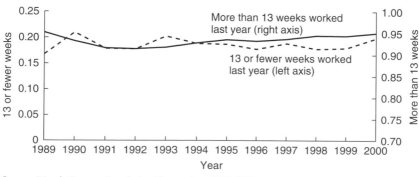

Sources: March Current Population Survey data, 1989–2000.

Figure 5.8. *Fraction of Less-Educated Men Employed Last Week Conditional on Weeks of Work Last Year, 1989–2000*

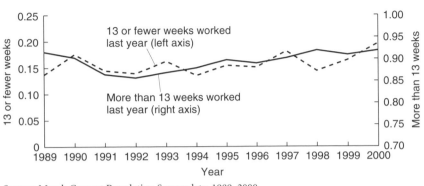

Sources: March Current Population Survey data, 1989–2000.

If increased female employment is crowding out increased male employment via increased hiring of women relative to men, then one would expect male rates of transition into employment to be smaller when female transition rates are greater. Of course, simple time-series evidence is of limited use here, given that men and women are both affected by economic conditions. We therefore again use cross-sectional and over-time variation at the MSA level to investigate the relationship between male and female transition rates.

Figure 5.9. *Fraction of Black Men Employed Last Week Conditional on Weeks of Work Last Year, 1989–2000*

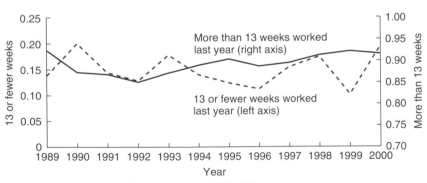

Sources: March Current Population Survey data, 1989–2000.

Our basic approach is to create separate samples for all men reporting a particular employment status last year—a sample of men who worked less than full-time last year and a sample who worked full-time last year. For each man, we define a dummy variable indicating whether he worked full-time last week, so the average of these dummy variables provides the probability of current full-time employment among the sample. Within each sample we regress this dummy variable on a set of explanatory variables.

The main variable of interest will be the average transition rate for women within an MSA. This is the fraction of women within the MSA who are now working full-time, conditional on the same starting labor market status as for the corresponding male sample. Hence, the regression on the sample of men who were not working full-time in the last year uses as an independent variable "the probability within the same MSA that women who were not working full-time last year now work full-time." Similarly, the regression for the sample of men who did work full-time last year uses as a independent variable "the probability within the same MSA that women who worked full-time last year continue to work full-time."[20]

Controlling appropriately for local changes in economic conditions is an important but difficult task. If economic differences across MSAs in underlying transition rates were fixed over time, we could simply use MSA fixed effects. Nationwide economic changes that affect all employment transitions in a given year could be absorbed using year dummies. But, as before, it is reasonable to believe that the impact of changes in female transition rates on male transitions differs across labor markets. In particular, area-level differences in male and female occupational structure could confound any crowding-out effects of female transitions. MSA-level fixed effects will not solve this problem if the impact of changes in female transitions is greater when, say, gender differences in industrial structure are smaller.

We address this concern by interacting female transition rates with the MSA-level industry segregation index used in our analysis of identifiable markets. With segregation of male and female workers across industries, we would expect male transition rates to be less affected by female transition rates in highly segregated areas. Since the expected effect of female transitions under the substitution hypothesis is to reduce transitions into employment for men, the expected sign of the coefficient on the interaction term is positive.

Other variables included in these regressions are men's race (black or white) and Hispanic background, their age, and their educational attainment, as well as average MSA-level values of these variables for women. The gender segregation index is also interacted with all these women's average characteristics.[21] Also included are the one-year-lagged values of the unemployment rate and its interaction with the segregation index. Last, a set of year dummies and their interactions with the segregation index are included. To obtain reasonably precise estimates of MSA-level average variables for women, we create these averages across all women in the sample at all educational levels.

We use data on the same 208 MSAs used in our analysis of identifiable markets and use all the data on men and women within these MSAs. Our data are based on the years 1989 to 2000 (hence, data for "last year" are for calendar years 1988 to 1999). The resulting sample has 234,308 observations on all men. All regressions are weighted using the March supplemental weights.

The results based on the probability of working full-time last week conditional on the hours a week worked in the previous year are presented by educational attainment in table 5.4 and by race and ethnicity in table 5.5. Columns 1 and 2 show the results among prime-age workers, while columns 3 and 4 show results among younger workers only.

Look first at columns 1 and 2 in table 5.4. Among prime-age male dropouts and high school graduates, the point estimates on the "probability of full-time work among women" variable are negative for only one of the four transitions into full-time employment among these less-educated workers. This suggests that, in a completely unsegregated MSA, more frequent transitions into full-time status for women are associated with more frequent transitions for men—exactly the opposite of the substitution hypothesis. The sign on the interaction with the segregation index is positive in two cases and negative in the other two, suggesting no systematic impact in more- or less-segregated MSAs. Moreover, the coefficient estimates are generally small and are all statistically insignificant.[22] For the prime-age group with more than a high school diploma, the coefficient estimates for the "main effect" do not have the expected sign, while the interaction effects are positive but statistically insignificant.

Among younger workers in table 5.4 (columns 3 and 4), the coefficient on the variable "probability of full-time work among women" is positive for high school dropouts and negative for high school graduates and more-educated young men. These coefficients are small, however, and insignificant in every case. The interaction with the segregation index also shows mixed signs but is insignificant in all estimates.

Table 5.4. *Estimated Probability of Full-Time Employment among Men, Conditional on Employment Status in Previous Year, by Education Level, March 1989–2000*

	Prime-Age Men (25–54)		Younger Men (20–34)	
	Less than full-time	Full-time	Less than full-time	Full-time
Less than high school education				
Mean of dependent variable	0.10	0.75	0.15	0.71
Probability of full-time work	0.33	0.01	0.67	0.36
among women[a]	(0.59)	(0.37)	(1.44)	(0.43)
Ind Segregation Index • Prob of	−0.81	0.40	−1.03	−0.75
full-time work among women	(1.67)	(1.06)	(4.69)	(1.28)
Number of observations	6,916	23,283	3,898	12,100
High school education				
Mean of dependent variable	0.12	0.82	0.19	0.78
Probability of full-time work	−0.81	0.15	−0.43	−0.30
among women[a]	(0.65)	(0.25)	(1.03)	(0.33)
Ind Segregation Index • Prob of	2.85	−0.04	1.60	1.06
full-time work among women	(1.84)	(0.74)	(3.31)	(0.99)
Number of observations	8,070	58,210	4,818	28,248
More than high school education				
Mean of dependent variable	0.16	0.86	0.16	0.80
Probability of full-time work	0.08	0.09	−0.27	−0.37
among women[a]	(0.84)	(0.15)	(0.61)	(0.23)
Ind Segregation Index • Prob of	0.57	0.11	1.37	1.14
full-time work among women	(2.52)	(0.44)	(1.98)	(0.70)
Number of observations	10,491	109,125	10,899	41,769

Sources: Current Population Survey Outgoing Rotation Groups, 1989–2000.

Notes: Data based on all males in 208 MSAs. Standard errors in parentheses are robust to arbitrary-form within MSA-year cells. All specifications include demographic covariates and year fixed effects.

[a]Average probability of full-time work last week among all women within an MSA, conditional on zero or part-time work last year (column 1) or full-time work last year (column 2). This average includes all women in all educational groups.

The results in table 5.5, stratified by race and ethnicity, are basically similar. Here the coefficient on the "probability of full-time work among women" variable is negative in a few specifications and positive in others, but none of these estimates is negative and statistically significant. For prime-age Hispanic men, the effect of women moving into full-time work on men's movement into full-time work appears to be positive and significant. The coefficient estimates for the interaction term are generally larger than in table 5.4, but they are never statistically significant and rarely of the right sign. There is no evidence that the effects are bigger among younger men than among prime-age men. In fact, most of the estimated coefficients are smaller among the younger group of men.

Tables 5.6 and 5.7 show the probability that men work last week, conditional on their weeks of labor market involvement in the previous year.[23] Table 5.6 estimates these transitional probabilities by skill group, and table 5.7 estimates them by race and ethnicity. Again, columns 1 and 2 show estimates for prime-age men, while columns 3 and 4 show estimates for younger men only.

In 4 of the 12 specifications in table 5.6, there are significant effects of "probability of any employment last week among women" on male employment. However, in three of these four cases the coefficient estimate is positive—again suggesting the opposite of the substitution hypothesis. The interaction effects are also significant in four cases, but in only one of these is the coefficient positive, the expected sign. The only case in which the coefficient estimates are significant and consistent with the substitution hypothesis is for younger men with more than a high school diploma. The results for this group are not likely to have been driven by welfare reform changes.

The results in table 5.7 are similarly mixed, with no group showing significant evidence consistent with the substitution hypothesis. In both tables 5.6 and 5.7, there is little evidence of notably different effects of women's employment changes on men's employment changes among younger workers versus prime-age workers.[24]

All in all, the results in this section suggest no evidence that women crowd out men in transitions to full-time employment (conditional on last year's full-time status) or to employment (conditional on last year's labor force attachment.) While it can be very difficult to infer causality from regressions such as these, the estimates suggest that any crowd-out effects are dominated by trends in local labor markets, even after controlling for a host of labor market variables.

text continues on page 116

Table 5.5. *Estimated Probability of Full-Time Employment among Men, Conditional on Employment Status in Previous Year, by Race and Ethnicity, March 1989–2000*

	Prime-Age Men (25–54)		Younger Men (20–34)	
	Less than full-time	Full-time	Less than full-time	Full-time
Black men				
Mean of dependent variable	0.10	0.78	0.12	0.73
Probability of full-time work	−.097	0.12	0.11	−0.89
among women[a]	(0.99)	(0.44)	(1.30)	(0.62)
Ind Segregation Index • Prob of	3.43	0.04	1.13	2.78
full-time work among women	(2.80)	(1.24)	(3.96)	(1.81)
Number of observations	4,499	16,948	3,107	7,710
Non-Hispanic white men				
Mean of dependent variable	0.14	0.85	0.18	0.79
Probability of full-time work	−0.42	0.10	−0.47	−0.08
among women[a]	(0.46)	(0.15)	(0.73)	(0.23)
Ind Segregation Index • Prob of	1.66	0.13	1.57	0.44
full-time work among women	(1.35)	(0.45)	(2.34)	(0.69)
Number of observations	14,296	134,364	10,532	52,323
Hispanic men				
Mean of dependent variable	0.17	0.80	0.22	0.79
Probability of full-time work	2.06*	0.38	−0.91	0.02
among women[a]	(1.21)	(0.36)	(2.02)	(0.47)
Ind Segregation Index • Prob of	−5.65	−0.82	3.82	0.05
full-time work among women	(3.86)	(1.07)	(6.52)	(1.43)
Number of observations	5,229	30,958	4,418	18,344

Sources: Current Population Survey Outgoing Rotation Groups, 1989–2000.

Notes: Data based on all males in 208 MSAs. Standard errors in parentheses are robust to arbitrary-form within MSA-year cells. All specifications include demographic covariates and year fixed effects.

[a]Average probability of full-time work last week among all women within an MSA, conditional on zero or part-time work last year (column 1) or full-time work last year (column 2). This average includes all women in all racial and ethnic groups.

*Difference significant at the 0.10 level.

Table 5.6. *Estimated Probability of Any Employment among Men, Conditional on Number of Weeks Worked in Previous Year, by Education Level, March 1989–2000*

	Prime-Age Men (25–54)		Younger Men (20–34)	
	13 or fewer weeks	More than 13 weeks	13 or fewer weeks	More than 13 weeks
Less than high school education				
Mean of dependent variable	0.15	0.88	0.24	0.86
Probability of employment	−0.48	1.00**	−0.11	−0.55
among women[a]	(0.48)	(0.46)	(0.89)	(0.60)
Ind Segregation Index • Prob of	1.45	−2.55*	0.21	1.57
employment among women	(1.39)	(1.31)	(2.76)	(1.87)
Number of observations	5,787	24,412	3,179	12,819
High school education				
Mean of dependent variable	0.18	0.92	0.28	0.89
Probability of employment	0.59	0.32	−0.13	0.67**
among women[a]	(0.58)	(0.26)	(0.89)	(0.28)
Ind Segregation Index • Prob of	−1.98	−0.59	0.93	−1.65*
employment among women	(1.65)	(0.77)	(2.75)	(0.85)
Number of observations	6,391	59,889	3,359	29,707
More than high school education				
Mean of dependent variable	0.21	0.95	0.23	0.92
Probability of employment	1.06*	−0.04	0.88	−0.45*
among women[a]	(0.59)	(0.12)	(0.73)	(0.23)
Ind Segregation Index • Prob of	−2.99*	0.16	−2.65	1.51**
employment among women	(1.79)	(0.35)	(2.37)	(0.74)
Number of observations	6,539	113,077	6,183	46,485

Sources: Current Population Survey Outgoing Rotation Groups, 1989–2000.

Notes: Data based on all males in 208 MSAs. Standard errors in parentheses are robust to arbitrary-form within MSA-year cells. All specifications include demographic covariates and year fixed effects.

[a]Average probability of any employment last week among all women within an MSA, conditional on 13 or fewer weeks last year (column 1) or more than 13 weeks last year (column 2). This average includes all women in all educational groups.

*Difference significant at the 0.10 level; ** difference significant at the 0.05 level.

Table 5.7. *Estimated Probability of Any Employment among Men, Conditional on Number of Weeks Worked in Previous Year, by Race and Ethnicity, March 1989–2000*

	Prime-Age Men (25–54)		Younger Men (20–34)	
	13 or fewer weeks	More than 13 weeks	13 or fewer weeks	More than 13 weeks
Black men				
Mean of dependent variable	0.14	0.89	0.19	0.85
Probability of employment among women[a]	−0.21	0.95	−0.31	0.43
	(0.66)	(0.64)	(1.33)	(0.96)
Ind Segregation Index • Prob of employment among women	1.06	−2.37	1.03	−0.90
	(2.04)	(1.93)	(4.35)	(3.09)
Number of observations	3,862	17,585	2,458	8,359
Non-Hispanic white men				
Mean of dependent variable	0.18	0.94	0.26	0.91
Probability of employment among women[a]	0.77**	0.10	0.09	−0.05
	(0.39)	(0.13)	(0.65)	(0.22)
Ind Segregation Index • Prob of employment among women	−2.46**	−0.19	0.02	0.32
	(1.13)	(0.39)	(2.05)	(0.68)
Number of observations	9,894	138,766	6,182	56,673
Hispanic men				
Mean of dependent variable	0.23	0.91	0.34	0.90
Probability of employment among women[a]	0.43	0.24	−1.05	−0.31
	(0.98)	(0.36)	(1.41)	(0.45)
Ind Segregation Index • Prob of employment among women	−1.18	−0.39	2.71	1.21
	(3.09)	(1.00)	(4.43)	(1.43)
Number of observations	3,915	32,272	3,027	19,735

Sources: Current Population Survey Outgoing Rotation Groups, 1989–2000.

Notes: Data based on all males in 208 MSAs. Standard errors in parentheses are robust to arbitrary-form within MSA-year cells. All specifications include demographic covariates and year fixed effects.

[a]Average probability of any employment last week among all women within an MSA, conditional on 13 or fewer weeks last year (column 1) or more than 13 weeks last year (column 2). This average includes all women in all racial and ethnic groups.

**Difference significant at the 0.05 level.

Conclusion

This chapter has searched for evidence of substitution over the 1990s between male and female workers. All the estimation techniques used here have some interpretational difficulties; in no case do we want to claim that we have clearly estimated causal effects. Yet we cannot find any evidence of displacement or substitution between less-educated male and female workers in the labor market.

To a large extent, the discussion in this chapter underscores the difficulties inherent in studying the substitution hypothesis empirically. One would have expected that crowd-out effects, should they exist, would have been discernible during the last business cycle: both the strong secular trend in female labor force participation and enormous reductions in the welfare rolls should have provided enough increases in female competitors to observe crowd-out. Yet the strength of macroeconomic performance in the last several years of the 1990s—when the welfare rolls were plummeting—was unprecedented. Untangling these two effects is extremely difficult.

Even with these problems, however, these estimates suggest than any substitution that occurred was probably minor. The techniques used here are likely to have uncovered evidence of female/male substitution if those effects were substantial in metropolitan labor markets. While we cannot entirely rule out the possibility of displacement and substitution among less-educated male and female workers with this analysis, we can say that any effect that did occur was relatively small and clearly not sufficient to adequately explain the declines in labor force participation observed among less-educated men in the 1990s.

NOTES

The authors thank Heidi Shierholz and Elizabeth Scott for excellent research assistance.
    1. For a summary of these legislative changes, see Blank and Ellwood (2002); for a summary of their estimated effects, see Blank (2002).
    2. In contrast, Eissa and Hoynes (1998) indicate that these changes had small negative effects on the incentives for married women to work.
    3. This estimate of the growth in child care subsidies is a minimum. It is based on federal programs that provide direct subsidies to welfare recipients and does not include state child care subsidy dollars, which have also expanded. Nor does it include expansions

in the dependent care tax credit, which benefits families with incomes high enough to owe taxes. See Loprest, Schmidt, and Witte (2000) for more details on child care subsidy changes.

4. All children under age 6 in families with incomes below 133 percent of the federal poverty level have access to Medicaid; 23 states use higher income cutoffs. All children up to age 19 in families with incomes below 100 percent of the poverty level are also covered by Medicaid; 26 states use higher income cutoffs. For more details on Medicaid expansions, see Gruber (2003).

5. For instance, the methodologies used to measure the impact of the economy and of welfare reforms typically use year fixed effects, which makes it impossible to separate the effects of minimum wage changes and EITC changes that were enacted everywhere at the same time.

6. Of course, it is always possible that unemployment among men would have fallen faster or wages risen faster in the absence of such strong increases in female labor supply.

7. In the 2000 Current Population Survey Outgoing Rotation Groups (CPS-ORG) data, the occupational gender segregation index is 0.48 for workers with more than a high school diploma and 0.57 for those with a high school diploma or less.

8. We are not concerned with changes in MSA boundaries during this period. Our interest is the metropolitan labor market. As MSAs grow, their relevant labor market necessarily expands.

9. The monthly CPS sample collects employment information. The ORG sample is composed of the Outgoing Rotation Groups (one-quarter of the CPS sample); these individuals are also asked for wage information.

10. Ideally, one would like to repeat the analysis in table 5.1, as well as in tables 5.2 and 5.3, for subgroups differentiated by race or ethnicity. Unfortunately, there are too few data observations within most MSA-gender-skill-year cells (tables 5.1 and 5.2) or within most state-gender-skill-year cells (table 5.3) to further differentiate by race.

11. Table 5.2 regresses changes in male labor supply on changes in female labor force participation. We have also regressed levels of male labor supply on changes in female labor force participation and a lagged dependent variable and found similar results.

12. This is known as a Duncan index and computed as $(.05) \times \Sigma_i(M_i - F_i)$ for each MSA in each year. M_i is the proportion of the male labor force employed in industry i and F_i is the proportion of the female labor force employed in industry i. (We calculate the index across 23 major industries in each MSA.) The measure indicates the proportion of women (or men) who would have to change industries for the industry distribution of men and women to be the same. Values range from 0 to 1, with 1 indicating total segregation.

13. Since the dependent variable in these regressions is the change in participation rates, fixed effects are removing systematic differences in labor force participation trends.

14. For a more extensive and nuanced discussion of the relationship between welfare reform and male labor supply (including specific attention to black men), see Lewis (2002). Bartik (2000) also estimates some models of this sort.

15. We use three age categories, while Schoeni and Blank used four.

16. Schoeni and Blank use March CPS data, which provide fewer observations and are likely to be noisier, but Schoeni and Blank were interested in AFDC receipt, family income, and poverty measures as well as labor force participation. These data were

available only in the March CPS, which limited Schoeni and Blank to that data source with fewer observations per cell.

17. In econometric terms, these regressions are reduced form specifications in which we use welfare reform dummies as instrumental variables. If these reduced form results were more compelling, one could use the welfare reform instruments to estimate the causal effect of female labor supply on male labor supply.

18. The extent to which TANF policy changes affected outcomes is the subject of ongoing research. Schoeni and Blank (2000) indicate that the economy accounts for much of the female labor force participation increases post-1996.

19. Men who do not work full-time include both those working part-time on their usual weekly job and those who have been out of the labor market for all of the previous year. Relatively few men do not report any hours a week on at least one job in the previous year; 16 percent of high school dropouts, 7.5 percent of high school graduates, and 4 percent of men with more than a high school diploma have no reported work in the previous year.

20. Obviously, men's transition rates between any one employment state and another will be associated with the other transition rates. Hence, the specifications estimated here are reduced form, so we have already solved out the full model.

21. In econometric terms, one can write down analogous gender-specific reduced-form models for transition rates. The underlying algebra shows that one must also control for interactions between average women's characteristics and the segregation index.

22. Standard errors were estimated using a robust method to account for correlation of unobservables over time within MSAs.

23. The dependent variable in tables 5.6 and 5.7 (and the key independent variable on women as well) is now defined as "employed last week," and not full-time employment.

24. We estimated the same models, instead defining strong labor force attachment by having worked at least 26 weeks last year. The results are qualitatively identical to those reported in tables 5.6 and 5.7.

REFERENCES

Bartik, Timothy J. 2000. "Displacement and Wage Effects of Welfare Reform." In *Finding Jobs: Work and Welfare Reform,* edited by David Card and Rebecca M. Blank (72–122). New York: Russell Sage Foundation.

Blank, Rebecca M. 2000. "Fighting Poverty: Lessons from Recent U.S. History." *Journal of Economic Perspectives* 14(2): 3–19.

———. 2002. "Evaluating Welfare Reform." *Journal of Economic Literature* 40(4): 1105–66.

Blank, Rebecca M., and David T. Ellwood. 2002. "The Clinton Legacy for America's Poor." In *American Economic Policy in the 1990s,* edited by Jeffrey Frankel and Peter Orszag (749–800). Cambridge, MA: MIT Press.

Blank, Rebecca M., and Lucie Schmidt. 2001. "Work, Wages, and Welfare." In *The New World of Welfare,* edited by Rebecca M. Blank and Ron Haskins (70–102). Washington, DC: Brookings Institution Press.

Blundell, Richard, and Thomas MaCurdy. 1999. "Labor Supply: A Review of Alternative Approaches." In *Handbook of Labor Economics,* vol. 3A, edited by Orley C. Ashenfelter and David Card. New York: Elsevier.

Eissa, Nada, and Hilary W. Hoynes. 1998. "The Earned Income Tax Credit and the Labor Supply of Married Couples." Working Paper E99-267. Berkeley: Department of Economics, University of California, Berkeley.

Eissa, Nada, and Jeffrey B. Liebman. 1996. "Labor Supply Response to the Earned Income Tax Credit." *Quarterly Journal of Economics* 111(2): 605–37.

Ellwood, David T. 2000. "The Impact of the Earned Income Tax Credit and Social Policy Reforms on Work, Marriage, and Living Arrangements." *National Tax Journal* 53(4, pt. 2): 1063–1105.

Grogger, Jeffrey. 2003. "The Effect of Time Limits, the EITC, and Other Policy Changes on Welfare Use, Work, and Income among Female-Headed Families." *Review of Economics and Statistics* 85(2): 394–408.

Gruber, Jonathan. 2003. "Medicaid." In *Means-Tested Transfer Programs in the United States,* edited by Robert Moffitt (15–77). Chicago: University of Chicago Press.

Lewis, Jeff. 2002. "The Effects of Welfare Reform on Economic Outcomes of Low-Education Men." Unpublished manuscript.

Loprest, Pamela, Stefanie Schmidt, and Ann Dryden Witte. 2000. "Welfare Reform under PRWORA: Aid to Children with Working Families?" *Tax Policy and the Economy* 14:157–203.

Meyer, Bruce D., and Dan T. Rosenbaum. 2001. "Welfare, the Earned Income Tax Credit, and the Labor Supply of Single Mothers." *Quarterly Journal of Economics* 116(3): 1063–1114.

Moffitt, Robert A. 1999. "The Effects of Pre-PRWORA Waivers on AFDC Caseloads and Female Earnings, Income, and Labor Force Behavior." In *Economic Conditions and Welfare Reform,* edited by Sheldon H. Danziger (91–118). Kalamazoo, MI: W. E. Upjohn Institute for Employment Research.

Schoeni, Robert F., and Rebecca M. Blank. 2000. "What Has Welfare Reform Accomplished? Impacts on Welfare Participation, Employment, Income, Poverty, and Family Structure." Working Paper 7627. Cambridge, MA: National Bureau of Economic Research.

6

Did Spatial Mismatch Affect Male Labor Force Participation during the 1990s Expansion?

John A. Foster-Bey Jr.

The United States experienced almost unprecedented economic growth in the 1990s. During this expansion, unemployment rates reached historically low levels in every part of the country and the absolute number of jobs soared. In addition, the low unemployment levels and job growth were achieved in conjunction with extremely low inflation rates—something that many economists believed could not occur over an extended length of time. Almost all segments of the population benefited from the lower unemployment. Poverty rates went down, the economies of several beleaguered cities improved dramatically, and scores of former welfare recipients moved successfully into employment.

Despite an apparently positive economic picture, some issues were not resolved by the robust economic expansion. For one thing, income inequality increased. During the early phases of the economic expansion, average wages either did not grow or grew at an infinitesimal rate. Only highly skilled and highly educated workers saw their wages rise commensurate with their productivity increases. Another issue was the continuing large gap in employment rates between white and black workers. Finally, the increase in labor force participation for men—especially low-skilled men with a high school education or less—was slower than expected.

The declining and stagnant labor force participation among men was in many ways difficult to understand. The question, then, is why did strong demand in the labor market not draw more potential male workers into the labor force? There are many possible answers.

Blue-collar jobs have traditionally provided above-average wages for less-educated men. As such, men have been disproportionately employed in these sectors (table 6.1). During the 1970s and the 1980s, there was concern that the United States was losing blue-collar jobs through de-industrialization.[1] That is, the U.S. economy was shifting from a production base to a service base

While much of this concern and analysis focused on the loss of blue-collar jobs in the economy as a whole, urban development specialists were particularly concerned that blue-collar jobs were not only declining, but also moving. Blue-collar jobs were leaving their traditional locations in central cities and moving to "greenfield" sites in the suburbs.[2] The results were growing demand for low skilled, less-educated workers in the outer suburbs and a large supply of such workers in central cities and inner-ring suburbs. That is, the locations of jobs and potential workers became disconnected.

This chapter explores how the decentralization of blue-collar jobs in metropolitan areas during the 1990s may have reduced labor force participation among less-educated men.[3] This phenomenon is generally referred to as spatial mismatch hypothesis and was originally posited by John Kain in the 1960s (Kain 1968; Kain and Persky 1969). According to Kain, spatial mismatch became a problem because many low-skilled workers faced limited mobility options. Housing costs in the suburbs were too high for workers to move closer to jobs, and regional transportation systems could not take workers from their central-city residences to suburban job sites efficiently.

Since Kain's original formulation, several other writers and researchers have examined how the shift of jobs from the urban core to the suburban periphery in metropolitan areas has affected employment for minorities and other low-skilled, less-educated workers.[4] William Julius Wilson (1987, 1996) is probably most responsible for recent interest in the spatial mismatch hypothesis. Wilson observed that the decline of industrial job opportunities in central cities close to minority communities might have led to a host of social and economic problems—turning low-income, working-class communities into underclass ghettos.[5]

Despite the compelling case that both Kain and Wilson make for the impact of the spatial mismatch hypothesis, attempts to document and measure the effects of spatial mismatch have been mixed (Arnott 1998;

Table 6.1. *Male Employment by Economic Sector for Select Metropolitan Areas, 1999 (percent)*

	Atlanta	Chicago	Dallas–Fort Worth	Denver	Detroit	Houston	Philadelphia	San Francisco–Oakland
Blue-collar	36.20	35.70	37.30	30.50	43.40	36.00	29.00	29.15
Trade	21.90	20.00	19.00	18.80	3.00	20.00	19.20	17.85
Finance, insurance, and real estate	4.90	6.60	6.50	4.90	3.90	3.40	5.50	5.25
Services	19.40	22.00	20.40	23.20	19.30	20.50	25.70	26.05
Government	8.10	9.20	6.80	13.90	7.20	6.40	11.80	9.35

Source: Author's calculations based on Bureau of Labor Statistics data.

Dickens and Blank 1999). However, most research seems to consistently show that central cities and inner-city neighborhoods have been steadily losing employment since the 1960s. A recent study examining changes in the employment shares of central cities from 1993 to 1996 found that central cities were continuing to lose employment market share to their suburbs (Brennan and Hill 1999). Despite mixed findings on the existence and the impact of spatial mismatch, it seems reasonable to suspect that low-skilled job seekers in central cities have been affected by the urban core's loss of employment market share.

This chapter examines whether spatial mismatch in the blue-collar sector of eight large metropolitan areas was related to falling labor force participation rates among less-educated men—especially minority men. The chapter focuses on three questions:

- Did spatial mismatch in the blue-collar sector occur during the 1990s?
- Was spatial mismatch related to the declining labor force participation rates of less-educated men?
- What are the implications of spatial mismatch?

To determine the existence and impact of spatial mismatch on labor force participation, a special merged data set was constructed for eight metropolitan areas—Atlanta, Chicago, Dallas–Fort Worth, Denver, Detroit, Houston, Philadelphia, and San Francisco–Oakland. These eight urban regions were selected for their diversity along several dimensions. All eight are large multicounty metropolitan areas, allowing comparisons between the central county and suburban counties. They also represent different regions of the country. In addition, the cities have different racial and ethnic populations, making it possible to assess whether job decentralization has greater impact on certain racial or ethnic groups. (For example, Chicago, Detroit, and Philadelphia have large black populations, while Denver and Houston have large Latino populations.) Finally, the eight cities represent different metropolitan types—some are highly dense and monocentric, while others are less dense and less centrally concentrated.[6]

Assessing the Existence of Spatial Mismatch

Before determining if spatial mismatch is implicated in declining male labor force participation, it is important to separate spatial mismatch from its effects. Two conditions must hold for spatial mismatch to occur. First, the demand for labor in the urban core should decline relative to the suburbs. In this case, blue-collar labor demand in the central city should fall compared with the outer suburbs. Two indicators measure declining labor demand: the loss in employment market share by the urban core to the suburban periphery[7] and a relative decline in real wages for blue-collar jobs in the urban core. Second, the target population must be highly concentrated in the urban center and lack geographic mobility.[8]

This section addresses its research questions in three steps. First, it determines whether labor demand in the blue-collar sector declined in the eight metropolitan areas in the sample. Second, it asks whether low-income racial minorities and less-educated potential job seekers were disproportionately concentrated in the urban center of the sampled metropolitan areas. Third, the section calculates spatial mismatch indices for the eight metropolitan areas.

Tracking Changes in Relative Labor Demand in the Blue-Collar Sector

To ascertain whether labor demand in the blue-collar job sector fell in the eight sample metropolitan areas during the 1990s economic expansion, two measures are examined: the change in job share in the blue-collar sector between the urban core and the suburbs, and the relative change in real wages in the blue-collar sector between the urban core and the suburbs.

CHANGE IN JOB SHARE

Two indicators are used to measure the change in relative job share. The first indicator measures the change in the absolute number of blue-collar jobs between the urban core and the suburbs. From 1990 to 1997, the suburbs gained more blue-collar jobs than the urban core in five of the eight metropolitan areas. All net new blue-collar jobs in Atlanta, Chicago, Denver, Detroit, and Houston occurred in the outer suburbs. In contrast, all net new jobs in the blue-collar sector in Philadelphia, San Francisco–Oakland, and Dallas–Fort Worth were in the central counties (table 6.2). The results are therefore mixed. While the urban cores in most of the eight areas under review were losing jobs—not just relatively, but in absolute terms—to the suburbs, three of the eight gained jobs in their urban cores.

Table 6.2. *Change in Blue-Collar Sector Job Share and Relative Wage Growth for Selected Metropolitan Areas, 1990–97*

	Atlanta	Chicago	Dallas–Fort Worth	Denver	Detroit	Houston	Philadelphia	San Francisco–Oakland
Net new job gap 1990–97	−57,310	−144,484	15,284	−52,256	−60,985	−10,945	2,999	18,259
Job availability gap 1990	1.82	0.99	2.11	1.77	0.99	2.76	0.78	1.19
Job availability gap 1997	1.66	0.86	1.93	1.37	0.88	2.56	0.73	1.36
Job availability growth gap 1990–97	−8.8%	−13.7%	−8.5%	−22.6%	−11.1%	−7.2%	−6.4%	14.3%
Wage growth gap 1990–97	2.2%	−2.7%	−2.0%	4.4%	−7.9%	−7.1%	−8.7%	6.1%

Sources: County business patterns and census county population and poverty estimates for 1990–97.

The second indicator is the change in the job availability index, which measures the number of available jobs in the blue-collar sector for every 100 potential job seekers.[9] Examining the job availability index indicates whether more blue-collar jobs were available in the urban core or the suburbs. In 1990, only Chicago, Detroit, and Philadelphia had fewer blue-collar jobs available in the urban core than in the suburbs. Even in Chicago and Detroit, the urban core and the outer suburbs had almost the same level of job availability. But by 1997, relative blue-collar job availability in the urban core declined in all but one of the eight metropolitan areas (San Francisco–Oakland).

This finding suggests that while the majority of central counties in the sample had higher blue-collar job availability than the suburbs, the demand for workers in the urban core in the sector may have weakened during the 1990s. Potential new entrants into the central-county labor market may have perceived work in the blue-collar sector as declining. If individual labor market decisions are grounded as much in the perception of change as in a static analysis, then potential job seekers will respond to opportunities based on the perception of growing demand, not just total job availability. The declining blue-collar job availability suggests that an individual seeking a job would have seen fewer employment opportunities in the urban core in seven of the eight metropolitan areas. This relative decline in demand could have discouraged many less-educated male workers interested in blue-collar work from entering the labor market.

RELATIVE CHANGE IN REAL WAGES

The net new job and job availability data tend to support the assertion that the urban core lost job share to the suburbs in the blue-collar sector. This loss of blue-collar job share may have been mitigated by the fact five metropolitan areas—Atlanta, Dallas–Fort Worth, Denver, Houston, and San Francisco–Oakland—had more blue-collar jobs in the urban core than in the suburbs in both 1990 and 1997.

However, the loss of job share alone, while compelling, is not enough to ascertain whether labor demand in the blue-collar job sector in the urban core declined relative to the suburbs. If real wages in the urban core were falling relative to the suburbs, that drop would tend to support the assertion that relative labor demand in the urban core fell. While the wage picture is somewhat mixed, from 1990 to 1997, five of the eight metropolitan areas experienced a decline in real wages in the blue-collar sector. The declines ranged from 2 percent to almost 9 percent.

DID LABOR DEMAND FALL?

Falling labor demand is calculated using a simple general equilibrium model. The changes in job availability and real wages are added for each metropolitan area. If the sum of the two indicators is negative, it supports the assertion that labor demand fell.

Of the eight metropolitan areas, only San Francisco–Oakland experienced increases in the share of jobs and in real wages in the blue-collar sector, suggesting that labor demand increased. Houston, Chicago, Dallas–Ft. Worth, Detroit, and Philadelphia experienced a loss of job share and falling real wages in the urban core. The loss provides strong evidence that labor demand in the blue-collar sector fell during the 1990s.

Denver and Atlanta have mixed results: both urban cores lost job share, but real wages rose. This suggests that the blue-collar labor market in these two urban cores may have adjusted to the loss of job share. However, when the relative changes in job availability and real wages are summed for Denver and Atlanta, the result is negative—supporting the hypothesis that labor demand in the blue-collar sector probably fell.

Estimating Geographic Concentration

The literature on spatial mismatch assumes not only that labor demand falls, but also that a target group—in this case, less-educated, low-skilled men—is highly concentrated in the urban core. The key assumption is that this geographic concentration leads to limited mobility and therefore reduces access to employment outside the urban core.

This section uses three proxies to test whether geographic concentration was evident and increased over time among less-educated men, especially minority men. The first proxy is the racial concentration ratio, which is useful because less-educated men make up a disproportionate share of the adult black and Latino population. The 1990 racial concentration ratios for all eight metropolitan areas varied from 1.99 in Philadelphia—meaning minorities were almost twice as likely to reside in the central county than in the outer suburbs—to 1.05 in Houston—meaning minorities were only slightly more likely to reside in the central county than in the suburbs. However, racial concentration increased in all but one metropolitan area—San Francisco–Oakland—between 1990 and 1997 (table 6.3).

The second proxy is the poverty concentration ratio, which is useful because less-educated men make up a large share of poor adults. The

Table 6.3. *Change in Population Concentration Ratios for Central Counties in Select Metropolitan Areas*

	Central County to Suburban Share Ratio		Percent growth, 1991–97/2000
	1990	1997/2000	
Concentration of adult minority population, 1990–97			
Atlanta	1.75	1.79	2.2
Chicago	1.27	1.29	1.7
Dallas–Fort Worth	1.17	1.19	1.8
Denver	1.86	1.87	0.2
Detroit	1.73	1.74	0.6
Houston	1.05	1.06	0.8
Philadelphia	1.99	2.00	0.9
San Francisco–Oakland	1.18	1.17	−1.1
All eight metropolitan areas	1.37	1.38	0.7
Concentration of low-income adults, 1990–97			
Atlanta	1.38	1.47	5.9
Chicago	1.26	1.28	2.0
Dallas–Fort Worth	1.04	1.10	6.0
Denver	1.64	1.67	1.6
Detroit	1.53	1.51	−1.1
Houston	1.04	1.06	2.4
Philadelphia	2.00	1.98	−0.9
San Francisco–Oakland	1.23	1.20	−2.5
All eight metropolitan areas	1.30	1.31	0.9
Concentration of less-educated adults, 1990–2000			
Atlanta	0.87	0.86	−1.2
Chicago	1.05	1.07	1.9
Dallas–Fort Worth	1.01	1.05	4.0
Denver	1.13	1.21	7.0
Detroit	1.10	1.14	3.6
Houston	0.99	1.02	3.0
Philadelphia	1.21	1.26	4.1
San Francisco–Oakland	1.07	1.06	−0.9
All eight metropolitan areas	1.04	1.08	3.8

Source: Author's calculations based on census county population and poverty estimates from 1990 to 1997.

Note: Adults are 15 to 64 years old.

poverty concentration ratio also varied greatly in 1990. It ranged from 2.00 in Philadelphia to 1.04 in Houston and Dallas–Fort Worth. From 1990 to 1997, poverty concentration increased in five of the eight metropolitan areas. The exceptions were Detroit, Philadelphia, and San Francisco–Oakland. Note, however, that even with a modest decline Philadelphia had a very high level of poverty concentration—1.98.

The third and final proxy is the education concentration ratio, used to assess whether less-educated adults disproportionately reside in the urban core.[10] The education concentration ratio varied from 1.21 in Philadelphia—meaning less-educated adults were 21 percent more likely to reside in the central county than in the suburbs—to 0.87 in Atlanta—meaning less-educated adults were more heavily concentrated in the Atlanta suburbs. Of the eight metropolitan areas, all but two—Atlanta and San Francisco–Oakland—increased their concentration of less-educated adults between 1990 and 1997.

According to these results, the geographic concentration of less-educated, low-income minority men increased during the 1990s. Whether these rising concentration ratios translated into growing mobility limits depends on other factors, such as the regional housing market and transportation system.

Estimating Spatial Mismatch

Having found indications that the urban core in all but one of the eight metropolitan areas was losing job share in the blue-collar sector to the suburbs and that the geographic concentration of low-income, less-educated minorities increased, the final step is to determine if spatial mismatch occurred in the eight metropolitan areas.

The spatial mismatch literature suggests that changes in job availability, changes in real wages, and population concentration measures are all related. Given this, a spatial mismatch index (SMI) is calculated for each metropolitan region. The index is a linear combination of five indicators: the relative change in blue-collar *job availability* between the urban core and the suburbs, the relative change in real blue-collar *wages* between the urban core and the suburbs in the blue-collar-sector, the change in the *concentration of racial minorities*, the change in the *concentration of low-income individuals*, and the change in the *concentration of less-educated adults*. Falling wages, the loss of job share, and rising concentration ratios increase spatial mismatch. Rising wages, relative job gains, and falling concentration ratios reduce spatial mismatch. A negative SMI indicates spatial mismatch.

Using the SMI, all but one of the eight metropolitan areas—San Francisco–Oakland—experienced spatial mismatch during the 1990s (table 6.4). Of the seven metropolitan areas experiencing spatial mismatch, Denver was the most affected, while Philadelphia was the least affected. The question is to what extent did spatial mismatch in the blue-collar sector result in falling male labor force participation in these metropolitan areas.

Measuring the Impact of Spatial Mismatch on Male Labor Force Participation

A primary question motivating this chapter is whether spatial mismatch is implicated in the decline (or slow improvement) in labor force participation for less-educated men. Two approaches are used to examine the relationship between spatial mismatch and male labor force participation. First, the LFPG—the urban–suburban gap in the growth in male labor force participation from 1990 to 2000—is calculated for each metropolitan area. The metropolitan area is then analyzed to verify a relationship

Table 6.4. *Spatial Mismatch Index for Select Metropolitan Areas (percent)*

	Urban–Suburban Gap 1990–97		Concentration Ratios 1990–2000			Spatial mismatch index
	Job availability	*Real wage gap*	*Racial*	*Low-income*	*Less-educated*	
Atlanta	−8.8	2.2	−2.2	−5.9	0.01	−13.7
Chicago	−13.1	−2.7	−1.7	−2.0	−0.02	−18.8
Dallas–Fort Worth	−8.5	−2.0	−1.8	−6.0	−0.04	−20.3
Denver	−22.6	4.4	−0.2	−1.6	−0.07	−27.0
Detroit	−11.1	−7.9	−0.6	1.1	−0.04	−14.6
Houston	−7.2	−7.1	−0.8	−2.4	−0.03	−13.4
Philadelphia	−6.4	−8.7	−0.9	0.9	−0.04	−10.4
San Francisco– Oakland	14.3	6.1	1.1	2.5	0.01	25.0

Source: Author's calculations.

between the LFPG and the SMI. Second, spatial mismatch is compared with the absolute change in male labor force participation in the urban core.

These approaches find no relationship between the SMI and the change in the LFPG. Of the seven metropolitan areas experiencing spatial mismatch, only one—Denver—also had declining male labor force participation rates (table 6.5). After controlling for race and ethnicity, the results remained varied. Relative labor force participation among white and Hispanic men fell in only two of the seven metropolitan areas where the SMI indicated spatial mismatch. Only three metropolitan areas that experienced spatial mismatch also had declining labor force participation rates among black men.

In some instances, however, the LFPG may be slightly misleading. Because the LFPG measures relative changes between urban and suburban men, the LFPG can be positive even when labor force participation is declining in both the urban core and the suburbs. This is exactly what

Table 6.5. *Urban–Suburban Gap in the Growth of Male Labor Force Participation by Race and Spatial Mismatch Category for Select Metropolitan Areas, 1990–2000*

	Spatial mismatch index (%)	*Male Labor Force Participation Growth (%)*			
		White	*Black*	*Hispanic*	*All*
Spatial mismatch–consistent results					
Atlanta	−13.7	3	8	14	3
Chicago	−18.8	0	6	12	2
Dallas–Fort Worth	−20.3	0	2	−15	2
Denver	−27.0	−3	−1	6	−2
Detroit	−14.6	−5	6	34	1
Houston	−13.4	3	−2	−6	2
Philadelphia	−10.4	7	−1	6	5
San Francisco–Oakland	25.0	3	17	15	3
Correlation with SMI		−0.11	0.87	0.22	−0.05
Statistically significant at 5% level?		No	Yes	No	No

Source: Author's calculations based on 1990 and 2000 census data and 1990 and 1997 county business patterns and population estimates.

happened in these eight metropolitan areas. Labor force participation in the urban core declined in all but two areas—Denver and San Francisco–Oakland. In the suburbs, labor force participation declined or remained unchanged in seven areas (table 6.6). Given this discrepancy, it seems appropriate to compare spatial mismatch not just with the relative change in labor force participation (the LFPG) but also with the absolute change in male labor force participation in the urban core.

In six of the seven metropolitan areas with spatial mismatch, average male labor force participation from 1990 to 2000 actually declined in the urban core—albeit at a slower rate than in the suburbs (see figure 6.1 and table 6.6). Denver was the only exception. In San Francisco–Oakland— the one metropolitan area in the sample without spatial mismatch— average male labor force participation in the urban core increased.

After controlling for race and ethnicity, the results become more complex. For white men residing in the urban core, absolute labor force participation declined in all the metropolitan areas experiencing spatial mismatch except Denver. Black men residing in the urban core experienced absolute declines in labor force participation in only three metro-

Table 6.6. *Change in Male Labor Force Participation by Race and Spatial Mismatch in Central Counties of Select Metropolitan Areas, 1990–2000*

	Spatial mismatch index (%)	Male Labor Force Participation Growth (%)			
		White	Black	Hispanic	All
Atlanta	−13.7	1	−5	10	−1
Chicago	−18.8	−3	3	−5	−2
Dallas–Fort Worth	−20.3	−2	4	0	−1
Denver	−27.0	9	1	10	7
Detroit	−14.6	−3	−1	12	−1
Houston	−13.4	−3	−1	0	−2
Philadelphia	−10.4	−6	5	−7	−1
San Francisco–Oakland	25.0	2	16	4	2
Correlation with SMI		−0.04	0.78	−0.04	−0.01
Statistically significant at 5% level?		No	Yes	No	No

Source: Author's calculations based on 1990 and 2000 census data and 1990 and 1997 county business patterns and population estimates.

Figure 6.1. *Impact of Spatial Mismatch on Changes in Male Labor Force Participation in the Urban Core, 1990–2000*

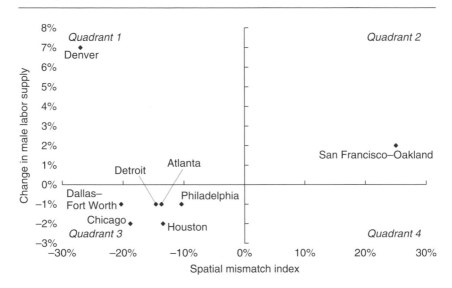

politan areas—Atlanta, Detroit, and Houston—of the seven with spatial mismatch. Hispanic men living in the urban core saw absolute declines in labor force participation in Chicago and Philadelphia.

Examining absolute changes in male labor force participation suggests a fairly strong relationship between spatial mismatch in the blue-collar sector and male labor force participation. The findings also suggest the impact of spatial mismatch on male labor force participation differs by race and ethnicity. Contrary to expectations, it appears that during the 1990s white men were more likely to experience falling labor force participation in metropolitan areas with spatial mismatch in the blue-collar sector. While black and Hispanic men in the urban core also suffered falling labor force participation in several metropolitan areas with spatial mismatch, this impact was limited to fewer metropolitan areas.

Implications

The results presented in this chapter strongly indicate that spatial mismatch in the blue-collar sector affected large metropolitan areas during the 1990s economic expansion. Most metropolitan areas examined in this chapter experienced some form of falling labor demand in their urban core relative to their suburbs in the blue-collar job sector. Only San Francisco–Oakland lacks any real indications of spatial mismatch.

A central question motivating this chapter, though, is whether spatial mismatch in the blue-collar sector is associated with falling male—especially less-educated males'—labor force participation. The data provide varying support for this hypothesis. The blue-collar spatial mismatch appears unrelated to the urban–suburban gap in labor force participation rates for the average male residing in the sample metropolitan areas. Yet, when the spatial mismatch indicator is compared with just the change in labor force participation for the average male residing in the urban core, the relationship appears strong.

When changes in labor force participation are controlled by race and ethnicity, the image becomes more complex. Across the sampled metropolitan areas, spatial mismatch had very different effects on white, black, and Hispanic men. In general, blue-collar spatial mismatch is associated with much smaller improvements in relative labor force participation and declines in absolute labor force participation for white men residing in the urban core. For Hispanic men residing in the urban core, spatial mismatch has little relationship to changes in either relative or absolute labor force participation. Compared with Hispanic men, black men residing in central areas have a slightly stronger relationship between spatial mismatch and changes in labor force participation.

This finding is surprising, since the literature suggests spatial mismatch most affects low-skilled, low-income, relatively immobile minorities. One explanation for these results may be that the study could not control for income levels. As a result, the impact on low-skilled, low-income minorities may have been swamped by positive results for higher-skilled, higher-income minorities. Given the disproportionate share of low-skilled, low-income individuals among the minority male population, however, it was anticipated that low-skilled, low-income individuals would affect the aggregate minority labor force participation figures more than the comparable white figures.

Generalizing from these results is subject to several limitations. The major limitation of this study is the sample size. The small sample renders dubious the validity and reliability of any statistical analysis. It also raises concerns about whether the sample is sufficiently representative of the nation's large metropolitan areas. While the eight metropolitan areas in the sample cannot claim to be statistically representative of all large metropolitan areas in the country, they provide broad regional balance. The sample includes the Northeast, the Midwest, the Southeast, the Southwest, the Mountain West, and the West Coast.

Despite these limitations, several implications can be drawn from the findings. First, it is important to recognize that while spatial mismatch in the blue-collar sector affected these metropolitan areas in considerably different ways, it was, and probably still is, affecting several regions of the country—not just the Northeast or Midwest.

Second, spatial mismatch in the blue-collar sector appears unrelated to the urban–suburban gap in the growth in labor force participation for the average male. However, it may help explain the decline in male labor force participation in the urban core. The relationship between spatial mismatch and the decline in labor force participation for men in central metropolitan areas seems strong. The impact of this relationship differs by race and ethnicity, and seems most pronounced for white men.

Blue-collar jobs may be available in a metropolitan region, but because of mobility barriers, low-skilled potential workers in the urban core may withdraw from the labor force because the jobs seem inaccessible. It might be useful to explore whether regional (i.e., metropolitan-level) intermediaries could effectively connect potential labor supply to potential labor demand. Interesting examples of such intermediaries are available all over the country.

The observed relationship between the loss of job share in the urban core to the suburbs and falling male labor force participation, however, may operate through disparate mechanisms. On the demand side, employers may be responding to perceptions of competence grounded in race and class. Based on the data on educational attainment and the racial and poverty concentration ratios, a large share of the working-age population in the selected urban cores is low-income, poorly educated racial and ethnic minorities. Even without ascribing racial prejudice, statistically this workforce hardly appears skilled. If employers were seeking to fill skilled blue-collar occupations, the urban core would not appear a desirable location for business expansion. (Surprisingly, the impact of such decisionmaking may actually fall hardest on white men.)

From another perspective, the concentrations of race, class, and low education may be associated with unobserved factors such as central counties' high business-related taxes, high crime rate, or local development policies that make it difficult for businesses—especially manufacturing facilities—to expand. If such issues create an unfavorable business climate, employers may choose not to invest or even to disinvest in central counties. Employers may see these unfavorable conditions as the issue, and not the racial and class composition of the urban core's population.

On the supply side, less-educated men may choose to stay out of the labor market for several reasons. Less-educated men may not recognize available employment opportunities because they lack either sufficient knowledge or contacts with the labor market to find work effectively. As a result, they believe no work is available and decide to forgo looking for employment. In some metropolitan areas, such as Atlanta, low-skilled black men may perceive that employers hold racial or class bias that keeps them from hiring less-educated blacks. These perceptions may not be factually based, but if held strongly enough they may stop men from pursuing possible employment.

Many less-educated men face various constraints from lack of private transportation, substance abuse problems, and criminal records. All these factors may make them less attractive to employers and, as a result, may discourage these men from seeking employment. Finally, less-educated men may have unrealistic perceptions of their labor market value. As a result, they may find entry-level wages for individuals with their education and job skills insufficient. This leads them to demand an unrealistically high reservation wage[11] and then withdraw from the labor market when they are unable to obtain it for the work they are qualified to perform.

Policy prescriptions must involve more than just connecting unemployed workers in one part of a region with jobs in another part. Indeed, most experiments to address spatial mismatch have focused on using transportation and, sometimes, housing options to bridge the mobility divide between the location of jobs and the residences of potential job seekers. Unfortunately, few of these experiments have produced compelling results.

The real issue may be that certain workers have difficulties connecting with desirable employment because of skill deficits and negative attitudes about race and class on both sides of the labor market. Policies aimed at improving mobility by providing transportation or increasing housing choices alone may not resolve these deficits and barriers. Any successful policy to address spatial mismatch must also address the skills deficits of many job seekers and the barriers created by negative perceptions related to race and class.

NOTES

1. Several authors have chronicled the impacts of de-industrialization on workers and communities. See Bluestone and Harrison (1984) and Wilson (1987, 1996).

2. "Greenfield" generally means locations where no prior industrial development has occurred.

3. Blue-collar jobs are those in manufacturing, construction, and transportation.

4. These writers and researchers include Cooke (1996), DeRango (2000), Ihlanfeldt and Sjoquist (1998), McLafferty and Preston (1992, 1996), Pastor and Marcelli (2000), Raphael (1998), Taylor and Ong (1995), and Weinberg (1998).

5. Other writers and researchers also chronicled the transformation of low-income, working-class black communities into underclass ghettos. See Jargowsky (1997), Massey and Denton (1993), and Mincy and Ricketts (1990).

6. See the appendix for more detail on the data set.

7. That is, the urban core loses market share to the suburbs in terms of job location. The result is more new jobs located in the suburbs than in the urban center. This shift can occur even when the absolute number of jobs in the urban core increases.

8. The lack of mobility may result from either the unavailability of suitable housing for the target population near the new jobs or inadequate public or private transportation.

9. See the appendix for how potential jobs seekers were calculated.

10. All three ratios measure how much of a metropolitan area's minority, low-income, and less-educated populations reside in the urban core. See the appendix for more detail.

11. The reservation wage is the minimum wage an individual is willing to accept to perform a particular task.

REFERENCES

Arnott, Richard. 1998. "Economic Theory and the Spatial Mismatch Hypothesis." *Urban Studies* 35(7): 1171–85.

Bluestone, Barry, and Bennett Harrison. 1984. *The Deindustrialization of America: Plant Closings, Community Abandonment, and the Dismantling of Basic Industry.* New York: Basic Books.

Brennan, John, and Edward W. Hill. 1999. "Where Are the Jobs? Cities, Suburbs, and the Competition for Employment." Washington, DC: The Brookings Institution.

Cooke, Thomas J. 1996. "City-Suburb Differences in African American Male Labor Market Achievement." *Professional Geographer* 48(4): 445–58.

DeRango, Kelly. 2000. "A Note on Commutes and Spatial Mismatch Hypothesis." Working Paper WP00–59. Kalamazoo, MI: W. E. Upjohn Institute for Employment Research.

Dickens, William T., and Rebecca M. Blank. 1999. "Rebuilding Urban Labor Markets: What Community Development Can Accomplish." In *Urban Problems and Community Development,* edited by Ronald F. Ferguson and William T. Dickens (381–436). Washington, DC: Brookings Institution Press.

Ihlanfeldt, Keith, and David L. Sjoquist. 1998. "The Spatial Mismatch Hypothesis: A Review of Recent Studies and Their Implications for Welfare Reform." *Housing Policy Debate* 9(4): 849–92.

Jargowsky, Paul A. 1997. *Poverty and Place: Ghettos, Barrios, and the American City.* New York: Russell Sage Foundation.

Kain, John F. 1968. "Housing Segregation, Negro Employment, and Metropolitan Decentralization." *Quarterly Journal of Economics* 82: 175–97.

Kain, John F., and Joseph J. Persky. 1969. "Alternatives to the Gilded Ghetto." *Public Interest* 18 (Winter).

Massey, Douglas, and Nancy Denton. 1993. *American Apartheid: Segregation and the Making of the Underclass.* Cambridge, MA: Harvard University Press.

McLafferty, Sara L., and Valerie Preston. 1992. "Spatial Mismatch and Labor Market Segmentation for African-American and Latina Women." *Economic Geography* 68(4): 406–31.

———. 1996. "Spatial Mismatch and Employment in a Decade of Restructuring." *Professional Geographer* 48(4): 420–30.

Mincy, Ronald, and Erol Ricketts. 1990. "Growth of the Underclass, 1970–1980." *Journal of Human Resources* 25(1): 137–45.

Pastor, Manuel, and Enrico Marcelli. 2000. "Men 'n the Hood: Spatial, Skill, and Social Mismatch for Male Workers in Los Angeles." *Urban Geography* 21(6): 474–96.

Raphael, Steven. 1998. "The Spatial Mismatch Hypothesis and Black Youth Joblessness: Evidence from the San Francisco Bay Area." *Journal of Urban Economics* 43: 79–111.

Taylor, Brian D., and Paul M. Ong. 1995. "Spatial Mismatch or Automobile Mismatch? An Examination of Race, Residence, and Commuting in U.S. Metropolitan Areas." *Urban Studies* 32(9): 1453–75.

Weinberg, Bruce A. 1998. "Testing the Spatial Mismatch Hypothesis Using Inter-City Variations in Industrial Composition." Unpublished paper.

Wilson, William Julius. 1987. *The Truly Disadvantaged: The Inner City, the Underclass, and Public Policy.* Chicago: University of Chicago Press.

———. 1996. *When Work Disappears: The World of the New Urban Poor.* New York: Knopf.

Methodology

T he data set was constructed using county business patterns, local area unemployment statistics, county poverty and population estimates from the Census Bureau, and the metropolitan and state labor force and employment estimates from the Current Population Survey for Atlanta, Chicago, Dallas–Fort Worth, Detroit, Denver, Houston, Philadelphia, and San Francisco–Oakland. To obtain information on labor force participation by race and gender and data on educational attainment, the data set was supplemented with summary data collected from the 1990 and 2000 ten-year census. This data set allows for the construction of several job availability indicators and of population, poverty, employment, and labor force measures at the county and metropolitan levels.

This data set has several limitations. For the most part, it covers only the period from 1990 to 1997.[1] While this misses the last two to three years of the economic expansion, it still captures the heart of it. The data set also does not easily allow analysis at the subcounty level. As a result, the unit of analysis is the central county versus the outer counties. Because the central counties of many metropolitan areas also contain the inner suburbs, the extent of spatial mismatch may be concealed by higher levels of economic performance in the inner suburbs raising the performance of central-city counties. Finally, the data set gives us only a limited capacity to disaggregate and analyze data by demographic or human capital characteristics. This restricts our ability to directly control for differences in race, education, or gender. Even so, the chapter includes some observations on the impact of race and educational attainment on opportunity.

Measuring Spatial Mismatch

The literature on spatial mismatch suggests several approaches to measuring spatial mismatch. Arnott observes that a useful approach to test for spatial mismatch is a general equilibrium model (Arnott 1998). A general equilibrium model would be based on the theory that true spatial mismatch would reflect a reduction in labor demand in the urban core relative to the suburbs. Such a situation should result in both a relative fall in the number of jobs (decentralization) and a decline in real wages (wage growth gap)[2] in the urban core.

This chapter defines spatial mismatch as the confluence of two conditions: falling labor demand in the urban core's blue-collar sector, and the geographic concentration of a target population (in this case less-educated, low-skilled males) leading to limitations on mobility. The simple general equilibrium model is used to assess the existence of falling labor demand in the urban core. If labor demand declined, the availability of blue-collar jobs in the central county should decline relative to the outer suburbs, and relative blue-collar wages should also fall.[3]

The equilibrium model is based on several assumptions. First, the metropolitan area is composed of two separate geographic islands—the urban core and the outer suburbs.[4] Second, changes in labor demand affect both skilled and unskilled labor in the geographic area and in the target industry. Third, there are no mobility limitations on residents of the urban core seeking work anywhere within the central county. Fourth, the occupation and skill mix and the distribution of full-time and part-time employment remain constant between 1990 and 1997. Fifth, if the urban core is losing job share to the suburbs, then relative wages in the urban core would have to grow much faster than job loss to keep labor demand in the central county strong.

This simple labor demand model along with measures of target population concentration is used to develop an index (the spatial mismatch index) to measure spatial mismatch as a linear combination of five factors: the change in the urban–suburban gap in job availability, the change in the urban–suburban gap in real wages, the change in the proportion of racial minorities residing in a metropolitan region's central counties, the change in the proportion of a metropolitan area's poor residing in the region's urban core, and the change in the proportion of less-educated adults residing in a metro region's central area. The last three changes are multiplied by −1 to indicate that an increase in concentration contributes to spatial mismatch, while a decline reduces spatial mismatch. Using the index, spatial mismatch occurs when the index value is less than 0. When the index value is positive, it indicates that the urban core is gaining employment and avoiding or mitigating the impact of racial and class geographic concentration.

Key Variables

The Job Availability Gap

The job availability gap (JG) is the ratio of job availability in the urban core to job availability in the suburbs. Job availability measures how many jobs in the blue-collar sector are available for every 100 potential job seekers in both the urban core and the outer suburbs.[5] The JG is calculated for both 1990, the start of the study period, and 1997, the last year of the study.

The Net New Job Gap

The net new job gap (NNJG) is the urban–suburban gap in new jobs in the blue-collar sector. The NNJG is calculated using the following formula: net new blue-collar jobs in the urban core minus net new blue-collar jobs in the suburbs. If the NNJG is negative, the suburbs have gained the majority of net new jobs in the blue-collar sector.

Measuring Mobility Limitations

All the literature on spatial mismatch suggests that for declining relative labor demand in the urban core to have a negative effect, workers must also suffer from limited mobility. Potential job seekers in the urban core must find it difficult to move their residences closer to available jobs in the suburbs or to travel daily from their current central residences to suburban jobs. There is no really good direct measure of limited mobility, but researchers have often used commuting times and commuting distance as proxies.

The data are not available to calculate either commuting time or distance for the study period covered in this chapter. But because the subject group—low-skilled, less-educated males—is disproportionately concentrated in three overlapping groups—low-income individuals, racial and ethnic minorities, and less-educated adults—concentration ratios for race, poverty, and educational attainment are calculated and used as proxies for mobility. In the absence of an effective regional public transportation system and a limited supply of low-cost and affordable housing in job-rich suburbs, the literature suggests that high and growing levels of residential concentration on the basis of race, class, and educational attainment would most likely indicate at least a potential limit on mobility (Massey and Denton 1993).

The concentration ratios are calculated using the following formulas:

Racial concentration (RC) is calculated for 1990 and 1997. If the number of nonwhites is greater than zero, then RC = (share of metropolitan area's nonwhite adult population in the urban core)/(share of metropolitan area's total adult population in the urban core).

The formula for the *poverty concentration ratio (PC)* for 1990 and 1997 is the following: if the number of poor is greater than zero, then PC = (share of metropolitan area's poor adult population in the urban core)/(share of metropolitan area's total adult population in the urban core).

The *less-educated ratio (LER)* for 1990 and 2000 is derived from the following calculation: if the number of less-educated adults is greater than zero, then LER = (share of metropolitan area's less-educated adults in the urban core)/(urban core's share of the metropolitan area's total population).

Where

Adults = all individuals 15 to 64 years old;
Nonwhites = all nonwhite and Hispanic adults 15 to 64 years old;
Poor = all individuals 18 and older with family incomes below the poverty level; and
Less-educated = individuals 25 years old and over with no more than a high school diploma.

A ratio of 1 means that the central county's share of either minority, low-income, or less-educated adults was the same as the county's share of the metropolitan area's adult population. For example, a ratio of 1.10 implies that the central area's share of the minority or low-income adult population is 10 percent higher than its share of the metropolitan population. The critical assumption here is that if these three groups are disproportionately concentrated in the urban core, then the area is most likely to suffer from spatial mismatch.

Male Labor Force Participation

Finally, this chapter attempts to determine whether there is any evidence that spatial mismatch and limited mobility have actually limited labor market success for low-skilled, less-educated males. Ideally, spatial mismatch findings for 1990–97 would be compared with the growth in labor force participation for less-educated males controlled for education, income, and race and ethnicity over the same period. Unfortunately, the data do not allow for this direct comparison. Instead, the change in labor force participation for all males from 1990 to 2000, controlled for race and ethnicity, will be used.

The hypothesis is that there should be a negative relationship between spatial mismatch and both the percent change in male labor force participation in the urban core and the change in the urban–suburban gap in male labor force participation. As spatial mismatch increases, relative and absolute male labor force participation should decline.

The following equations are used to measure change in male labor force participation. The growth in male labor force participation (GLFP) for the urban core and the suburbs is measured as the percentage of change in the male labor force participation rate (LFP) for white, Hispanic, and black men from 1990 to 2000. The equation for each racial/ethnic group in the suburbs and the central county would take the following general form:

$$GLFP_{males} = \left(LFP_{all\ males\ 2000} / LFP_{all\ males\ 1990} - 1 \right) \times 100.$$

The urban–suburban gap in the GLFP is the labor force participation growth gap (LFPG). The LFPG is measured by subtracting the average GLFP for all males residing in the suburbs from the GLFP for all males in the central counties controlled for race and ethnicity. If the LFPG is negative, then male labor force participation in the urban core has not kept up with the suburbs. The equations to control for race and ethnicity would take the following forms:

$$LFPG_{all\ males} = GLFP_{urban/all\ males} - GLFP_{suburban/all\ males}$$

$$LFPG_{white\ males} = GLFP_{urban/white\ males} - GLFP_{suburban/all\ males}$$

$$LFPG_{black\ males} = GLFP_{urban/black\ males} - GLFP_{suburban/all\ males}$$

$$LFPG_{Hispanic\ males} = GLFP_{urban/Hispanic\ males} - GLFP_{suburban/all\ males}$$

Concepts and Terminology

Most of the research on spatial mismatch uses the central city and the suburbs as the units of analysis. The geographic unit of analysis in this chapter is the metropolitan area's central urban county (or counties) and the suburban counties outside the central county (or counties). The chapter refers to the central county as the urban core. The urban core may contain the inner suburbs as well as the central city. "Central areas" and "urban" are used interchangeably with urban core. "Outer suburbs" is used interchangeably with suburbs.

The urban core in three of the eight metropolitan areas examined in this chapter contains two counties, while the other five metropolitan areas contain one central county. A central county is included in the urban core if it contains all or part of a major central city. For example, the two central counties that contain the central cities of Dallas and Fort Worth are included in the Dallas metropolitan area. The two counties containing the central cities of San Francisco and Oakland make up the San Francisco–Oakland metropolitan area's urban core. Fulton and DeKalb counties are included in the Atlanta metropolitan area's urban core because they make up the central city of Atlanta. The other five metropolitan areas—Chicago, Denver, Detroit, Houston, and Philadelphia—contain a single county in their urban core.

The blue-collar job sector includes all jobs in manufacturing, construction, and transportation. Males are disproportionately employed in this sector. The chapter uses blue-collar jobs, blue-collar job sector, and jobs in the blue-collar sector interchangeably.

NOTES

1. The summary data from the 1990 and 2000 censuses allow analysis of county and metropolitan labor force participation and employment over the whole decade.

2. In their analysis of Los Angeles, Pastor and Marcelli (2000) focus on the relationship between changes in wages and changes in employment. If a change in employment demand reduces employment in a defined geographical area, then wages should fall.

3. The average payroll per job is used as a proxy for average wages.

4. Arnott (1998) uses the idea of two islands: the central city and the suburbs. In this chapter, the urban core or the central urban county is one island, and the outer suburbs are the other island. The urban core comprises the central city and in some instances the inner suburbs.

5. Potential blue-collar job seekers = (Number of working-age males × % males working in blue-collar industries for 1999) + (Number of working-age females × % females working in blue-collar industries for 1999).

7

Low-Income Black Men on Work Opportunity, Work Resources, and Job Training Programs

Alford A. Young Jr.

Despite social scientific research's close attention to low-income black men, a paucity of information exists about how these men perceive the worlds of work and work opportunity, and how they believe they can navigate those environments. More specifically, no research has documented what low-income black men believe are the types of jobs available in their own or surrounding communities, the relevant skills and capacities needed for securing these jobs, and how often low-income black men think about or use publicly supported workforce development programs in their efforts to securely position themselves in the workforce.[1]

This chapter aims to fill this gap by examining the views of 26 black men from inner-city Detroit (age 18 to 24). Each man is designated as low-income because he has not been gainfully employed for more than half of any given year since his 16th birthday.[2] The households in which the men were raised included parents or guardians whose work experience ranged from consistent unemployment to stable semiskilled or skilled blue-collar employment (e.g., factory laborer, automobile plant worker, store clerk or cashier, or security guard). The employment experiences of parents or guardians did not result in the transfer of significant material benefits or resources to these men.

This analysis focuses on how these men judged their involvement in job training and placement programs. A healthy portion of the discussions, however, centered on their views of work and work opportunities in Detroit, as well as their personal work histories and experiences looking for work. These personal histories and experiences place the men's views on job training and placement programs in a broader context.

The findings are categorized according to various focal points of the discussions with the young men. The chapter begins with an overview of the men's employment histories. It then turns to their outlooks on the worlds of work and work opportunity, followed by their assessment of skills and resources relevant to securing stable and desirable employment. The chapter concludes by considering the men's experiences with and evaluations of job training and placement programs.

Although some men had briefly enrolled in other job training or placement services, each man in the survey group has participated in the Michigan Works! job training and placement program as well as the Youth Opportunity (YO) program, a job training and social services initiative.[3] Hence, although living in or near poverty, these men are actively seeking work or the training that could lead to it. Consequently, they can be considered "best case" types for an analysis of how urban-based, low-income black men think about work and the potential and possibilities of work. Table 7.1 profiles the 26 men.

It is no secret to urban researchers, policy advocates, and policy analysts that throughout the 20th century, Detroit contained one of the largest constituencies of urban-based, low-income blacks (Farley, Danziger, and Holzer 2000; Sugrue 1996). By the end of the 20th century, Detroit had become a sphere of poverty and destitution for many blacks. According to 1990 Census data, approximately 30 percent of Detroit residents earned cash incomes below the poverty level.

The decline in the automobile sector has been the principal source of diminished manufacturing-centered labor market prospects for Detroit-area residents. From 1970 through 2000, manufacturing jobs declined from 36 percent to only 20 percent of the labor market in the Detroit metropolitan area (Farley et al. 2000). In inner-city Detroit, manufacturing jobs decreased 50 percent between 1960 and 2000, dropping from 200,000 to 100,000 jobs. Black men (age 24 to 65) have endured a particularly challenging experience in Detroit, with 6.9 percent of the black male population unemployed in 1997.

Clearly, then, the men in this study were born and raised in an urban area that no longer offers many blue-collar labor market prospects that men of their educational stature were previously able to secure. It is within this socioeconomic context that the men talk about good jobs, the

Table 7.1. *Participant Demographics*

ID	Age	Fellow residents in current household	Education	Work history	Children
Kevin	22	Mother, sister	HS diploma	custodian, fast food	
Carlton	19	Mother, stepfather	HS diploma	none	
Greg	19	Mother, her boyfriend	HS diploma	none	
John	23	Grandmother	HS diploma	van driver	
David	18	Mother, brother	Some HS	laborer	
Vince	21	Girlfriend	Some HS	fast food, security guard	1
Sam	20	Grandparents	Some HS	dishwasher, fast food	
Stan	21	Mother, aunts	HS diploma	welder	2
Don	18	Mother, grandmother	HS diploma	none	
Derrick	21	Mother, sister	Some HS	fast food, mechanic	1
Bob	19	Mother, sisters	Some HS	fast food, construction	1
Jerry	24	None	HS diploma	forklift operator	
Henry	18	Mother, father[a]	HS diploma	lifeguard	
Brian	20	Mother, brother	HS diploma	fast food, store clerk	
Ron	20	Mother, siblings	HS diploma	cashier, custodian	
Darryl	22	Mother, stepfather, brother	HS diploma	fast food, mover	1
Steve	22	Mother	Some HS	custodian, mover	
Ray	18	Mother, father	HS diploma	fast food	
Eric	21	Mother, sisters	Some HS	none	
Harold	21	Wife, child	HS diploma	recreation center staff	1
Mark	23	Mother	HS diploma	car wash, laborer	
Ben	20	Mother	HS diploma	store cashier	
Curt	19	Mother, stepfather, siblings	HS diploma	fast food	
Ricky	20	Mother, stepfather, sister	Some HS	custodian	
Terry	19	Mother, siblings	HS diploma	none	1
Daniel	20	Mother	HS diploma	store clerk, orderly	

HS = high school

[a] intermittent member of household

opportunity structure in Detroit, and the institutions and programs that they use in hopes of improving their employment prospects.

Before considering what the surveyed men said, it should first be understood that they do not always accurately depict Detroit's contemporary labor market structure, nor do they always elucidate accurately how good jobs are found or what it takes to keep a good job. Instead, the commentary illustrates how these men think about work and their experiences training for and trying to be placed in jobs. Whether accurate or not, the men's views, claims, and accounts shed light on how they have responded to work opportunities (or the lack of them) in their pasts, and how they may function with such opportunities (or their absence) in the future. Hence, their views and opinions serve to shed light only on their own capacity for better incorporation into employment, and not on any objective reading of work and work opportunity in Detroit.

Work Histories and Experiences

As young men between the ages of 18 and 24, the survey group members do not have long or rich work histories. As shown in table 7.1, most of their employment experiences are in the fast food industry, although a few of the men have encountered other labor market experiences (custodial work, semiskilled labor, and the like). Their rather short-term exposure to this limited arena of work prospects is a critical factor in how they respond to work opportunities. In essence, the men are less tolerant or accepting of employer demands if the job is low-paying (e.g., less than $8.00 an hour). This attitude results in consistent job turnover for these men; they either leave jobs or are fired. Sometimes, circumstances the men do not create bring about the dismissal. At other times, it results from their negative interaction with colleagues and bosses. In other cases, business failures bring about an end to employment.

When discussing their work experiences, the men explain that employers in the fast food industry and other low-skilled, low-paying sectors do not find it worthwhile to invest extensive time working out problems or conflicts with employees when an ample supply of potential employees is available. The men feel that employers believe employee dilemmas are most effectively rectified by dismissing employees and immediately hiring new ones, rather than by negotiation or mediation. The men explain that their responses to these work opportunities and their conduct on the job is somewhat based on the understanding that their employers consider them expendable.

The men also are performing work that brings them little material return and involves extraordinarily routine, often highly uninteresting tasks. These circumstances are compounded by some of the men's experience with unstable labor markets in the municipal economy throughout the late 1990s and the early 2000s. In short, the men with work histories rarely work at jobs that are more than minimally gratifying, and almost all are in employment sectors that consist of rapid employee turnover, if not complete business closings. These conditions result in both the men's strong sense of precariousness concerning work and in their general unwillingness to adapt fully to the demands of employers, who are generally seen as indifferent to their workers and unwilling to provide satisfactory wages:

> **Sam:** Now, see, I'm the type of person, I have walked off jobs because of the way a person talks to me. . . . The way you talk to me can make and break a relationship, and I will walk off a job, knowing I need the money, you're not going to talk to me like a peon. . . . You can talk at me or you can talk to me. I guarantee you talk at me, we're going to have a problem. . . . But you talk to me, and we can resolve this.

A rich social scientific literature details the value black men place on being respected in public interaction, whether at work or other settings (Anderson 1990, 1999; Billson 1996; Majors and Billson 1992). While this chapter is not the place to critically assess that literature, one assertion from this work is that how black men express their desire for respect, and how they respond when such respect is not forthcoming, contribute to their problems establishing robust work histories. The comments made by the men in this study affirm that they share this plight with many other black men.

Even when the men have positive relations with employers, past experiences lead them to hold firm to the idea that unforeseen circumstances could cause problems in their jobs. These and similar accounts demonstrate that these men generally do not trust the world of work to deliver what they desire:

> **Curt:** [*On working at McDonald's*] I moved up fast along their business because I was a hard worker, the managers loved me, I

came in and I could catch on to everything in like maybe two or three days. They had me running the grill area as the grill team leader at my first site that I was working at. Then I got transferred up the street and they had me working up under somebody, and I was like, "I can't work up under somebody right now. I have a higher position than they do, I make more than they do, so I need to step up." Then, they was like, "Well, that means you need to learn cash," and then they taught me cash and I learned it in three days. He was like, "Well, I'm going to recommend you for management." Uh, before he could recommend me for management, the negative came in.

That "negative" was the stealing of money out of **Curt's** cashier drawer during an intensely busy period at work. **Curt** said that although the theft was caught on a security monitor, he was still relieved of his job on the grounds that he was irresponsible for letting a fellow employee access his cashier's drawer.

Brian reported a similar situation from his brief employment in the fast food industry:

I worked in McDonald's and I was an assistant manager, and then because of an incident that happened that I wasn't even a part[y] to, I wasn't even working that day, but I was working at a McDonald's in the suburbs, and it was only three black people that worked there, and I was one of the three, and some money came up missing, and since I'm a cashier, I'm the first person they looked at— when it turned out one of they, uh, the actual manager was stealing money—and I got bumped back out to a crew member. . . . I worked there, I would say, for another two months after that happened, and then I quit [after] about eight months.

Often the lack of trust between employer and employee is supplemented by problems with coworkers or a workplace with low morale (the result of either the mundane work or the minimal wages). Regardless, these jobs do not strike the men as particularly fulfilling, either materially or emotionally. Hence, situations and circumstances arise that often force the men into leaving or otherwise help them decide not to invest much time and effort into their jobs. No man with work experience found great pleasure in any of his jobs, and no one expressed regret about leaving any particular job. All men, however, firmly hold onto ideas about better jobs and better overall qualities of life that they want to encounter.[4]

Ideal and Acceptable Goals and Desires Concerning Work

The ultimate desire for each man is a middle-class blue-collar or white-collar job. These jobs include working at a factory or plant in a unionized job sector or achieving a college education and becoming a business executive. The precise objective held by each man is a product of his personal history. That is, each man determines ideal goals as a consequence of what he has encountered in past work situations.

For instance, some men want to own a business because they have worked in this arena. Intimate and consistent exposure to their bosses provided them with coherent images of an employment status that they reconstruct into a future goal or desire. Others want to become white-collar professionals as a result of exposure to attorneys in the criminal justice system or to other business people who frequented the fast food establishments where the men have worked. In other cases, ideas about ideal jobs come from some exposure to or training for lower-tier sectors of certain industries (e.g., deciding on a career in computer science after having some basic training in data entry or after expecting to receive some computer-based training in the near future).

The men are not yet old enough to have experienced long-term bouts of unemployment. They also have had only a few disappointing or turbulent interactions with potential and actual employers. Thus, they do not yet consider themselves perpetual victims of Detroit's poor-quality labor markets. Instead, they steadfastly maintain hopes and desires for white-collar or skilled blue-collar work that could firmly embed them into the American middle class:

> **Don:** I want to be an engineer. . . . I'm going to school now for computer information systems. . . . Working for myself, entrepreneur . . . computer engineering like Bill Gates. Something like that . . . hopefully working for Microsoft, or some big computer company, then start my own company.
>
> **Derrick:** [I want to have] my own business—an architect or a mechanic. Something where I can run it the way I want it to be ran, and pay people what I want to pay them. Somewhere I got my own

rules like, "Okay, you got to be here at this time, and this and this," and basically just help out the community.

Daniel: I want to be a criminal lawyer . . . because sometimes I feel people are proven—not proven—some people are found guilty when they're actually not. Just it's a lot.

Terry: I want to be dir—a film director. . . . I want to get on the radio too. I want to get a show on the radio or something too, so . . . you know, I'm working on that in school, and I'm doing little side things to work my way into the biz, so people know my name, whatever.

The men hold these idealistic aspirations largely because, as young men in their late teens or early twenties, they lack sustained exposure to the world of work, and thus are not as disillusioned or frustrated as older, urban-based low-income black men have become (Young 2004). None of the men in this study has acquired anything more than a few years of struggling to find and maintain good jobs. They are also either living with their parents or guardians or not very many years removed from living with such people. Hence, the security of having at least some parental support, coupled with the absence of utter despair resulting from many years of few to no work prospects, means the men can still dream of bigger and better lives, and feel that such dreams could come true.

As stated earlier, another critical factor in the men's ability to talk about specific occupations is that past experiences or encounters have given them ideas about those arenas. **Don** enrolled in a computer school and thus conceived of a high-status position in computer technology because he had learned that this was the upper bounds of possibility for those in that industry. Like a few of the men, **Daniel** has had some trouble with the law. His encounters with the police and the juvenile justice system provided him with consistent exposure to attorneys. This was one of his few consistent encounters with people in a high-status white-collar profession. Thus, he was able to embrace that profession as an ideal goal for himself despite lacking the educational credentials he would need to become an attorney. In fact, each man rationalizes his ultimate desires by tying in some personal connection with the employment sector that exemplifies that desire. This is the case despite very little apparent preparation for such pursuits (after all, most of these men have only a high school education, and some have just a few years of high school).

When asked what they would find comfortable or satisfactory rather than ideal, the men speak almost exclusively about skilled blue-collar jobs rather than the white-collar world. They believe this level of employment could provide economic stability, if not vast riches. They also focus on jobs of this caliber because they are interested in working in sectors that provide fringe benefits, some kind of promotion plan, and union membership (the last factor of slightly less interest than the other two):

Steve: A good-paying job with good benefits. A full-time job, not a part-time job, something I can get medical, you know, health insurance, because you never know what can happen to you and for you to be working some penny-ante job and don't have no benefits and something happen to you, you know what I'm saying, then you just ass out. You know, and it could be serious enough to where you [become] ass out for life.

Terry: Forty hours a week at least, you know what I'm saying? Being able to do what you want to do—not what you want to do, but being able to have the freedom to do your job . . . without somebody dictating how you got to do something. . . . And a salary is better than anything per hour because a salary, regardless, you sick, whatever, you're going to get your check.

The common connection between the ideal interest and the satisfactory one is that both provide economic stability and security, as well as delivering to the men a clearly respectable status in the larger social world.

The other major point of interest in discussions about ideal and acceptable interests in the world of work is wages. The men generally state that a job worth doing is one that pays a minimum of $7.00 to $8.00 an hour. Anything less does not allow them to meet their needs and interests, nor motivates them to develop a sincere commitment to their employer. The men also argue that minimum-wage and near minimum-wage jobs require work expectations beyond their expected pay scale. Consequently, they do not feel excited by or firmly committed to such work. Slightly more than half of the men speak of their unwillingness to work for wages they determine are insufficient. Most of these men know jobs exist at the bottom end of the pay scale, and many move into (and, often, back out of) these jobs, but the general perspective is that these options simply are not worthwhile:

> **Vince:** Right now, I ain't going to lie, right now I'll take anything—least $8.50 though. I know that's the least I can . . . I can work with $8.00, but I'll take $8.50 and whatever. I even take the $7.00 job right now. . . . Because they ain't even hiring, except McDonald's. [*"So $7.00 is the cutoff point, though?"*] Really, I ain't going to take no $7.00. I'm saying I will . . . but, man, I . . . about $8.50. I got family wants. . . . I'd a been had a job if I would have took $7.00 an hour. . . . I really . . . I can't afford to lost jobs like I had been. I mean, a lot of jobs, a lot of these low-paying jobs, they don't want to pay you right. So, you know, in turn, I'm the type of person, I might be mad and then just quit, not to deal with the problem. But then I got rent at home to pay. You know, and I pay $500 a month. . . . So you know, can't just quit no job like that no more.

> **Darryl:** You know, a lot of places are hiring, but then you got to think . . . do you want . . . $5.50 an hour? Come on, now. . . . I'm not fittin' to just get out here and work myself, enslave myself, you know, for minimum wage.

> **Steve:** At this point in time, I don't have any skills or trades, you know what I'm saying, I can show you that I'm good with this, but [without formal certification] I can't say that with my skills and my knowledge, you can't pay me less than $18 an hour. You know, so right now I don't have that, and I don't have that to take to some of these companies. So, you know, whatever they can start me off, but I won't work for anything under $8.00. Anything under $8.00 I just won't work for. . . . Unless I just had to.

Steve's statement illustrates a particularly important point about the men's desires and goals concerning work. His stated willingness, yet unwillingness, to work for a wage below $8.00 an hour is consistent with how about 20 of the other men talked about acceptable baseline wages. They often say they will take whatever they could get, but a sentence or two later say that certain wages are wholly unacceptable. This seemingly contradictory talk is consistent with their statements about problems with certain past work experiences, such as the fast food industry, where some men eventually find jobs but abandon them (if not be dismissed) as soon as problems or tension arise.

Approximately five men do not discuss aspirations or desires at any length. Instead, they say they are prepared to accept whatever opportunities might come their way:

> **Darryl:** Well, right now I'll take anything. Anything. Anything. I'm not a picky person now, so, you know, what we say then, there was a time you wouldn't catch me out here till now. "I'm not fittin' to do this, I'm not fittin' to do that." But now, you know, I just seen how growing up, how work was for my moms working and, you know, they didn't really make a lot of money then, and you know what I'm saying? So now I won't take nothing for granted anymore. And I say you got to get out here and do whatever you got to do.

The basic story, then, about goals concerning work is that the men generally aim quite high in terms of ultimate desires and interests. When asked what they would accept or find comfortable, they focus on stable blue-collar employment that includes fringe benefits and possibilities for promotion. The men believe work is usually available, but not the kind of work that would allow them to meet their personal or family needs. In essence, like many Americans, these men aspire to have careers rather than simply any form of available work. They express desires to control their economic destiny, as well as the pace and quality of their workdays. Their desired jobs provide emotional satisfaction as much as material rewards, and the material rewards include fringe benefits as well as a good salary.

In addition to the financial rewards associated with good jobs, the men believe a job is good if it holds some intrinsic appeal. Good jobs allow for some measure of personal growth and development, as well as the chance to garner some public respect and acclaim:[5]

> **Vince:** A good job is a job that you satisfied with, something that you feel you could build on and graduate to bigger and better things, I guess. . . . I mean, if you making seven dollars a hour, but that's what you happy with and it's doing for you, then it's a good job.

> **Sam:** My definition of a good job is something you enjoy doing because you don't look at it like work then . . . even if the pay might

be crappy, you still like doing it. . . . You can have a job paying you a lot of money, but you catching shit every day. . . . Me, I'd rather have a job that pay all right and some [enjoyment from it as well]. . . . Because the difference between a job and a career is a job is something you just go do repeatedly day after day. . . . I think it dulls you out. You know what I'm saying? It just dulls you out. Because like you're really not being challenged. And that's one thing, if I'm not being challenged, I draw back and I just get lazy.

Curt: If I don't like what I'm doing, I'll be real depressed, always upset, and my attitude towards the job would be a whole lot different. And I might end up losing that job because I have a whole lot of aggression and they don't want aggressive people working right now. They need you to be assertive, but they don't want you to be aggressive.

Derrick: If you got a job that pays well and you're not satisfied, you'll be unhappy with the job. Then, after a while, you'll be unhappy with yourself and the people working around you and you'll wind up arguing with somebody or hurting somebody, so it's better to have something you enjoy doing.

The commentary about income mattering less than the qualities of a job might seem contradictory to what the men said earlier about low-paying jobs. The matter becomes clear, however, when it is understood that each man's enjoyable or fulfilling jobs are precisely those that pay more than the fast food industry or unskilled labor sectors. Hence, while the quality of the job matters more than income, a job of sufficient quality happens to pay more than the jobs these men are accustomed to working (if they have, indeed, worked in the first place).

Family Desires, Expectations, and Pressures Concerning Work

Only one man in the survey group is married and living with his child. The rest of the men reside in the home of a parent or guardian, except one man who lives alone. The 25 men who do not reside with a wife or partner express clear interests in marriage and family. Each man says he would accept, if not fully expect, a wife or long-term partner who provides financial support for the household. Only two or three men speak explicitly about wanting to be the sole breadwinner for his future family or household. While the others clearly are committed to being the principal breadwinner, they do not mind if their spouse or partner works as well.

The men also desire long-term partners who are committed to supporting them emotionally as they navigate the work world. By this, the men mean they desire spouses and partners who are not overly consumed by material interests and who understand that job stability can ebb and flow. Accordingly, the men want spouses and partners who are clear about the possibility of having to work through tensions or surprises that might occur throughout the men's work lives. Clearly, these men generally eschew the idea that spouses or partners should stay at home while the man brings home the money. Otherwise, they are as traditional in their views as many American men are about family goals and desires.

The fathers in the group offer a slightly different perspective on work prospects from those without children. The fathers are more willing than those without children to take lower-paying jobs. The men without children state that they do not have to accept the worst-paying jobs precisely because they are not obliged to support anyone other than themselves. Even if fathers speak against working in extremely low-paying jobs, they are more likely to waver between stating that they eventually would or would not accept this kind of work. Their understanding of child support mandates and their own interest in providing materially for their children are the sources of this wavering:

> **Terry:** Like if I got to get a job, it's got to be a good job, where I can get, you know, make a lot of money because I mean "Friends of the Court" [*his child support arrangements*] ain't my friend, you know what I'm saying? Straight up. I don't have no friends at Friend of the Court. . . . And so, you know, that check, you know what I'm saying?—got a check got to be worth it, you know what I'm saying?—so I can have at least something left over. You know. I going to spend it on her anyway.

> **Darryl:** [*On how having a son affected his work life*] Like I say, me, then now, me having a son is really . . . I'm not going to say change, but it just me looking at a lot of things more differently, you know what I'm saying? . . . It made me want to get out here and do better, just knowing that I have a son out here, you know what I'm saying so . . . that's why I'm really trying hard as I can as far as trying to get

a job, because I know I got my little man out here. You know, then I don't want to leave all the pressure on her [his partner], you know. Like I say, my girl work 10, 11 hours a day, you know, seven days a week. So, you know, I got to be able to bring something to the table. You know what I'm saying? So I think me having my son has really helped me out as far as me want to . . . being more persistent with everything as far as trying and putting more effort in everything.

While not always successful in finding or holding jobs, all fathers speak assertively about the need to acquire a job. Their views reveal that finding work is as much about establishing a positive identity for themselves and their children as it is about their capacity to become material providers.[6]

The commentary thus far has centered on the men's values, goals, and desires concerning work and work opportunity. We now turn to their sense of what is going on in the world of work, especially in Detroit, and how they relate this to their particular circumstances as young unemployed or underemployed black men.

Views on Work Opportunity in Inner-City Detroit

The rise and fall of good employment opportunities in Detroit has been tied to the automobile industry. This understanding is not lost on these men. In fact, much of the anxiety and tension about dealing with low-paying jobs comes from the men's sense of the automobile industry as the site of better work opportunities in Detroit—if not now, then at least earlier. For these men, the work most acceptable to them either is no longer available (at least not in the quantities that it was earlier) or now requires education or credentials that were not previously necessary. The men believe that these educational levels or credentials stood far above what they currently possess:

> **Steve:** Even the cities outside of Detroit is built around the big three [automobile manufacturers], you know what I'm saying. This is—the big three is our big money here in Detroit. It supplies smaller businesses and smaller businesses keep the bigger businesses up and running, you know what I'm saying. It's not Ford that's keeping Ford up and running, it's all Ford's smaller groups,

you know what I'm saying, because they [Ford] can't make every part. So, small companies keep this world up and running, you know what I'm saying. Small businesses, you know, that keep us up and running. It's not Ford, you know, and it's not Chrysler or General Motors, you know, it's these little plants like Bud and those cutting plants, or the pressing plant, you know, the little plant that makes these little screws, you know, that you would never know. Without this screw, the car won't perform.

Daniel: It's not as easy today as getting in Chrysler and Ford, you know, back then, so you have to get in school. It's just harder now. They not hiring, they not doing. You know, back then the cars were selling and everything. . . . Basically, they used to come looking for you, when you got out of high school, they used to want you.

Terry: Jobs not being there. . . . I mean, why would they need you to do something they can pay . . . they can pay an electric bill to do, you know what I'm saying? What they use you for, you know? A computer can do your job. You know what I'm saying? Straight up. Especially in the automotive industry. For sure. Soon as they start getting computers and all that stuff, they start firing people, you know what I'm saying?

A few of the men mention they missed out on earlier chances to take advantage of the automobile manufacturing arena:

Steve: My mama wanted me . . . to come straight out of high school and get into that plant out there, you know what I'm saying? That was her biggest goal . . . to get me out there on that floor straight out of high school . . . which would have been good. But I probably wouldn't even have known how to act making that type of money at 18, you know what I'm saying. So, I'm not saying it was a good thing or a bad thing, but I'm saying it was a bad experience that I didn't finish high school like I was supposed to. So, now I'm working on that, and once I get through with that, you know, it's all type of worlds going to open up for me.

Talking further about the structure of contemporary work opportunity, these men accurately depict many of the transformations unfolding in late-1990s labor markets. They consistently talk about the availability of low-skilled and low-paid job prospects, especially in the fast food industry. Regardless of whether the men are disgusted with the wages in the fast food industry, most of these men garnered work experience in this employment sector. The men tend to move in and out of that sector rather quickly, however, because, as mentioned earlier, fast food offers no true stability or a way to provide sufficiently for themselves and their significant others.

Without the Big Three (Ford, Chrysler, and General Motors) as the driving force behind labor market opportunities, the men see contemporary work opportunity in Detroit as consisting of available jobs that either lack the salary and benefits package that would allow the men to effectively support themselves and significant others or demand a level of education or credentials beyond these men:

Derrick: Well, it's not that hard [to find a job right now]. So far as Burger King and McDonald's, fast food, you can always get a job at them places, but mostly everybody else want to go to a higher level, better pay, stuff like that.

Carlton: I'm like, "McDonalds!" I'm sick making that daggone chump change!

Vince: I ain't going to lie. I turned down a couple of them [jobs]. I turned down—I think it was Armco Security. Because I had worked in security, I worked in a plant for a year . . . and then when I get to Armco, they want to send me to a little Rite-Aid [drug store], and they going to tell me some stuff like for my first week or two I'm going to make $5.15. And I'm going to make the base pay and then I move up, and if I do good at a Rite-Aid, then they going to send me—they'll send me to a better-paying site for the people with experience. And I'm like, I turned it down, because I'm like I got experience and I'm not about to sit up in no Rite-Aid or none of that.

Steve: The black people, you know what I'm saying, we don't have the trades. There's not that much skilled plumbers here, you know what I'm saying, black skilled plumbers here to take on the jobs [available in Detroit]. It's not much skilled pipers or welders, you know what I'm saying, and that makes them take the jobs outside the city, you know what I'm saying? . . . There's jobs out here like that where you can make $27 an hour or $30 an hour, $40, $50 overtime, and work only six or seven months a year, you know what I'm saying.

A quarter of the men state that good jobs simply are not available in Detroit and that residing in the city itself is a major obstacle to finding good work:

> **John:** Go to the suburbs, dog . . . unless you want a plant job, because there ain't really no good jobs here in the city right now.

Ideas and Strategies about Attaining Good Jobs

In talking about how to attain and maintain a good job, the men uphold the basic contours of the Protestant work ethic. They speak of hard work, commitment, a positive attitude, and sufficient education as the basic tools for attaining good work. Again, this view is consistent with those of most Americans (Hochschild 1995). However, these men also speak about prior work experience as critical to finding good jobs:

> **Daniel:** Just keep going to school. . . . You know, regardless. . . . That seem the way to go. Today it is, anyway.

> **Terry:** [*"And what do you think it takes to get a good job?"*] Good attitude. Education, sometime. Just to know how. Like I said, who you know, depends.

> **Curt:** Outside of a degree and everything, you have to be willing to work, and be willing to go through some rough jobs before you get your good job. You have to take time to look at all aspects of a job. You can't just say they pay good and that's a good job. No, you have to look at if they pay good, yeah, but how is the personality of the persons you're going to be working around. Who has the snotty attitude? How is the supervisor acting towards others? How is the owner of this business? What is their attitude towards life?

> **Don:** It's kind of difficult [to find a good job]. You have to have a little experience.

Hence, while they believe in a work ethic that stresses hard work and initiative, the men do not believe such traits alone will deliver on good jobs. In fact, the men are critical of the assertion that the unemployed and underemployed are lazy:

Daniel: [*"What do you think about the following statement? 'The hardest working people have the best jobs'?"*] That's not true. . . . I work hard. That's not the best job.

Terry: [*"What do you think about this statement? 'People who can't keep a steady job or are unemployed are lazy'?"*] Sounds like somebody . . . something some rich white man saying. Hell no . . . because I lost my job you think I'm lazy? . . . Because somebody won't hire me means I'm lazy? You know, I might be out here trying hard and hell, there just might not be nothing out here right now. Does that mean I'm lazy? Well, who are you to put me in, and, you know what I'm saying, in that type of realm, where I'm lazy, you know, I'm lazy like that, you know. The hardest working people work for the people with the best jobs . . . straight up. That's who keep the people with the best jobs in they jobs.

Mark: There's people out here working and doing these general labor jobs . . . sweating, pulling muscles in they back, going home sore, can't move and got to get up and go back to work and do the same thing. Then you got people that do nothing but stay at a desk all day. . . . Making three, four thousand dollars a week, and just sitting at a desk. Well, probably at a computer terminal. Only thing they going to have is elbow problems. That's about it. . . . People who can't keep a steady job are lazy? . . . That's not true . . . Now you have some people who just don't want to work. . . . Then you have some people who are unemployed and it's not because they want to be unemployed. It's just they having a hard time finding a job. Or they might not have even found their niche, what they good at. They might even have found something that they like, enjoy doing. . . . And that's . . . that's the case . . . well, that is . . . I don't think it's a case of somebody being lazy.

Aside from these points of emphasis, however, the men make clear that maintaining a certain level of self-respect is vital. This is stated not so much as a necessity for securing or keeping a good job, but as a way for a man to maintain some inner comfort given the demands and expectation of the work world. Of course, commitment to this point of view often causes some of the problems these men experienced at work:

> **Terry:** Don't kiss nobody's ass [at work]. Be yourself. Because you kiss ass, they run over you. You know what I'm saying? Be yourself, let them know. You got boundaries too. Let them know, you know what I'm saying? Because the way they got the law set up now, you know, you just as equal as them, you know what I'm saying? Anything they do to you and you come back ten times worse at them, you know what I'm saying? So be yourself, do you, you know.

Personal Skills and Resources for Work

None of the men who professed to having any specific skilled-laborer capabilities have received formal certification or licensing. Also, none has received more than a high school diploma. Thus, regardless of whether these men possess the skills needed for success in the blue-collar work world, they could describe their social skills and competencies as indications of what they could offer to the world of work. Without anything else to offer, almost all of them mention social rather than technical skills when asked about their skills and resources for work:

> **Curt:** Um, well, I have excellent people skills. Um, management skills, I'm good with that. I can run any shift that they put me on. Um, let's see. My talents. I move pretty quick, I learn pretty fast. I was head cashier for the store I was working at for Burger King. . . . I learned that you got to move fast in the workforce now, especially with the jobs I've had, mostly Burger King and McDonald's. . . . I know I had to move fast, I had to learn fast, work hard, and I had to take a lot of stuff off people, because you got to have humility sometimes. She said, "Sometimes the customers are going to try to run with the ball, but you just got to try and take it for a second, because when you take it, it makes them feel real crunchy. And, if you argue back with them, you lose a customer, then you get yourself reprimanded by me." So, I was like, "That's not worth it anyway."

> **Mark:** I can cooperate with people. . . . I love working in a team environment. . . . Teamwork.

Terry: I'm a team player and I think I learned that from working in some of the summer programs we used to work in teams, you know. . . . You get the job done, you get to work in teams, and, you know what I'm saying? But I also . . . I can also do it by myself, you know.

About six men claim they could do basic construction work or machine repair (usually automobile), but they do not have the necessary credentials to formally enter these employment arenas. Further, the absence of formal credentials and lengthy work histories leaves some men with little else to refer to other than soft skills when discussing what they can bring to the workplace. They cannot discuss in depth how they function in work environments other than the fast food industry and a few other arenas. Without such a foundation to draw upon, by default these conversations emphasize personal attributes.

Obstacles to Finding Work

There has been considerable discussion thus far of the obstacles standing between these men and good jobs. However, it is important to distinguish two categories of obstacles, because they directly relate to the men's views on the virtues and benefits of job training and placement programs (or what they tried to buffer themselves against by taking advantage of such programs). The first category consists of problems the men identify as self-imposed. Most often cited is their insufficient education for the contemporary work world. Educational credentials that had been sufficient for certain jobs are no longer all that one needs:

Vince: It's like well, Fords and all that, you ain't had to have no education or nothing to get them jobs. But now, you got to have a education to get everything. They might make it around make you have to get, to have a diploma to get a McDonald's job now. . . . Because I remember, lot of people, lot of the jobs they had, they'll tell me, "Well, when I was working here, you ain't had to have no education to get this job."

Sam: You're going to need at least a GED or a high school diploma to flip burgers in McDonald's. That's how it's starting to look . . .

[You need] at least a diploma under your belt to open the door and get your foot in the door. . . . Like I said, don't even have a high school diploma. . . . Yeah. So you can barely get at Foot Locker, or be able to get a job at Sports Authority, or barely get a job at Tim Horton's or McDonald's or Burger King.

Mark: [*On obstacles to trying to find work*] But, well, one obstacle I did have back in the past is I haven't had any training in nothing [*laughs*]. . . . I didn't have any training in anything. So it does make it difficult to get a job, if you ain't got no kind of paper.

Curt: Um, qualifications. Like, I'm young and I just got out of high school in 2001, so I don't have many qualifications. I mean, a lot of them say a high school diploma is needed. I have a high school diploma. I have a certified high school diploma. Then, they say, "We need you to have at least two years of work experience." And, since I was in high school, I didn't do too much working when I was in high school because I wanted to get out with at least a 3.0. I achieved that and, um, then I had to try and go play catch up with everybody else. And now, most jobs say, "We need you to at least have an associate's degree in this field." So, now I have to go back to school. I'm in college now.

The second category consists of problems that are externally produced (either by the geographic location of higher-quality employment opportunities or by social forces and factors that inhibited the men's access to good jobs). One much-cited problem, and one that works against securing employment in suburban regions, is the lack of transportation. This is a particular factor because the men believe some good job prospects might be found outside Detroit.

Vince: Say if you ain't got no transportation, it ain't worth it. Or some of the jobs don't even be in the town. I be looking at an employment guide—Canton, Michigan, and you know, farther than the surrounding cities of Detroit. And they want . . . only paying eight dollars. It ain't worth your time [to go if you do not have your own transportation].

Terry: Transportation is like one of the biggest problems, right. . . . Like getting to and fro, you know what I'm saying? It's like . . . and what else would be a big problem? And money, man. I mean, it's just like . . . they be like . . . they be wanting you to do stupid jobs way the hell out somewhere for, you know, $4.00 . . . for $6.50 an hour, you know what I'm saying? . . . Even if I got a car, that's gas money. . . . You know what I'm saying? To go back and forth out there, you only make $6.50 a hour? Not right, you know.

Another common obstacle the men mention is that, as young black males, they are not desired by employers:

Derrick: Well, for one, I go to a couple of interviews, and I feel like they won't give me the job, because they look at me and think, "You look more like a thug, street man, this and this," accuse me of this and this. . . . Well, they kind of said it to me, but not in those exact words, but, you know, they beat around the bush with it.

John: My case manager said this job it paying $12.00 a hour instead of a mattress company, or whatever, out in West Hell somewhere. And, "They're hiring big time, they're hiring big time, you need to get out there." So I was like, "Cool." I jumped on it and I went out there. And a white lady came and she was like . . . she looked at me, and I said, "Yeah, I here to fill out a application for a position. I heard you guys were hiring." And [she] said, "Oh, I don't . . . I don't think we're hiring." And I'm like, "Well, I just called. We just called out here this morning and we talked to a gentleman and he said you all were hiring." And she was like, "Well, I'll take your application," you know. So I fill out the application, you know, with a smile. I stayed really nice. I asked her name, she kind of smiled. I don't know, I think maybe I filled out my application and it went straight to the shredder or something.

When speaking about barriers to finding and keeping work, these men elucidate employers' views on potential hires of black men, as supported by recent research. Various studies have either explicitly or implicitly affirmed that black men are viewed as liabilities in the workplace (Holzer 1996; Kirschenman and Neckerman 1991; Moss and Tilly 2001; Wilson 1996). This research argues such men have acquired that image either as a result of outright racism, an enduring sense that they are most likely to lack the appropriate credentials or skills for the job, or some combination of the two. Beyond promoting these views on the obstacles confronting black men, many men in this study point out that women are the preferred prospects in certain circumstances.

> **Terry:** Black women got it easier than black men. . . . You know what I'm saying? Because a woman is always going to be a woman, no matter what, you know what I'm saying? And any man, any real man, you know what I'm saying, is attracted to a woman, you know. So first of all, it's a female, you know. So she got it. And then by me . . . by me being a male, it's like, you know, here come another . . . oh, here comes another nigger, you know what I'm saying? "Can I help you, Bro?" you know what I'm saying? "Here comes his attitude," you know, "about life." "He done had shit because of the man. It's not my fucking fault, you know what I'm saying?" Shit like that [is what employers think when confronted with black men looking for work].

For some men, the litany of obstacles is compounded by the lack of social ties to people in the workforce. The significance of durable social ties to those firmly embedded in employment is well documented in research, especially in the case of low-income blacks (Falcón 1995; Fernandez and Weinberg 1997; Granovetter 1995; Taylor and Sellers 1997; Wilson 1987, 1996). Apart from access to resources provided by job training and placement programs, such ties are minimal. Accordingly, many men say their principal job search strategy is little more than walking around their neighborhoods to determine where work is available:

> **Derrick:** Like, I'll see people on the street that own their own little business like roofing and all that, and I ask them do they need help and stuff like that. [*"So, roofing is one type of job. Any other types of jobs?"*] No, not just roofing, but it's just anything that got something to do with working with my hands, because I love working with my hands.

Others feel the high numbers of unemployed people indicate just how hard it has become to get a job—the competition for positions has become more intense:

> **Terry:** You go for interviews, there's 400 people in there for one job, you know what I'm saying? The odds ain't too good. . . . Man,

if you don't know somebody who could hook you up or . . . I don't know. It just depends who you are. If you . . . if you that man—you know what I'm saying?—you're going to get the job. But if you just a Plain Jane like everybody else, slim next to none, you know what I'm saying?

Darryl: Well, I just think the economy right now is just messed up to where, you know, ever since that September 11th, man, it's just, as far as jobs, it's just been dropping, you know.

The major self-induced obstacles concerned the men's failures to maintain positive attitudes or appropriate temperaments given their tribulations finding work. They explain these problems emerged largely from their experiences and manners of conduct in their neighborhoods, and readily admit these attitudes and temperaments do not transfer well to the world of work:

Mark: The area I might need the most improvement in is how to hold my . . . keep my composure sometime. Like if somebody say something out the way or disrespectful to me, it's . . . I got to . . . I have to learn how to just walk away sometime instead of responding to the ignorance that some people say.

In fact, about a third of the men talk about their inability to withdraw from the streets as one source of their problems attaining the work they desire:

Steve: If I would have stayed on my job and quit BS'ing in the streets, I would have been like that, you know what I'm saying, I would have had better places.

The preceding sections have explored a range of problems and tensions concerning young black men's quest to find and keep good jobs. The excerpts from our interviews richly depict the kinds of lower-income black men that come through the doors of job training and placement programs. The commentary captures the historical and social forces that have shaped complex people needing a range of services. This depiction provides a basis for investigating how and why these men discuss their experiences with training programs the way they do. It is to this discussion that we now turn.

The Virtues of Job Training and Placement Programs

As participants in job training and placement programs, these men obviously believe these programs are worth pursuing and hope to improve their employment prospects. Hence, these men constitute a skewed sample of underemployed and unemployed urban-based young black men. With that in mind, these men are well situated to comment extensively about the utility and shortcomings of job training and placement programs.

For the most part, the men feel their involvement in Michigan Works! and YO was beneficial. The evidence they provide to support this claim centers as much, if not more, on the relationships the men established with program personnel (trainers, counselors, and so on) as with the program's ability to deliver jobs.[7] For many men, the value of these programs remains in the interactive dimension precisely because they know good jobs are scarce. Hence, the men greatly appreciate the chance to immerse themselves in institutional settings that provide emotional and social support, empathy, and encouragement.

In essence, delivery of emotional and social support took on great importance because, as men with little financial, social, or economic capital to draw on in order to advance their lives, they come to these programs looking not only for specific jobs but also for a sense that they are worthy of support and services. Hence, program staff are valued for making the men feel validated as people striving to better their lives and for acknowledging the men's efforts. This is evident in staff members' willingness to understand the men's plight as unemployed and underemployed people or to provide extra attention as the men discussed their insecurities, hesitancies, and anxieties about transferring into stable work opportunities:

> **Derrick:** The staff is real cool. You can talk to them about anything you want, personal, or in-school, or out-of-school problems. They're pretty cool. They'll help you. They stay worried about you. They always ask me, like every day, "When you finish your GED, what's your next step? What's your next plan?" So, they're really concerned. . . . [*Okay. And, what has YO provided in terms of resources, skills, or information?*] Oh, okay, well, they got a poetry class in here and they help you write poetry emotionally and spiritually. They have you stand up and read, you know what I'm saying,

how it's supposed to be read. They gave us free memberships to the YMCA and we can go over there and work out and play basketball or whatever. Um, let me see. They have movie night up here like every week so students can come, like some days after everybody's finished, you can just come up here and watch movies and chill out. And they have a lot of classes so far, like last week we had this speaker come in here and talk to us about STDs and then they talked to us about how to treat females—I forgot the name of the class. There are a lot of programs up here. They taught us how to properly wash cars.

As Derrick's remarks make clear, the interpersonal connection is as meaningful for him as the transmission of work-related skills. He and the other men feel a sense of respect and value as a result of efforts to enhance their sense of social inclusion. For the Youth Opportunity program in particular, some men also greatly appreciate the social outreach, which brought heightened feelings of value and dignity.

Steve: They're [*the Youth Opportunity program*] trying to help me get my GED. That's more than I can ask for right now, you know. They help me in one-on-one training with teachers. They're on me, you know, if I'm slacking off, they call me, make sure I'm on my business. They try to keep me on my toes, you know. I never been in a program like that. Even in high school, your teacher didn't call you up, "Where have you been for the last week?" You know, they don't care. You know, all through high school, the teachers always told us, "Well, I got mine," and that's been with every teacher, not just one, like your third-grade teacher. They said that all through school, since preschool, you know, "I got my education, you're going to have to get yours." And, then, dealing with the public schools, like that, that's how a lot of them basically felt, you know what I'm saying. . . . Yeah, people at YO are different. It's a different type of environment. They want to see you do better, they want to see you succeed in life.

Don: It was nice [using the Youth Opportunity program services]. Treat you well. People are nice. Eat here. Have movies sometimes here. There are classes.

Brian: Everybody I came across was extremely helpful. They actually care here. I can't speak for other programs, but here, they actually want you to be successful, and they make the effort to help you to get there. . . . Yeah, you get more personalized attention. That's what I like about it. You get more individual attention. And some people may need that, so that's what I like about it.

For the majority of the men, success in the program also is predicated on their willingness to bring the appropriate attitudes and dispositions with them. These men say the programs work only for those that are truly prepared to accept and abide by the rules and objectives. Consequently, every program is not suited to every individual:

Sam: I mean, you can put a glass of water in front of them, but you can't make them join. . . . People who really need it and really want it [get the most out of job training programs]. . . . You have a person who really don't care and just want to be doing something to do something, they really all don't get the same fulfillment, same . . . from a person who really would appreciate it, person who wants it, you know. So I'm saying people who really . . . that's who really benefit from it, the people who really show that effort. . . . And show that drive and that . . . you know what I say? determination . . . again, persistence, you know what I'm saying? So that's who I think really benefit from it.

Derrick: [*On the people that benefit most from these programs*] Ones who want to go do something with their life. Ones who don't want to just sit around and wait for somebody else to take care of them.

Henry: Anyone who don't really want to be here, I wouldn't recommend you come down.

Curt: The person with the attitude that, "I'm going to do what I have to to make it in the workforce. I'm going to step over these obstacles, and if I need a little help, I'm going to get it while it's here. . . ." I believe anybody can pursue it if they want to, but you have to go in there with the right attitude.

Most of the men argue that demonstrating patience while interacting with program staff is crucial to feeling that these programs eventually meet some of their needs and interests. For one thing, patience helps the men handle that the programs cannot necessarily deliver immediately on jobs, much less so on the jobs these men most desire to have. Further, programs that include training and development initiatives, rather than just a one-stop placement approach, require participants to complete formal training sequences before being placed in a job. Thus, unemployed or underemployed men have to endure a few weeks of training and development rather than see more immediate possibilities for bettering their lives. Once they have completed the initial phase, however, the men say that having case workers that take a sincere interest in them makes all the difference:

> **Sam:** Once you get past that, though, everything runs pretty smoothly . . . think that depends on the staff that's working too. Because you have some people that's really for the . . . really for the youth, and then you have some that are just there for the paycheck. . . . It depends on the staff.

To be sure, these men value the programs for more than social and emotional support. The men also appreciate the material rewards and benefits from participating in these programs:

> **Darryl:** Um, basically really how to keep a job, how to get a job, how to fill out a résumé properly, how to react in certain situations if you work from a job site and, you know, you and another co-worker end up, you know, in feud or whatever. . . . It really taught me how to really just be a people person, you know . . . eye contact as far as, you know, job interview, you know, that's real important. Lot of people might not believe it. Hand movement, body movement, period, you know.

> **Steve:** They help you speak to people, or they help you answer some of the questions an interviewer will throw at you, you know. And, uh, pretty much it will help you polish how to think, what to say, how to react when they say certain questions. . . . They tell you to try not to have any pause in your speech, try to know what you want to say and just say it . . . and use professional words.

> **David:** They got a little GED preparation on the computer. They got a lot of stuff here . . . Ah, computers, internet. . . . [my instructor] taught me stuff that I was supposed to learn back in tenth grade . . . like math . . . how to use correctional English. . . . I feel that I learned

something, you know what I'm saying? . . . And if you show them that you down with learning and you will come up a better man.

Vince: [The program staff] tell you about all the different type of career paths you can go through there. What you'll be learning and what you're expected to learn in each field. . . . Your learning level in computers don't stop here because they upgrade computers, they make something different every year, new applications so you'll get outdated real quick if you ain't keeping up on the newest computer technology.

Derrick: I mean, they give you rewards, but you're rewarding yourself as far as doing what you got to do so far as getting your GED, coming in here and you're staying out of trouble. And they reward you with stuff like movie night where we can eat pizza and watch movies. They got a game room down there where you can go chill, play games, and they take us out like Cedar Point, and they take us camping and stuff like that. So, you are getting rewards all the way around. [However,] the biggest reward is accomplishing your goals.

In short, delivering formal work-related skills with a sense of care and concern for the personal growth of the clients is what these men considered the positive aspects of job training programs. Taking into account the range of views on job training and placement programs, it is not insignificant that the men participated in programs that offered more than one-stop services. Thus, some problems common to one-stop programs do not concern these men. These problems include inadequate time for conversing with staff and inadequate space in facilities so participants and clients could feel comfortable working through matters that left them tension-filled and anxiety-ridden.

However, as young men not yet immersed into work, the men in our survey group are unable to comment on whether the programs affect longer-term stability in the world of work (and, indeed, such a query would require another study). Further, the fact that human relations are crucial for client satisfaction with this training and placement program indicates how often exclusion from work opportunities results in psychological and social wounds in addition to economic ones. Accordingly, how well a job training and placement initiative treats these needs and interests could affect client satisfaction.

Problems and Inadequacies with Job Training and Placement Programs

By far, the most significant problem the men identified with the programs is the inadequate funding to serve a larger population or enhance services:

> **Sam:** The intake process to me . . . that's where you usually have the most problems with this [usage of job training and placement programs]. . . . People [*staff*] don't have that much time. They usually have someone out the door. . . . Like come in and you're probably here for like four, maybe five hours, taking tests and filling out aps [*applications*]. . . . People have so much to do. If they leave and they didn't finish that process, it's so hard to get them to come back in and get past that [the initial paperwork rush].

> **David:** I don't think that job training programs have the resources that they really need . . . to accurately prepare people for the job. But I do think that they are a help in the sense that they kind of prepare people mentally. [*On what the programs need*] More resources. . . . Like more money to buy . . . buy equipment and, you know, books and, you know, make it more like a . . . more like a school. You know what I'm saying?

> **Henry:** I figure, I believe they could'a did a little more. But given the circumstances that the youth development specialist had received, they can . . . they can only do as much as they can. They bosses be giving them so much paperwork, they really don't have too much time to deal with the participants. . . . I actually would like to see they [*sic*] go to lunch with the participants.

> **Derrick:** I really didn't think they would be able to do it, you know, have so many programs running at one time on different days, but they managed to pull it off. I mean, they need to do this in some high schools, too, you know, high schools, middle schools, catch the kids while they're young, before it's too late. . . . How they got it here, this setup, it's only for students and their partners, where if they had it set up like anybody from 14 to 21, then that would be more better, because I know a lot of people who want to come, but they're not in the zone [*the YO geographic catchment area*].

About 10 men also state that they would have preferred further skills training. Although the programs provide opportunities to learn certain skilled trades, they do not go far enough in providing formal certification or in-depth experiential learning:

Henry: They teach you the skills, but they don't give you no experience on the skills. You see what I'm saying? . . . Like this A-Plus Certification, far as they teach you how to build a computer, but they only teach you how to build one computer, and that's the computer you take home. Why not have you build, you know, multiple computers, break it down and do it again so you're going to have experience and you actually know exactly what you [need to] know.

About a quarter of the men are concerned that participating in job training programs could stigmatize participants by tracking them into jobs occupied by socially marginalized people:

Vince: Most of the people who work there is like drug addicts and, you know, just fresh out of prison, just couldn't find nothing.

Irrespective of their views about how the program operates and who is likely to use it, the goal for these men is to use the program to establish a baseline work history and then move on to better opportunities. For those (such as **Vince**) who feel such programs are havens for the destitute, the determination to remain involved centers on the idea that once these men establish a work history, they will be able to distinguish themselves from the ex-convicts, substance abusers, or other social types they identify as typical clients of social service and employment agencies. Hence, more significant than feeling stigmatized, the major problem for these program is the limitation on resources and service provision that resulted from financial constraint.

Discussion and Conclusion

This inquiry of 26 low-income young black men from Detroit reveals that these men have very clear opinions about their interests and goals concerning the worlds of work and work opportunity. It also reveals that the men have many suggestions about the specific roles job training and place-ment programs can play in helping them meet those interests and goals.

These men, unlike many young men of the early 1990s and the 1980s, believe that numerous jobs are available in their municipal region (Bour-gois 1995; Venkatesh 2000; Wilson 1996; Young 2004). The men doubt, however, that the jobs available would enable them to provide basic necessities for themselves or their children. As a result of the low finan-cial returns from this work and the absence of intrinsic value and chal-lenge associated with it, the men feel uninspired by and generally uncommitted to these jobs. Given the vast pool of potential hires and how quickly workers could be replaced, these men also feel that employ-ers do not value or commit to them as individual workers, thus exacer-bating the problems and tensions associated with working these jobs.

The mind set of these men about the available jobs is also conditioned by their knowledge that skilled, blue-collar labor prospects, specifically those in the automobile manufacturing sector, were once the leading work opportunities in their city. To the men, such jobs seem the "right" kind of jobs, especially because they include fringe benefits, a formally scheduled work arrangement, and opportunities for promotion and advancement. Lacking long-term exposure to the frustrations and disappointments of navigating unemployment or poor work prospects, these men also hold firm to ideal visions of securing positions in the white-collar professional world or owning a business.

All the men desire a future household that includes a wife or partner and children. They plan to support, if not encourage, their spouses or partners to work. As for present-day family circumstances, the fathers are more willing than the men without children to take jobs at lower wages. Maintaining this commitment, however, does not mean that the fathers end up more willing to endure conflicts or tension while at work. Thus, they move in and out of jobs according to the same general pat-terns as the men without children do.

In terms of strategies and techniques for getting jobs, the men speak about education, good work ethics, and maintaining a positive outlook and proper demeanor as key resources. When asked about their best personal resources, however, they mention little other than soft skills—social inter-active capabilities and the capacity to uphold the right attitude on the job.

The men generally regard the current work opportunities in Detroit as poor quality, and point out that poor-quality jobs demand higher levels of education or more credentials than had been previously necessary. The men believe better jobs could be found in the suburbs, but they generally lack transportation for getting to those jobs. For many men, accessible transportation would not help them overcome what they consider employers' negative attitude toward young black men, and they have no elaborate or detailed ideas about how to confront this problem. Perhaps the most significant problem with finding good jobs is knowing that many other people also need such work. Consequently, the men feel they have little chance of standing out, either as potential employees or valued workers to be kept on a job if employee- or business-related problems arise.

For these men in particular, job training and placement programs are helpful when they provide counseling and support in addition to information. These men want to feel cared about and understood by the staff of these programs, especially given that they found neither affect in the employment sectors to which they have been exposed thus far (if they have worked at all). The men typify that portion of urban, young black men that is committed to participating in these programs. Thus, they know that any form of success is predicated on having a certain level of patience in dealing with staff and in having job opportunities come their way. They also know that they have to be assertive at the appropriate times. (Whether they actually have functioned or will function this way is a topic that lies beyond the purview of this analysis.) They also have enough experience with these programs to know that funding for them is not extensive, and that many programs, events, or activities cannot reach all of those who might best benefit from them.

All this must be taken as the perspective of men who have involved themselves in job training and placement programs. Consequently, what they regard as positive aspects may not be realized or considered by men who have not committed themselves to these programs, and what the men surveyed regard as negative may be acknowledged with even greater intensity by men who are less pleased or less involved in these programs. Moreover, and perhaps most important, a study of this nature does not thoroughly assess what it may take to get more such men into the doors of these agencies. This is every bit as critical as what occurs once the men get there.

With these caveats in mind, some key points of consideration can be forwarded about the relationships among perceptions of work opportunities, resources for work, and experiences in job training and placement programs. First, the challenge of simply getting men into work may run up against the men's desires to develop a career or a logical pattern of experience and upward mobility. Some men may accept that almost any form of job placement, as menial as that first job may be, is the foundation for developing a career in employment. Others will not find this to be the case. Accordingly, they may continue to experience the kind of despair or frustration with employers that casts them further into socioeconomic marginality.

Second, many men simply want a meaningful wage that allows them a decent chance to make ends meet. This demands that some consideration of the status of wage levels and fringe benefits—and the means for advancing them—in lower-tier employment take on greater importance in the assessment of labor market dynamics and the situation of low-income black men. As other chapters in this volume make clear, a significant number of black men are not going to work at available jobs if they cannot earn what they interpret as an appropriate wage, for various reasons. Hence, it is not only the men themselves, but also the social structure and design of work and work benefits that must continue to be critically assessed if work programs intend to improve the social conditions of low-income black men.

Third, these men desire the opportunity to acquire the credentials—and in some cases, the educational prerequisites—that have escaped them in the past. Men who are able and prepared to engage education must have some means of doing so, and their efforts should connect tangibly with opportunities for work. Once these men are exposed to tangible links between educational opportunities and employment prospects, they may be more eager and effective at engaging in schooling, especially if it results in formal certification or credentials in specific skills and trades, and then in the opportunity to work in those trades.

Of course, everything presented here is easier to articulate than it is to implement. This is especially the case given the high numbers of young black men with exposure to the criminal justice system, which heightens the insecurities of an already unwilling employment sector to incorporate these men into its midst (Mauer 1999; Miller 1996). A utopian agenda does, however, provide a road map. If employers, politicians, and other crucial parties provide sufficient interest in, support for, and understanding of the outlooks and interpretations of urban-based low-income black men, perhaps some incremental steps along this road can be taken.

NOTES

1. Prior research has explored certain dimensions of this research agenda, including how such men think about their future quality of life, the kinds of jobs that they believe would help them achieve better lives in the future, and their sense of how to engage upward mobility (Freeman 1992; MacLeod 1995; Newman 1999; Sullivan 1989; Venkatesh 1994; Wilson 1996; Young 2000, 2004). Nevertheless, that research has not critically engaged how job training and employment programs may fit into the future-oriented thinking of low-income black men.

2. All interviews were conducted by two University of Michigan graduate students on site at Michigan Works!/Youth Opportunity program field offices throughout Detroit. Each interview took between 60 and 90 minutes. The core questions asked of each man explored the work histories of his immediate family members (especially during his childhood), recollections of the information provided by these family members about work and work opportunity (e.g., the skills and resources needed to find and maintain work, support and guidance in finding work), the work histories of each man, his evaluation of his work experiences, his assessment of his own skills and resources for finding and maintaining work opportunities, his most desired and expected future work opportunities, his views on the quality and structure of the modern urban labor markets, and his evaluation of the job training and placement programs that he had been involved with over the course of his life (which in all but a few cases were restricted to Michigan Works! and the Youth Opportunity program).

3. Prior contacts with staff at both agencies enabled me to conduct this research. The Youth Opportunity program (often referred to by its participants and staff as YO) is a social program funded by public and private grants to implement initiatives aimed at helping Detroit-based low-income black and Hispanic youth age 16 to 24 improve their employment prospects. The Youth Opportunity program provides some of the same longer-term services as Michigan Works!, but the YO agency specializes in providing social activities and exercises that develop occupational skill levels and work preparedness in adolescents and young adults. Emotional and social growth is as central to the mission of YO as is placing its participants in jobs. The central office for the Youth Opportunity program is located in the same building as the central Michigan Works! job placement center, and the staff of the two programs share clients and regularly interact with one another. Hence, all the men in this analysis made use of both programs despite their closer attachment to YO.

Michigan Works! is a state and federally funded job placement agency with offices located statewide. It aims to match job seekers to employers throughout the state. Michigan Works! provides services including such one-stop services as job postings, Internet access, the Michigan Talent Bank and Job Bank listings, résumé assistance, and basic information about occupational training, financial aid, community service agencies, and job search methods. Longer-term services include computer training, in-depth testing and assessment, and employability counseling. Michigan Works! also provides a range of services to employers, including providing interview facilities, helping to find qualified workers, and publishing job opportunities.

4. The notion that low-wage-earning black men are not inherently incapable of working hard at their jobs, but rather begin to emotionally disinvest in work that garners

little in terms of wages, upward mobility, and social prestige, was introduced in Elliot Liebow's classic study, *Tally's Corner* (1967).

5. In her review of studies on how Americans conceive of mobility and opportunity structures in American life, political scientist Jennifer Hochschild (1995) argues that this vision of desirable work is consistent with the outlook of most blacks as well as Americans more generally. Moreover, in Kevin Henson's (1996) study of temporary workers, such workers articulated the same views about what they ultimately desired from the world of work. Finally, in a comparative study of men in the United States and France, Michele Lamont (2000) portrays the extent to which working-class black and white American men hold such views.

6. A recent litany of research on low-income black fathers has uncovered a more complex understanding of the relationships among manhood, economic and social provisions, and parenting than has been the case in prior decades (Bowman and Forman 1997; Hamer 2001; McAdoo 1993; McAdoo and McAdoo 1994; Waller 2002). Most of this research argues that actual interaction between fathers and their children does not indicate clearly how often these men think about their children or how intensely they reflect upon their status (and sometimes failings) as fathers.

7. Of course, a caveat here is that, as active program participants while this study was conducted, none of these men came into the research having already been placed in a job. However, many do know of other men who were placed through the efforts of program staff. Accordingly, the men believed this outcome could unfold for them as well.

REFERENCES

Anderson, Elijah. 1990. *Streetwise: Race, Class, and Change in an Urban Community.* Chicago: University of Chicago Press.

———. 1999. *Code of the Streets.* New York: W. W. Norton.

Billson, Janet Mancini. 1996. *Pathways to Manhood: Young Black Males' Struggle for Identity.* New Brunswick, NJ: Transaction Publishers.

Bourgois, Philippe. 1995. *In Search of Respect: Selling Crack in El Barrio.* New York: Cambridge University Press.

Bowman, Philip, and Tyrone Forman. 1997. "Instrumental and Expressive Family Roles among African American Fathers." In *Family Life in Black America,* edited by Robert J. Taylor, James S. Jackson, and Linda M. Chatters (216–47). Thousand Oaks, CA: SAGE Publications.

Falcón, Luis. 1995. "Social Networks and Employment for Latinos, Blacks, and Whites." *New England Journal of Public Policy* 11(1): 17–28.

Farley, Reynolds, Sheldon Danziger, and Harry J. Holzer. 2000. *Detroit Divided.* New York: Russell Sage Foundation.

Fernandez, Roberto, and Nancy Weinberg. 1997. "Personal Contacts and Hiring in a Retail Bank." *American Sociological Review* 62(6): 883–902.

Freeman, Richard. 1992. "Crime and the Employment of Disadvantaged Youths." In *Urban Labor Markets and Job Opportunities,* edited by George Peterson and Wayne Vroman (201–37). Washington, DC: Urban Institute Press.

Granovetter, Mark. 1995. *Getting a Job: A Study of Contacts and Careers.* 2nd ed. Chicago: University of Chicago Press.

Hamer, Jennifer. 2001. *What It Means to Be Daddy: Fatherhood for Black Men Living Away from Their Children.* New York: Columbia University Press.

Henson, Kevin D. 1996. *Just a Temp.* Philadelphia, PA: Temple University Press.

Hochschild, Jennifer L. 1995. *Facing Up to the American Dream: Race, Class, and the Soul of the Nation.* Princeton, NJ: Princeton University Press.

Holzer, Harry J. 1996. *What Employers Want: Job Prospects for Less-Educated Workers.* New York: Russell Sage Foundation.

Kirschenman, Joleen, and Kathryn M. Neckerman. 1991. " 'We'd Love to Hire Them But . . .': The Meaning of Race for Employers." In *The Urban Underclass*, edited by Christopher Jencks and Paul E. Peterson (203–34). Washington, DC: Brookings Institution Press.

Lamont, Michele. 2000. *The Dignity of Working Men: Morality and the Boundaries of Race, Class, and Immigration.* New York City and Cambridge, MA: Russell Sage Foundation and Harvard University Press.

Liebow, Elliot. 1967. *Tally's Corner: A Study of Negro Streetcorner Men.* Boston: Little, Brown and Company.

MacLeod, Jay. 1995. *Ain't No Making It: Aspirations and Attainment in a Low-Income Neighborhood.* 2nd ed. Boulder, CO: Westview Press.

Majors, Richard G., and Janet Billson. 1992. *Cool Pose.* New York: Lexington Books.

Mauer, Marc. 1999. *The Race to Incarcerate.* New York: The New Press.

McAdoo, John Lewis. 1993. "The Role of African American Fathers: An Ecological Perspective." *Families in Society* 74(1): 28–35.

McAdoo, John Lewis, and Julia B. McAdoo. 1994. "The African American Father's Role within the Family." In *The American Black Male: His Present Status and His Future*, edited by Richard Majors and Jacob U. Gordon (286–97). Chicago: Nelson-Hall Publishers.

Moss, Philip, and Chris Tilly. 2001. *Stories Employers Tell: Race, Skill, and Hiring in America.* New York: Russell Sage Foundation.

Miller, Jerome G. 1996. *Search and Destroy: African American Men in the Criminal Justice System.* Cambridge: Cambridge University Press.

Newman, Katherine S. 1999. *No Shame in My Game: The Working Poor in the Inner City.* New York: Knopf and Russell Sage Foundation.

Sugrue, Thomas. 1996. *The Origins of the Urban Crisis: Race and Inequality in Postwar Detroit.* Princeton, NJ: Princeton University Press.

Sullivan, Mercer L. 1989. *Getting Paid: Youth Crime and Work in the Inner City.* Ithaca, NY: Cornell University Press.

Taylor, Robert Joseph, and Sherrill L. Sellers. 1997. "Informal Ties and Employment among Black Americans." In *Family Life in Black America*, edited by Robert Joseph Taylor, James S. Jackson, and Linda M. Chatters (146–56). Thousand Oaks, CA: SAGE Publications.

Venkatesh, Sudhir Alladi. 1994. "Getting Ahead: Social Mobility among the Urban Poor." *Sociological Perspectives* 37(2): 157–82.

———. 2000. *American Project: The Rise and Fall of a Modern Ghetto.* Cambridge, MA: Harvard University Press.

Waller, Maureen R. 2002. *My Baby's Father: Unmarried Parents and Paternal Responsibility.* Ithaca, NY: Cornell University Press.

Wilson, William Julius. 1987. *The Truly Disadvantaged: The Inner City, the Underclass, and Public Policy.* Chicago: University of Chicago Press.

———. 1996. *When Work Disappears: The World of the New Urban Poor.* New York: Knopf.

Young, Alford A., Jr. 2000. "On the Outside Looking In: Low-Income Black Men's Conceptions of Work Opportunity and the 'Good Job.'" In *Coping with Poverty: The Social Contexts of Neighborhood, Work, and Family in the African-American Community,* edited by Sheldon Danziger and Ann Chih Lin (141–71). Ann Arbor: University of Michigan Press.

———. 2004. *The Minds of Marginalized Black Men: Making Sense of Mobility, Opportunity, and Future Life Chances.* Princeton, NJ: Princeton University Press.

8

The Availability and Use of Workforce Development Programs among Less-Educated Youth

Demetra Smith Nightingale and Elaine Sorensen

This chapter examines how many young people participate in workforce development programs and the characteristics of those who receive these services through publicly funded programs, paying particular attention to young black men. The first section briefly summarizes public workforce development programs serving youth. So that we may understand the population that might benefit from those programs, the second section summarizes the educational attainment of young people overall, specifically analyzing those who have not gone to college. The third section examines the relationship between education and work, presenting evidence on the work experience and occupational status of less-educated youth.

Following is an assessment of how many noncollege youth one might expect to use or need government-sponsored workforce development program services and how many actually receive employment-related services, such as job search assistance or job training. Then, analysis of how the major federal employment and training programs funded under the Job Training Partnership Act (JTPA) served noncollege low-income young men and women in the late 1990s is presented.[1] The final section discusses implications for current and future policy options to improve the employment opportunity and labor market outcomes of less-educated young people, particularly black men.

Much of the analysis in this chapter uses two data sets. First, the 1999 National Survey of America's Families (NSAF), a large nationally representative survey of the civilian noninstitutionalized population under age 65, is used to examine the characteristics of young people and their reported use of education and training services. The main purpose of the NSAF is to track how the devolution of responsibility for social programs from the federal government to states affected the well-being of low-income children. As such, it oversamples low-income families and includes detailed questions about family income, well-being, and program participation. The NSAF is thus a good source of information on low-income people in general. The 1999 survey file includes 7,746 young adults between the ages of 18 and 24.

The second data set used in this chapter is the U.S. Department of Labor's Standardized Program Information Report (SPIR) data system, which includes information on all individuals who participated in JTPA programs nationwide. The SPIR data are used to examine the extent of actual participation in various JTPA-funded employment and training activities.

A Brief History of Workforce Development Policy

National workforce development policies for youth have evolved over the past three decades. In general, the programs and services offered to disadvantaged, mainly out-of-school youth have included subsidized work experience, such as summer jobs, short-term basic education, and job search counseling and assistance. The one major exception is the Job Corps, which, since 1965, has provided intensive comprehensive education; occupational training; health, counseling, and life-skills preparation; and employment services in a residential setting. Until the mid-1990s, aside from the Job Corps, programs for youth were funded at a fairly low level and services were brief (Lerman 2000).

The federal role in youth employment policy began in earnest in the 1960s, first under the Manpower Development and Training Act of 1962 (the MDTA) and then the Economic Opportunity Act of 1964, which created the Job Corps and the Neighborhood Youth Corps (which evolved into the Summer Youth Employment Program). The Comprehensive Employment and Training Act of 1973, which replaced MDTA, consolidated many separate employment-related programs and designated some federal funds specifically for youth employment and training and the summer youth jobs programs.

Reflecting growing national concern about the employment problems of disadvantaged youth, but acknowledging the difficulty in addressing those problems, Congress in 1977 authorized about $3 billion for use between 1978 and 1980 through the Youth Employment Demonstration Projects Act (YEDPA). YEDPA was enacted as part of the amendments to the Comprehensive Employment and Training Act, to find more effective service delivery models and approaches. A GAO report in 1980 noted that the passage of YEDPA "was an admission that, despite years of experience and the expenditure of billions of dollars for youth employment and training programs, no one knew how to solve the chronic youth employment problem" (GAO 1980, 2).

With the authorization of YEDPA in addition to the regular youth training and summer jobs programs, the federal government, through the Department of Labor's Employment and Training Administration (ETA), was by 1980 devoting over $2 billion a year for youth employment programs (Anderson and Sawhill 1980). For comparison, this would equal about $3.4 billion in constant 2000 dollars (i.e., adjusting for inflation). After 1981, though, federal funding for youth programs gradually declined. By 2004, federal appropriations for youth employment programs had declined to about $2.6 billion ($2.45 billion in constant 2000 dollars), or less than three-quarters of the 1980 funding level (Mikelson and Nightingale 2004).

The large decline in funding going to youth in the mid-1990s was a stark reaction to findings from the major national JPTA evaluation, which found that, while JTPA programs had some modest impact on the employment and earnings of adults, results for youth were generally disappointing (Orr et al. 1996). The policy response was rather dramatic, with sharp funding reductions for both youth training and the summer jobs program.

Funding for the Job Corps continued and even increased, in part because evidence of that program's positive impacts was accumulating. Funding for the summer jobs program was subsequently restored, but appropriations for regular youth programs remained low until the enactment of the Workforce Investment Act (WIA) in 1998, as policymakers considered how to improve services. In 2002, about 63,000 young people between the ages of 16 and 21 were served through WIA year-round and summer youth programs—more than 100,000 *fewer* than had been served in JTPA programs in 1980, a year in which another 750,000 summer job opportunities were available for disadvantaged youth (Anderson and Sawhill 1980; Mikelson and Nightingale 2004).

Among the latest policy responses to the youth employment "problem" are the Youth Opportunity Grants (YOGs), which support community-based comprehensive youth development strategies, and the Young Offender Initiative. Begun in the late 1990s, both initiatives encourage implementing integrated services and expanding capacity-building efforts in selected communities, drawing on some promising lessons from research on Job Corps, YEDPA, and earlier demonstrations (King 2004; Walker 2000). The Young Offender Initiative—a federal interagency cooperative effort involving the departments of Labor, Justice, Housing and Urban Development, and others—targets offenders up to age 25 and may eventually serve several thousand youth each year. Between 1998 and 2004, about 40,000–50,000 individuals a year received services under the YOG and Young Offender programs. Most were between the ages of 14 and 21 and participating in YOG-funded programs.

Thus, federally funded employment services have targeted disadvantaged youth in various ways over the years. Before examining the primary programs in more detail, it is important to better understand the characteristics of this population, namely youth with limited educational attainment.

Educational Investments among Young Adults

Formal education is the largest human capital investment in the early part of a young person's life. On the positive side, the vast majority of young people in the United States today have at least a high school education—only 20 percent have not completed high school (table 8.1). In addition, young black adults have similar high school completion rates as other young adults. On the negative side, young Hispanic adults have significantly lower high school completion rates than other racial and ethnic groups—35 percent of young Hispanic women and 39 percent of young Hispanic men have not completed high school.

Although the majority of 18- to 24-year-olds complete high school, most of them do not go on to college. Young Hispanic men and women and young black men have the lowest levels of college enrollment. For example, 81 percent of young Hispanic men, 73 percent of young Hispanic women, and 67 percent of young black men do not go on to col-

Table 8.1. *Educational Attainment of Those Age 18–24 (percent)*

	High school dropout	High school graduate	Some college	College graduate
All	20	37	33	10
Men				
Black	20	47	30	3
Hispanic	39	42	16	3
White	18	40	32	10
Other	7	30	43	20
Women				
Black	19	41	35	5
Hispanic	35	38	23	4
White	15	32	38	15
Other	17	29	38	16

Source: 1999 National Survey of America's Families.

lege (compared with 57 percent of all young people). Not surprisingly, college completion rates are relatively low among all youth between the ages of 18 and 24 since many are still in college. Nonetheless, table 8.1 shows that blacks and Hispanics have considerably lower college completion rates than people of other races in this age range.

It would be good news if most young people who did not follow the traditional path from high school to college continued to invest in their educations—for example, by enrolling in continuing education classes or community college courses. As shown in table 8.2, however, most high school dropouts and high school graduates did not attend school in 1998—only 39 percent of young high school dropouts and 24 percent of high school graduates were enrolled in school during that year.

The situation is particularly stark for young Hispanics. Only 24 percent of young Hispanic high school dropouts attended high school or GED classes during 1998. Even fewer young Hispanic high school graduates (17 percent among young Hispanic men) were enrolled in school that year.

The news is somewhat better for young black men. Just over 50 percent of young black men who had not completed high school had attended GED or high school classes in 1998, and 39 percent of young black men who had completed high school had been in school in the previous year.

Table 8.2. *Young Adults Who Took Classes in 1998 (percent)*

	High school dropout	High school graduate	Some college	College graduate
All	39	24	73	60
Men				
Black	51	35	44	—
Hispanic	24	17	50	63
White	45	24	76	64
Other	—	—	80	72
Women				
Black	39	17	69	73
Hispanic	25	14	66	69
White	44	28	79	55
Other	41	28	84	73

Source: 1999 National Survey of America's Families.

— sample size was too small to estimate the percentage.

Enrollment rates for high school dropouts tend to be much lower than for youth who have completed some college. Nearly three-quarters of young people who had completed some college were taking courses in 1998. Only young black and Hispanic men who had completed some college had school enrollment rates at or below 50 percent.

Work Experience and Occupational Status of Less-Educated Young Adults

One reason young adults are not attending school is because they are working. Eighty-five percent of less-educated young adults (18 to 24 years old with a high school education or less) were employed at some point in 1998 (table 8.3). Less-educated young men were considerably more likely to have worked in 1998 than young women. Black men had a lower employment rate (86 percent) than white (92 percent) and Hispanic men (88 percent), but their employment rate was higher than that of black women (78 percent). Two groups of less-educated young women had substantially lower rates of employment than other groups—only

Table 8.3. *Work Experience of Less-Educated Young Adults in 1998 (percent)*

	Did not work	*Worked part year*	*Worked full year*[a]
All	15	42	43
Men			
Black	14	51	35
Hispanic	12	38	50
White	8	41	51
Women			
Black	22	48	31
Hispanic	40	39	21
White	15	41	45
Other	41	38	20

Source: 1999 National Survey of America's Families.

Note: "Other" men are not included because their sample size is too small.

[a] Worked full year is defined as working at least 48 weeks.

about 60 percent each of Hispanic women and other minority women (not black or Hispanic) worked in 1998.

Although most less-educated young adults had worked at some point in the previous year, most of them (57 percent) had not worked year-round (at least 48 weeks). While full-year work was most common among white and Hispanic men and white women, only about half of these groups worked year-round. In contrast, only 35 percent of less-educated young black men and 31 percent of less-educated young black women worked all year. Hispanic and other minority women had even lower rates of full-year employment.

The occupational status of less-educated young adults who work is not concentrated in any particular area, as seen in table 8.4. The occupational status of certain subgroups, however, is highly concentrated. For example, over half of less-educated young black men who worked were employed as operators or laborers in 1998, while less than one-quarter of all less-educated young adults worked in these occupations. In contrast, only one-fifth of less-educated young black men worked as professionals, managers, clerical workers, craft workers, or in sales, while half of all less-educated young adults worked in these occupations.

Table 8.4. *Main Occupation in 1998 for Less-Educated Young Adults (percent)*

	Professional or managerial	Sales	Clerical	Service	Craft	Operator	Laborer	Farm
All	9	14	12	22	15	12	11	4
Men								
Black	5	5	5	24	5	19	36	1
Hispanic	9	9	4	16	26	15	13	8
White	11	10	6	14	25	16	13	6
Women								
Black	9	33	18	31	2	6	2	0
Hispanic	10	21	25	25	3	9	5	2
White	8	19	21	33	5	7	6	1
Other	11	26	7	17	20	16	3	0

Source: 1999 National Survey of America's Families.

Note: "Other" men are not included because their sample size is too small.

Participation in Workforce Development Activities among Less-Educated Young Adults

Since about one-fifth of 18- to 24-year-olds are high school dropouts and fewer than half of 18- to 24-year-olds are enrolled in college, many could benefit from employment and training or other activities designed to improve work skills. To examine how many less-educated young adults undertook job search or job training, we examined their responses to the following two questions in the 1999 NSAF:

> "During 1998, did you take classes or workshops to help [you] look for work, like job search assistance, job clubs, or world-of-work orientations?"

> "During 1998, did you take courses or apprentice programs that trained you for a specific job, trade, or occupation, excluding A.A. or B.A. degree programs, GED classes, or on-the-job training?"

The responses to these questions are likely to reflect activities funded or provided by a range of programs and agencies, including community colleges, nonprofit organizations, welfare or food stamp agencies, private training institutions, and schools.

Only 10 percent of less-educated young adults reported that they received job training and only 7 percent reported that they received job search assistance in 1998 (table 8.5). In addition, receipt of these services varied by race and ethnicity. Less-educated young nonblack and non-Hispanic minority women are the least likely to participate in either activity. Hispanics also tend to have lower participation rates than blacks and whites. Less-educated young blacks are more likely to participate in job search assistance, and less-educated young whites are more likely to participate in job training.

We also examined how many less-educated young men are nonresident fathers.[2] Only 9 percent of less-educated young men were nonresident fathers in 1998. However, less-educated young black men were about four times as likely as other less-educated young men to be nonresident fathers (table 8.6). Nearly one-quarter of less-educated young black men were nonresident fathers.

Very few less-educated young nonresident fathers reported receiving either job search assistance or job training. For example, just 2 percent of young, black, less-educated nonresident fathers reported receiving job

Table 8.5. *Less-Educated Young Adults Who Reported Receiving Job Training or Job Search Assistance in 1998 (percent)*

	Job training	Job search assistance
All	10	7
Men		
Black	6	13
Hispanic	6	6
White	13	6
Women		
Black	10	15
Hispanic	8	8
White	11	5
Other	2	3

Source: 1999 National Survey of America's Families.

Note: "Other" men are not included because their sample size is too small.

training, and 3 percent reported receiving job search assistance. The survey did not address why individuals did or did not participate in various activities, but young nonresident fathers who seek services may be more interested in obtaining a job immediately than in participating in a training program. Young nonresident fathers may also be less aware of training opportunities as other youth, or may not be offered those services.

In summary, young black men are similar to other youth in many respects. About 80 percent of 18- to 24-year-olds have at least a high school education, regardless of race or gender, and most of those without college report that they are working. Young black men, however, are less

Table 8.6. *Young Less-Educated Nonresident Fathers Receiving Job Training or Job Search Assistance in 1998 (percent)*

	Black	Hispanic	White
Nonresident fathers	23	4	6
Nonresident fathers who report receiving			
Job training	2	3	2
Job search assistance	3	1	1

Source: 1999 National Survey of America's Families.

likely to attend college than other young population groups. In addition, less-educated young black men (i.e., those without college) are less likely than other young men to work year-round and are more likely than other young adults to be concentrated in laborer and operator occupations.

On a somewhat promising note, less-educated young black men are more likely to be enrolled in classes and more likely to receive job search assistance than other groups. That is, while young black men are more economically disadvantaged than white men and less likely to attend college, substantial percentages have completed high school and their labor market activity is high. Both qualities could provide a foundation for targeted skills development services and programs, which may help improve their longer-term economic opportunities.

Who Is Served by Workforce Development Programs?

To better understand the types of services young adults receive and to examine the receipt of services from a program perspective, data from the JTPA SPIR system maintained by the U.S. Department of Labor's Employment and Training Administration were analyzed.[3] Until 1998, JTPA was the largest source of federal employment and training funding. The WIA replaced JTPA in 1998; many of the same work-related services, job training, and job search assistance are now funded under WIA. Programs funded under WIA or JTPA are not the only places individuals might receive job training or job search assistance. Other programs—such as those offered through the vocational education system, secondary schools, community colleges, and various private and nonprofit training institutions—include employment-related services and occupational training. However, since JTPA represented the core of federal employment and training funding for the economically disadvantaged until the end of the 1990s, it is useful to examine participation in its programs.

JTPA Context

Before discussing youth participation in JTPA, three introductory points are important. First, the federal employment and training system is fairly small. JTPA primarily targeted services to economically disadvantaged adults and youth, dislocated workers, and others with employment difficulties. JTPA (and now WIA) represents the largest single source of federal employment and training funding, with a congressionally authorized budget in 2002 of about $3.5 billion for adult and youth programs combined. However, resources are fairly limited compared with the population that might benefit from workforce development activities. Estimates suggest, for example, that there was only enough JTPA funding to provide services to between 1 and 2 percent of those eligible (Loprest and Barnow 1993; Sandell and Rupp 1998). As a result, nationwide, about 300,000 persons received services under the adult, youth, or dislocated worker components of JTPA each year in the late 1990s. That represents only a very small portion of those who presumably could have been served if more resources were available. The federal funding level for WIA is similar to what was available under JTPA.

The second important point is that funding for JTPA's regular youth and adult programs did not increase throughout the 1990s. While total federal funding for JTPA increased by about 28 percent (adjusting for inflation) between fiscal years 1993 and 2001, the increase was essentially for dislocated worker programs—that is, programs for those who lost their jobs due to firm closing or permanent reductions in workforce—in which few young adults are served.

The third point is that job search assistance and other services designed to help individuals move immediately into a job have generally been found to have positive effects on employment; and job training, particularly occupation-specific on-the-job training, results in higher wage rates and longer job retention.[4] As noted earlier, research has found somewhat less positive results for youth than for adults. More specifically, while on-the-job training (OJT) has had some positive impact on *adults'* employment and earnings, the JTPA evaluation found no evidence of positive outcomes for youth from OJT or from any other services analyzed (Orr et al. 1996). There continues to be much discussion about these findings, including the possibility that the results reflect poorly designed operations and not employment services or training per se. Regardless of how effective or ineffective JTPA services were found to be for youth, the system did offer the full range of employment and training services to economically disadvantaged persons, and it is informative to understand how many less-educated young adults participated.

Young People in JTPA

Since JTPA represented the main source of federal funding for disadvantaged persons until 1999, program year (PY) 1993 and 1998 SPIR data were analyzed to examine the young adults in these programs.[5] In PY 1998, 230,000 people under the age of 35 were served through JTPA programs. This total includes 30,000 14- to 17-year-olds and 86,000 18- to 24-year-olds and represents approximately 1 percent of individuals in each age group nationwide in households with incomes less than 150 percent of the federal poverty level.

Given the gradual reduction in federal funding for JTPA, it is not surprising that about 30 percent fewer youth under 35 were in JTPA in 1998 than in 1993 (the number of JTPA participants of all ages decreased by about 11 percent over that period). As noted in table 8.7, the most dramatic declines in services occurred for those between the ages of 14 and 24. Even if one were to assume that another 50,000 14- to 21-year-olds participated in YOG and Young Offender programs, this would still mean that about 20 percent fewer youth under 24 were served in 1998/1999 than in 1993.

Young adults also represented a smaller share of all JTPA participants (figure 8.1) in PY 1998 than in PY 1993, and adults 35 and older represented a larger share. This shift undoubtedly reflects the increased funding for services to dislocated workers (few of whom are young adults) over that period, compared with a reduction in funding for basic JTPA adult and young adult programs.

In general, more women than men participated in JTPA at all age groups, and the difference was greater in PY 1998 than in PY 1993, as shown in table 8.8. Some of the widening gender discrepancy may have been related to increased emphasis on welfare reform in the late 1990s and the related increase in employment services for young mothers. While welfare agencies have overall responsibility for work programs for welfare recipients, many JTPA agencies had contracts from welfare agencies to provide various employment and training services, and some programs enrolled individuals in both JTPA and welfare programs. The gender difference is particularly evident for those between 20 and 24.

Many of the young men in JTPA were fathers, although there is little information about their children or families. Of the young men age 14 to 34 who participated in JTPA in PY 1998, 25 percent (22,000) reported being the parent of a minor child living in the same household. The rate was somewhat higher for white and Hispanic men and lower for blacks (table 8.9). It is very likely that many other participants were nonresident fathers, although there is no information on this in the SPIR data files.

There is some evidence from the data, however, that JTPA placed relatively high priority on providing services to young adults from minority

Table 8.7. *Youth Age 14–34 Receiving JTPA Services in PY 1993 and PY 1998*

Age	PY 1993			PY 1998			Total change
	Men	Women	Total	Men	Women	Total	
14–17	41,767	42,000	83,767	14,298	15,763	30,061	−64%
18–19	21,900	28,293	50,193	10,833	16,016	26,849	−47%
20–24	28,436	45,258	73,694	21,134	37,628	58,762	−20%
25–34	49,882	72,188	122,070	41,737	72,642	114,379	−6%
35–60	81,579	83,375	164,954	89,763	118,877	208,640	+26%
Total 14–34	141,985	187,739	329,724	88,002	142,049	230,051	−30%
Total 14–60	223,564	271,114	494,678	177,765	260,926	438,691	−11%

Source: Analysis of U.S. Department of Labor's Standardized Program Information Report data for program years (PYs) 1993 and 1998.

Figure 8.1. *Age Distribution of JTPA Participants, PY 1993 and PY 1998*

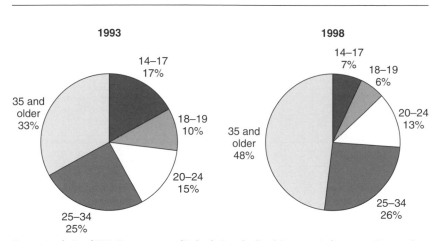

Source: Analysis of U.S. Department of Labor's Standardized Program Information Report data for program years (PY) 1993 and 1998.

groups. Compared with the total minority participants in JTPA, for example, minority young adults represented a larger share of their age group of participants (table 8.10). Thirty percent of men age 14 to 17 and 27 percent of men age 18 to 24 in JTPA were black, and similar shares were Hispanic.

Youth could be served by both JTPA adult programs and youth programs (since the target age groups overlapped), and the youth programs

Table 8.8. *Young Adults in JTPA by Gender and Age, PY 1993 and PY 1998 (percent)*

	PY 1993		*PY 1998*	
Age	*Male*	*Female*	*Male*	*Female*
14–17	49.9	50.1	47.6	52.4
18–19	43.6	56.4	40.3	59.7
20–24	38.6	61.4	36.0	64.0
25–34	40.9	59.1	36.5	63.5
35–60	49.5	50.5	43.0	57.0
All ages (14–60)	45.2	54.8	40.5	59.5

Source: Analysis of U.S. Department of Labor's Standardized Program Information Report data for program years (PYs) 1993 and 1998.

Table 8.9. *Male JTPA Participants Age 14–34 Who Are Fathers Living with One or More of Their Children, PY 1998 (percent)*

| Age | Race/Ethnicity | | | | |
	Black	Hispanic	White	Other	Total
14–17	2	3	1	2	2
18–19	4	9	5	6	6
20–24	15	27	24	18	22
25–34	31	47	43	38	40
Total 14–34	18	28	29	23	25

Source: Analysis of U.S. Department of Labor's Standardized Program Information Report data for program year (PY) 1998.

served both those who were in school and those who were not. Of all teenagers in JTPA in PY 1998, about 70 percent of those age 14 to 17 were in school when they entered a JTPA program, as were between 20 and 40 percent of 18- and 19-year-olds (table 8.11). Black and Hispanic teens in JTPA were more likely to be out of school than their white counterparts.

As one might expect, nearly all JTPA participants between the ages of 14 and 17 lacked high school diplomas, regardless of race (table 8.12). Of participants over the age of 18, minority young adults in JTPA had lower levels of education than white participants in the same age group. For example, 29 percent of black and 35 percent of Hispanic male JTPA participants between 20 and 24 years old had not finished high school, compared with 21 percent of white male participants.

It is useful to examine the experiences of those who participated in JTPA, since the services through these programs are fairly typical of the types of publicly supported employment-related services available. Young minority men in JTPA were more likely to receive a basic education and less likely to receive skills training than other groups. In addition, a higher percentage of young minority men and women, especially teenagers, received basic education services, possibly reflecting their lower educational levels (table 8.13). More women than men (of all races), however, received occupational skills training. Black and Hispanic men were the least likely of all groups to receive occupational skills training.

Black men were also less likely than other youth to participate in on-the-job training, the component that research suggests may be most

text continues on page 206

Table 8.10. *Race and Ethnicity of JTPA Participants by Age, PY 1998 (percent)*

| | Men | | | | | Women | | | |
Age	Black	Hispanic	White	Other	Total	Black	Hispanic	White	Other	Total
14–17	30	25	39	6	100	34	26	34	6	100
18–19	27	29	39	5	100	33	25	38	4	100
20–24	27	28	41	4	100	35	21	40	4	100
25–34	26	20	49	5	100	33	18	45	4	100
35–60	19	14	63	4	100	23	13	59	5	100
All ages (14–60)	23	19	53	5	100	30	19	47	4	100

Source: Analysis of U.S. Department of Labor's Standardized Program Information Report data for program year (PY) 1998.

Table 8.11. *JTPA Participants Age 14–34 Who Were in School When Entering JTPA, by Race, PY 1998 (percent)*

	Men in School				Women in School			
Age	White	Black	Hispanic	Other	White	Black	Hispanic	Other
14–17	71	69	73	76	67	74	75	77
18–19	36	29	22	38	27	22	24	33
20–24	6	4	5	7	9	5	7	9
25–34	4	2	3	5	7	3	5	7

Source: Analysis of U.S. Department of Labor's Standardized Program Information Report data for program year (PY) 1998.

Table 8.12. *Educational Level of JTPA Participants Age 14–34, by Race, PY 1998 (percent)*

	Men				Women			
Age	White	Black	Hispanic	Other	White	Black	Hispanic	Other
14–17								
Less than high school or GED	98	99	98	98	95	98	97	97
High school diploma or GED	2	1	2	2	5	2	3	3
Some college or vocational school	0	0	0	0	0	0	0	0
18–19								
Less than high school or GED	63	74	64	71	50	58	57	58
High school diploma or GED	35	25	34	26	45	40	41	37
Some college or vocational school	2	1	1	2	4	2	2	5
20–24								
Less than high school or GED	21	29	35	28	18	25	32	23
High school diploma or GED	62	58	56	53	62	58	56	56
Some college or vocational school	17	3	9	20	19	17	13	21
25–34								
Less than high school or GED	14	17	29	17	29	19	30	18
High school diploma or GED	57	60	54	46	59	55	53	49
Some college or vocational school	28	24	16	37	29	26	17	32

Source: Analysis of U.S. Department of Labor's Standardized Program Information Report data for program year (PY) 1998.

Table 8.13. *JTPA Services to Young Adults, PY 1998 (percent)*

Age	Men				Women			
	White	Black	Hispanic	Other	White	Black	Hispanic	Other
14–17								
Basic skills education	54	64	65	58	53	60	62	56
Occupational skills training	15	14	16	19	18	12	15	19
On-the-job training	1	0	2	2	1	0	2	2
Work experience or internships	35	23	42	49	33	26	45	53
Other	45	40	44	59	45	43	45	57
18–19								
Basic skills education	34	46	36	45	32	40	42	40
Occupational skills training	34	29	28	32	49	43	39	39
On-the-job training	5	2	8	3	2	2	6	2
Work experience or internships	27	20	36	37	19	17	29	33
Other	34	36	31	46	27	29	30	40

20–24

Basic skills education	14	19	16	25	16	22	27	24
Occupational skills training	58	53	47	52	68	64	57	62
On-the-job training	11	7	11	8	5	5	9	6
Work experience or internships	5	7	20	9	6	7	14	10
Other	9	14	8	16	11	12	12	19

25–34

Basic skills education	11	12	12	16	14	18	23	23
Occupational skills training	59	56	50	57	66	60	55	63
On-the-job training	10	8	12	9	6	6	9	6
Work experience or internships	1	2	12	2	3	3	10	3
Other	4	8	5	9	7	7	7	13

Source: Analysis of U.S. Department of Labor's Standardized Program Information Report program year (PY) 1998.
Note: Percentages in each category do not total 100 percent because some individuals participate in multiple activities.

promising in terms of increased employment and earnings. About two-thirds of JTPA participants in PY 1998 (all ages) entered employment at a median hourly wage between $6.00 and $8.00, with relatively higher employment rates and wages for older participants. The employment rates and wages, though, were lower for blacks and Hispanics than for whites in the same age groups (table 8.14).

What Are the Implications?

The information in this chapter indicates that young black men do less well in the labor market than young white men and have lower rates of college enrollment. A few factors, however, suggest that young black men have the foundation necessary to undertake more skills development than is currently occurring. Black men between the ages of 18 and 24 have a high school completion rate on par with their white counterparts, 85 percent of young black men without college work at some point during the year, and many (one-third to one-half) enroll in some type of education or class. That is, while young black men have some employment and educational deficits compared with their white counterparts, a fairly high percentage are willing to work and participate in further education or training (although their rates of employment and participation in education and training are lower than for young white men, and they are more likely to be concentrated in laborer occupations).

While young black men do participate in the primary federally funded job training programs, funding has been so limited that, like all groups, few have been able to participate. Those black men who did participate in JTPA, however, were more likely than young white men to receive basic education services or job search assistance, and their employment success and earnings were lower. While national studies of JTPA suggest that stand-alone training has been of limited assistance to youth, on-the-job training and any work-based, occupation-specific training may have more potential. Young black men, though, were less likely than other young participants in JTPA to receive OJT.

Therefore, one implication of the information presented in this chapter is that it may make sense to invest more in occupation-specific training that integrates education; in doing so, skills development may increase among young black men in particular. Integrating reading, mathematics, computer instruction, and other basic learning into the workplace

Table 8.14. *JTPA Participants Entering Employment, by Race, PY 1998*

	Men				Women			
Age	White	Black	Hispanic	Other	White	Black	Hispanic	Other
14–17								
Share entering employment	37%	27%	33%	29%	40%	30%	31%	32%
Median hourly wage	$6.00	$5.65	$5.75	$5.75	$5.75	$5.75	$5.75	$5.75
18–19								
Share entering employment	65%	55%	48%	44%	66%	57%	53%	59%
Median hourly wage	$6.50	$6.16	$6.00	$6.50	$6.25	$6.25	$6.00	$6.50
20–24								
Share entering employment	77%	69%	61%	65%	73%	69%	62%	64%
Median hourly wage	$8.00	$7.50	$7.00	$8.00	$7.25	$7.00	$7.00	$7.50
25–34								
Share entering employment	78%	73%	67%	70%	74%	71%	61%	68%
Median hourly wage	$10.00	$8.50	$8.25	$10.00	$8.00	$7.50	$7.30	$8.24

Source: Analysis of U.S. Department of Labor's Standardized Program Information Report data for program year (PY) 1998.

can efficiently improve an individual's future employment prospects. An integrated skills development strategy can simultaneously improve both basic skills (e.g., reading and mathematical ability) and employment or occupational skills, which should help individuals qualify for better jobs in demand occupations. A major appeal of OJT, which integrates employment with skills development, is that individuals receive a regular hourly wage during the training period. Men, especially fathers, generally prefer work to formal training, in part because they want and need immediate income. More young black men might participate in workforce development programs if they could combine wage-paying jobs with occupation-specific training.

While individuals with a college education earn more in the job market than those without college, there are some potentially good jobs for people, especially men, without college. Despite the rapid technological development in the U.S. economy, the Bureau of Labor Statistics estimates that about three-quarters of the projected new jobs over the next decade (net new jobs) will not necessarily require a college degree. An analysis of the growth occupations found that several offer relatively high wages (median hourly wage is equivalent to at least 200 percent of the poverty level for a family of three) and are generally full-time (Nightingale 2002).

The good news for men (and not so good for women) is that many of these jobs are in occupations that have been traditionally considered male jobs—machinists, technicians, and operatives. Individuals in these "good jobs" qualify by having relevant work experience or short-term on-the-job training; a few require postsecondary vocational training (often offered through community colleges). The categories of such "good jobs" include:

postsecondary training: sound technicians; electronics repairers; aircraft, automobile, and truck mechanics;

related work experience: first-line managers/supervisors; building and transportation inspectors;

long-term OJT (12+ months): plant operators; precision repairers; HVAC mechanics; police and patrol officers;

moderate-term OJT (1–12 months): equipment installation, operation, and repair; sales representatives; and

short-term OJT (1 month or less): mail carriers, sorters, and clerks; procurement clerks; sailors and fishers.

Thus, individuals, especially men without a college degree and those who do not wish to engage in higher education, can, with careful labor marketing planning and some occupation-specific training or work experience, find decent jobs. Individuals should be encouraged to seek out job opportunities in occupations, like those listed above, that are projected to have increased demand and appear to have some potential for wage growth. Workforce development programs could also expand the types of integrated work and training available, better target their offerings to these "good" jobs, and increase their efforts to attract young black men to these programs. Of course, the best path to higher income is still a college education, but in lieu of that it is important that individuals make good choices about which occupations to pursue to avoid stagnating in dead-end jobs in the low-wage labor market.

Finally, federal funding for workforce development and job training for the disadvantaged is low compared with the potential need and with earlier decades. The best way to increase the employment prospects of less-educated youth may be to expand federal funding of programs through WIA and special grants programs such as YOG; target the new funding to preparing youth for high-skilled, high-wage-potential jobs; and make special effort to ensure those programmatic options are accessible to young disadvantaged workers.

NOTES

1. The Workforce Investment Act of 1998 replaced the Job Training Partnership Act. However, at the time of the analysis conducted for this chapter, the most currently available participant data was from the JTPA programs, which in general provided services to youth similar to the programs authorized under WIA. The next section discusses this is more detail.

2. The data on nonresident fathers have been reweighted to adjust for the underreporting of nonresident fathers in national household surveys. The reweights do not adjust for nonresident fathers outside of the survey sampling frame, such as those in institutions. See Sorensen and Oliver (2002).

3. The SPIR data system was used until 1999. JTPA was replaced by the new Workforce Investment Act of 1998; the new reporting system, the Workforce Investment Act Standardized Record Data (WIASRD) system, was not yet available at the time of this analysis.

4. For a review of employment and training research, see Barnow and King (2000).

5. JTPA program years begin July 1. Program Year 1998 is the most recent year for which SPIR data from all states were available at the time of the analysis. Beginning in PY 1999, seven states chose to implement WIA early and therefore did not submit SPIR data.

REFERENCES

Anderson, Bernard E., and Isabel V. Sawhill. 1980. "Policy Approaches for the Years Ahead." In *Youth Employment and Public Policy,* edited by Bernard E. Anderson and Isabel V. Sawhill (137–55). Englewood Cliffs, NJ: Prentice Hall.

Barnow, Burt S., and Christopher T. King. 2000. *Improving the Odds: Increasing the Effectiveness of Publicly Funded Training.* Washington, DC: Urban Institute Press.

GAO. See U.S. General Accounting Office.

King, Christopher T. 2004. "The Effectiveness of Publicly Financed Training in Services: Implications for WIA and Related Programs." In *Job Training Policy in the United States,* edited by Christopher J. O'Leary, Robert A. Straits, and Stephen A. Wandner (57–99). Kalamazoo, MI: W. E. Upjohn Institute for Employment Research.

Lerman, Robert. 2000. "Employment and Training Programs for Out-of-School Youth: Past Effects and Lessons for the Future." In *Improving the Odds: Increasing the Effectiveness of Publicly Funded Training,* edited by Burt S. Barnow and Christopher T. King (185–208). Washington, DC: Urban Institute Press.

Loprest, Pamela J., and Burt S. Barnow. 1993. "Estimating the Universe of Eligibles for Selected ETA Programs." Washington, DC: The Urban Institute.

Mikelson, Kelly, and Demetra Smith Nightingale. 2004. "Estimating Public and Private Expenditures on Occupational Training in the United States." Unpublished manuscript, The Urban Institute.

Nightingale, Demetra Smith. 2002. "Economic Security and Job Opportunities for Low Skilled Workers." Unpublished manuscript, The Urban Institute.

Orr, Larry L., Howard S. Bloom, Stephen H. Bell, Fred Doolittle, Winston Lin, and George Cave. 1996. *Does Training for the Disadvantaged Work? Evidence from the National JTPA Study.* Washington, DC: Urban Institute Press.

Sandell, Steven, and Kalman Rupp. 1998. "Who Is Served in JTPA Programs: Patterns of Participation and Intergroup Equity." Research Report. Washington, DC: National Commission for Employment Policy.

Sorensen, Elaine, and Helen Oliver. 2002. "Policy Reforms Are Needed to Increase Child Support from Poor Fathers." Working Paper. Washington, DC: The Urban Institute.

U.S. Department of Labor, Employment and Training Administration. 2001. "Summary of Budget Authority, FY81 to Current, by Year Appropriates, 05/16/01." http://www.doleta.gov/budget/tephah.txt.

U.S. General Accounting Office. 1980. "CETA Demonstration Provides Lessons on Implementing Youth Employment Programs." HRD-81-1. Washington, DC: U.S. General Accounting Office.

Walker, Gary. 2000. "Out-of-School and Unemployed: Principles for More Effective Policy and Programs." In *The 21st Century Challenge: Moving the Youth Agenda Forward,* edited by Marion Pines (73–83). Public Policy Issues Monograph 00-02. Baltimore, MD: Sar Levitan Center for Social Policy Studies.

9

Improving Public Policies to Increase the Income and Employment of Low-Income Nonresident Fathers

Wendell Primus

Low-income noncustodial parents often face challenges complying with the child support system, finding and maintaining employment, and developing the long-term ability to support themselves and their children. Even those who are fully willing to pay child support find themselves navigating a difficult child support enforcement system, accumulating arrears, often retaining less than half their gross incomes, and facing high marginal tax rates with few work supports or incentives. During the last economic cycle, the employment of less-educated young black men declined, while the employment of less-educated young black women increased (chapter 2, this volume). In response to these concerns, this chapter proposes several policies aimed at nonresident fathers to increase employment and, in turn, enhance the well-being of their children.[1]

Substantial increases in the Earned Income Tax Credit (EITC), a program that supplements the wages of low-wage workers, has heightened financial rewards and increased employment for low-income single custodial parents (Dickert, Houser, and Scholz 1995; Eissa and Liebman 1996; Meyer and Rosenbaum 1999). But because the EITC is conditional on the presence of custodial children, these incentives are usually unavailable to noncustodial parents, or NCPs.[2] This chapter explores how similar earnings subsidies could be structured for noncustodial parents, recognizing that society expects them to pay child support and would not support earnings subsidies for NCPs without fulfilling that expectation.

For various reasons, policymakers are extremely reluctant to spend resources on noncustodial parents, even when the goal is increasing employment and work. Some are concerned that resources will be diverted from measures that increase the employment and income of single custodial mothers. Others worry that concentrating resources on noncustodial parents might encourage more fathers to leave their children. Thus, an earnings subsidy for NCPs must not increase marriage penalties or allow NCPs to avoid parental responsibilities. As this chapter demonstrates, marriage penalty concerns can be addressed and remedied. A careful combination of systemic child support changes and new policies geared toward NCPs and modeled after policies that increased earnings for low-income mothers during the 1990s can reward positive behavior and enhance the well-being of children and families.

Why the Child Support System Is Problematic for Low-Income Fathers and Their Families

To increase employment and earnings for low-income NCPs, it is important to understand the role of the child support system and its effect on low-income fathers. The child support system was created to enforce children's rights to receive financial support from both parents, regardless of the parents' marital status. Child support income can constitute a large part of families' budgets. On average, child support makes up more than a quarter of the annual income of low-income families receiving it (Sorensen and Zibman 2000). Unfortunately, even with an improved child support enforcement system, many low-income fathers do not pay child support regularly.

While some fathers are simply unwilling to support their children, many fathers want to be involved in their children's lives but face considerable barriers. Fathers of poor children are often poor themselves and unable to pay significant amounts of child support. The most disadvantaged low-income fathers are very similar to disadvantaged low-income single mothers: they are often young, lack high school diplomas and work skills, and have limited work experience (Richer et al. 2003). Many also struggle to cope with substance abuse, legal problems, and job discrimination, and lack affordable transportation and housing. Many have health issues that impede employment ("Forgotten Population" 2003). Although the economy has been strong for the past several years, and unemployment in 2000 fell to its lowest level in decades, employment levels for young black men have stagnated (Holzer and Offner, this volume). A growing number of states and cities are providing services to low-income fathers, but these efforts remain limited.

Payment of child support can also affect the quality of the relationship between noncustodial fathers and their children. Although it is unclear which factor is the cause and which is the effect, fathers who are actively involved in their children's lives are more likely to pay child support than fathers who are uninvolved (Zill and Nord 1996).

The current child support program uses many tools to enforce non-custodial parents' responsibility to pay child support. In recent years, the program's enforcement activities have been significantly strengthened at both the state and the federal levels, and a much higher percentage of low-income fathers are now affected by the child support system. The enforcement tools have become increasingly automated as well. Federal legislation passed in 1988 requires automatic withholding of child support obligations from the paychecks of noncustodial parents. To make wage withholding as effective as possible, legislation enacted in 1996 established the National Directory of New Hires, which allows the child support office to closely track NCPs' employment.

Once a noncustodial parent enters the child support enforcement system—either because his children receive TANF or because the custodial parent seeks assistance in collecting child support—states are authorized to take several additional steps. States can seize assets held in financial institutions and intercept periodic or lump sum payments from public sources such as unemployment compensation or lottery payments. They can place liens against real or personal property and suspend driver's, professional, occupational, and recreational licenses. The federal government may also deny the issuance of a passport if a parent has $5,000 or more of outstanding child support payments. Other enforcement techniques include withholding state and federal tax refunds payable to a parent who is delinquent in support payments and performing quarterly data matches with financial institutions to track down assets of delinquent parents (for a complete list, see U.S. House of Representatives 1998, 552–53). States can order noncustodial parents to engage in work activities and use civil contempt procedures to incarcerate NCPs who do not comply with court orders to pay child support.

While many collection techniques and sanctions are necessary and effective, certain aspects of the child support system are clearly problematic for low-income fathers who are willing, but unable, to provide the mandated payments. These include the size of the order, arrearages, modifications, visitation, and the economic disincentives.

Size of Order

Very low income noncustodial parents often cannot afford to pay enough child support to meet all their children's needs. According to the Maryland guidelines, for example, a noncustodial parent with two children and $15,000 of annual earnings in calendar year 2003 is required to pay $3,823 a year in child support. After child support, federal and state taxes, and work expenses are paid, and accounting for any government benefits the NCP is entitled to receive (food stamps, for example), this parent would have $7,744 left on which to subsist (table 9.1). This amount is approximately 81 percent of the poverty level for one person, even though gross earnings exceeded 156 percent of the poverty level. Similarly, an NCP earning $15,000 in California would pay nearly $5,210 in child support, leaving him at 75 percent of the poverty level. In Texas, the same NCP would pay $3,281, and his disposable income would be 95 percent of the poverty level. These examples also illustrate that the size of child support orders varies considerably among states.

When the state does not have income information for the noncustodial parent, child support orders are often imputed based on a set standard, such as minimum care for the children, earnings at minimum wage, or known employment history. In California, for example, many

Table 9.1. *Disposable Income and Poverty Level of Noncustodial Parents Earning $15,000 in 2003*

	California	Maryland	Texas
Disposable income	$7,163	$7,744	$9,092
Child support order	$5,210	$3,823	$3,281
Percent of earnings retained	48%	52%	61%
Disposable income as percent of poverty level	75%	81%	95%

Source: Author's calculations based on child support guidelines for each state.

Notes: The poverty level for a one-person household was $9,573 in 2003. Disposable income includes food stamps and EITC and subtracts federal and state income taxes, employee share of payroll taxes, child support, and work expenses (equal to 5 percent of income up to $750 a year).

orders are based on imputed income: Los Angeles County estimates that 70 percent of its proposed judgments are based on this standard (Roberts 2002).

An imputed order can be either too high or too low depending on the parent's actual income. Imputed child support orders do not solve the lack of information regarding NCPs and can cause higher nonpayment rates. A recent study by the Department of Health and Human Services Office of Inspector General found that

> where imputed income was used to calculate the amount of the child support obligation owed in cases established in 1996, almost half of the cases generated no payments toward the financial obligation over a 32-month period. In contrast, where cases were not based on imputed income, only 11 percent of cases received no payment during this time period. While it is possible that the parents for whom income was imputed were potentially less likely to pay anyway, imputing income does not appear to be an effective method of getting them to pay. (HHS OIG 2000, 3)

Imputed orders, when necessary, should be temporary, and resources might be better focused on outreach and determining the noncustodial parent's actual income in order to prevent arrearages (Roberts 2002).

Finally, the child support guidelines in Maryland, California, and Texas suggest that some orders exceed the amount that low-income NCPs are able to pay. Unfortunately, even when adding custodial parent income, the orders typically fall short of the cost of raising a child. Reducing the size of orders for low-income NCPs is an inadequate solution unless additional steps are taken to ensure that children in custodial families are not made worse off as a consequence.

Arrearages

One direct consequence of nonpayment of child support is that noncustodial parents accumulate large child support arrearages, or debts. Of fathers who owed child support in 1999 in Maryland, 82 percent had accumulated an arrearage (table 9.2). These arrearages averaged about $6,834 (Primus and Daugirdas 2000a). In Baltimore City alone, the child support arrearages owed by NCPs totaled about $407 million. In

Table 9.2. *Prevalence and Size of Arrearages among Cases with Support Orders, Noncustodial Parents in Maryland and Oregon, Fiscal Year 1999*

	Maryland	Maryland welfare cases	Oregon	Oregon welfare cases
Total cases	128,625	12,928	79,167	33,502
Cases with an arrearage	106,130	11,326	66,342	32,664
Percent of cases with an arrearage	82.4%	87.6%	83.8%	97.5%
Average arrearage per case with an arrearage	$6,834	$7,539	$6,301	$8,142
Of cases with arrearages, percent with arrearage > $10,000	20.9%	26.4%	18.4%	24.4%

Sources: Maryland and Oregon offices of child support enforcement.

Oregon, 84 percent of fathers who pay child support had accumulated an arrearage, with an average $6,301 balance.[3] For NCPs with spouses on welfare, the arrearage situation is even worse. In both Oregon and Maryland, the percentage of cases with an arrearage, the average amount of the arrearage, and the percentage of cases with an arrearage over $10,000 are all higher than average.

In some cases, these arrearages may have unintended effects. Arrearage policies may deter noncustodial parents from seeking stable employment, and very large arrearages may encourage some low-income NCPs to limit their employment to underground jobs that pay cash. This implication is supported by a substantial amount of ethnographic research: several studies document that fathers may quit jobs when they discover how much of their income is garnished for child support (Achatz and MacAllum 1994; Furstenberg 1992; Johnson and Doolittle 1996; Waller 1996).

The California arrearage study also highlighted several other issues. Of the $14.4 billion in arrearages, some 70 percent was owed to state and federal governments, while 30 percent was owed to custodial mothers. Most of the debt was over two years old. While 80 percent of the fathers had some or recent earnings, many had very low incomes or no income at all. Thus, the study concluded that little of these arrearages would ever be collectible (Roberts 2002).

Modifications

Modifying child support orders can be complicated and intimidating. First, if fathers are employed irregularly or seasonally, standard orders might not adequately reflect corresponding earnings adjustments, and fathers may not know how to navigate the CSE system to fit their child support payments to their fluctuations in income. Second, if the father is absent from child support hearings, the court establishes an imputed order that reflects the needs of the child, not the father's ability to pay. In California, if a noncustodial parent's income is unknown, the standard amount of child support is $423 a month for one child—well out of the range of many low-income fathers (Sorensen 2002). Third, some states modify orders when fathers are incarcerated, but some do not, citing "voluntary unemployment." All these situations can exacerbate the accumulation of arrearages.

Visitation

Historically, the child support enforcement system has resisted enforcing visitation rights. As a rule, fathers want to be involved in their children's lives, but the child support agency enforces only the payment of support. About half the fathers in the Parents' Fair Share (PFS) demonstration visited their children once a month. The findings from the PFS demonstrations show how difficult it is to increase the involvement of fathers in their children's lives. More recent programs have somewhat increased involvement for families that have low levels of conflict or have recently separated. But these programs also provided legal services to help fathers gain visitation.

Research from PFS and other ethnographic work has repeatedly suggested that both parents in low-income families are more comfortable with the noncustodial father taking part in his children's life when he has something to "bring to the table." Data from PFS show that fathers who earned more were more involved with their children. Although it is difficult to determine whether this relationship is causal—fathers who earn more, for example, may have other characteristics that make them more likely to visit their children—society's emphasis on fathers as providers suggests a strong link between how much fathers earn and how often they visit their children (Miller and Knox 2001).

Economic Disincentives

Under current federal law, arrearages collected from federal tax refund intercepts are applied first to the debt owed to state and federal governments and then to the debt owed to custodial families. At the state level, administrators decide whether to "disregard" child support income when determining the size of a family's monthly cash assistance. The 1996 federal welfare law repealed a requirement that states pass through and disregard the first $50 a month in child support payments to custodial parents and their children, rather than retaining the full amount as reimbursement for cash assistance. To ensure that custodial families are made better off financially when NCPs pay child support, states should be encouraged to disregard child support payments when calculating TANF benefits.

In states where the $50 disregard was eliminated, many noncustodial fathers (and custodial mothers) are discouraged and frustrated by the fact that child support payments yield no benefits for their children. In these states, child support payments are counted dollar for dollar against TANF benefits, effectively resulting in a 100 percent tax rate on those payments. Under these circumstances, fathers have no economic incentive to pay child support to their children because no matter how much they pay, their children are not better off economically. In 2000, the child support program collected a total of $17.9 billion in child support. Of the $8.2 billion collected for current and former TANF families, federal and state governments kept $2.4 billion as recovered welfare costs ($1.23 billion for former TANF families and $1.16 billion for current TANF families), or nearly one-third of child support payments (Turetsky 2002).

The Importance of Employment for Low-Income Noncustodial Parents

This chapter takes a comprehensive approach to policies directed at noncustodial parents because many of the problems low-income NCPs face are closely interrelated. This is especially true of employment issues and child support. Some noncustodial parents avoid employment because of child support sanctions. Others cannot pay child support because they are unemployed, and still others are employed but cannot afford their full child support order.

A basic reason many noncustodial parents do not pay child support regularly is unemployment or underemployment, which leaves them limited income from which to pay child support. As a result, many low-income NCPs amass large arrearages and become subject to child support enforcement polices. Some enforcement policies, such as incarcerating noncustodial parents or revoking their drivers' licenses if they do not meet their child support obligations, may make it more difficult for low-income NCPs to become employed.

About a third of all low-income noncustodial parents are black men, a group that has not made the employment strides seen by others in the past decade (Bell and Gallagher 2001). A recent analysis comparing the labor force participation rates of young black men and women found that their trends have differed markedly in recent years. Between 1992 and 1999, the labor force participation rate of black males between the ages of 20 and 24 who were not incarcerated *fell* from 83.5 percent to 79.4 percent nationwide, despite the strong economy. By contrast, the labor force participation rates of young black women rose dramatically during this period, from 64.2 percent to 78.8 percent (Holzer and Offner, this volume). One key factor explaining this increase in employment among women, especially low-income women with children, is the EITC (Meyer and Rosenbaum 1999).

A study from the Urban Institute examines the population of Americans between 25 and 49 who have neither children of their own living with them nor any work-limiting disabilities. This population, also known as ABAWDs (for able-bodied adults without dependents), includes many noncustodial parents. The Urban Institute study finds that they "appear to be quite a vulnerable population. Over a third are officially poor—one in seven extremely poor (below 50 percent of poverty)—and an equal number sometimes uncertain about being able to afford food" (Bell and Gallagher 2001). When the authors examined the low-income noncustodial fathers (below 200 percent of the poverty level) in this group, they found that the noncustodial fathers were more likely to work full-time than their childless counterparts (74 percent compared with 59 percent) but were no more likely to escape poverty despite their higher work effort.

The probability that a low-income noncustodial parent is involved with the child support system today is much higher than it was 10 or 20 years ago. This is because the child support system has become much more automated and the enforcement tools more effective. Also, paternity establishment rates have increased substantially. This increased enforcement could be driving more fathers into the underground economy.

Finally, economic security is a key aspect of sustaining relationships among both married and cohabiting couples; for cohabiting couples it is also key factor in the decision to marry or separate. Both qualitative and quantitative data support this contention. Ethnographic researchers found that when they asked low-income single mothers specifically about their economic criteria for marriage, nearly every one told them the father needed to have a "good job" (Edin 2000). The interviewed women had strong moral (and often religious) objections to marrying men whose economic situation would, in their view, practically guarantee eventual marital dissolution. Another recent study found that joblessness is a major impediment to father involvement and family formation (Gadsen and Rethemeyer 2001). New policies crafted to ensure NCPs have the ability, not just the willingness, to pay child support could result in fewer children in poverty and more fathers involved in their children's lives.

Low Retention of Earnings and High Marginal Tax Rates

The high marginal tax rates that low-income custodial parents with children face (especially as their earnings increase from roughly $13,000 to $20,000) are well documented (Primus and Daugirdas 2000b). This section uses hypothetical examples of low-income noncustodial parents in Maryland, California, and Texas to explore two aspects of income: the implicit marginal tax rates NCPs face, and the proportion of earnings they retain as disposable income after taking into account federal and state taxes, food stamps, work expenses, and child support.

Most means-tested benefits are targeted to families with children. In most cases, single adults are ineligible for these benefits because they do not have, or do not live with, their children. Noncustodial parents that live alone are generally ineligible for cash assistance.[4] The 1996 welfare law limited the receipt of food stamps for most able-bodied adults without dependents to three months in a three-year period while unemployed. In most cases, NCPs are also ineligible for health care coverage under Medicaid. The EITC for childless workers is less than one-tenth the size of the EITC for families with two or more children.

Disposable income is income left after federal and state taxes are paid, food stamp benefits are received, work expenses deducted, and the child support order is fully paid.[5] Child support payments in these illustrative examples are subtracted because noncustodial parents are required to pay child support (and risk penalties when they do not). In addition, in many cases NCPs' wages are garnished and the child support owed is automatically withheld from their paychecks and deducted from their disposable income.

Noncustodial Parents Who Pay Child Support Retain Approximately Half Their Earnings

Table 9.3 summarizes findings about disposable income and implicit marginal tax rates in California, Maryland, and Texas for calendar year 2003. Child support orders increase as earnings increase, but often with a considerable lag in time. The examples presented in this part of the analysis could also be thought of as "snapshots" of NCPs at different earnings levels rather than a description of one NCP whose earnings (and commensurate expenses) increase over time. Thus, the primary focus is on disposable income relative to earnings.

Table 9.3 shows that the disposable income of noncustodial parents with earnings between $10,000 and $25,000 usually equals approximately half of gross earnings. For example, the disposable income of an NCP with earnings between $15,000 and $25,000 is much less than 50 percent of gross earnings in California and slightly above 50 percent in Maryland. In Texas, low-income NCPs retain a slightly higher proportion of their earnings—between 60 and 68 percent—over the $10,000 to $25,000 range of earnings. Texas does not have a state income tax and its child support orders are somewhat smaller than Maryland's and California's.

A noncustodial parent living in California, Maryland, or Texas must have gross earnings between 115 and 215 percent of the federal poverty level (FPL) before his disposable income reaches 100 percent of the poverty level for one person ($9,573). At $15,000 in earnings, the NCP's disposable income ranges from $7,163 to $9,092, or between 75 and 95 percent of FPL. At $20,000 in earnings, an NCP's disposable income ranges from below the FPL in California (97 percent) to 125 percent of FPL in Texas.

The implicit marginal tax rates that low-income NCPs face can be quite high; the NCPs in these examples frequently face implicit marginal tax rates above 50 percent. Noncustodial parents in all three states face implicit marginal tax rates between 55 and 88 percent as their earnings increase from $5,000 to $10,000 to $15,000. Besides the child support

text continues on page 224

Table 9.3. *Disposable Income and Marginal Tax Rates of Noncustodial Parents in California, Maryland, and Texas, 2003*

	Gross Earnings				
	$5,000	$10,000	$15,000	$20,000	$25,000
California					
Disposable income	$5,581	$6,578	$7,163	$9,292	$11,492
Child support order	($833)	($2,766)	($5,210)	($6,695)	($8,162)
Percent of earnings retained	112%	58%	48%	46%	46%
Disposable income as percent of poverty level	58%	69%	75%	97%	120%
Maryland					
Disposable income	$4,977	$6,243	$7,744	$10,290	$12,766
Child support order	($1,440)	($2,742)	($3,823)	($4,784)	($5,768)
Percent of earnings retained	100%	62%	52%	51%	51%
Disposable income as percent of poverty level	52%	65%	81%	107%	133%

Texas

Disposable income	$5,167	$6,847	$9,092	$11,993	$14,893
Child support order	($1,250)	($2,277)	($3,281)	($4,248)	($5,214)
Percent of earnings retained	103%	68%	61%	60%	60%
Disposable income as percent of poverty level	54%	72%	95%	125%	156%

Marginal Tax Rates

California	80%	88%	57%	56%
Maryland	75%	70%	49%	50%
Texas	66%	55%	42%	42%

Marginal Tax Rates (if support orders constant and NCP does not receive food stamps)

California	23%	25%	28%	27%
Maryland	23%	40%	30%	30%
Texas	23%	25%	23%	23%

Source: Author's calculations based on child support guidelines for each state.

Notes: The poverty level for a one-person household was $9,573 in 2003. Disposable income includes food stamps and EITC and subtracts federal and state income taxes, employee share of payroll taxes, child support, and work expenses (equal to 5 percent of income up to $750 a year). Numbers in parentheses are deductions from gross income. The top two panels of the table assume child support orders increase immediately when income changes.

order, the main factors driving the high implicit marginal tax rates over this income range are a loss of food stamp benefits and tax liabilities.

Assuming the noncustodial parent does not receive food stamps and calculating marginal tax rates during the time lag before child support orders increase, the picture changes. The implicit marginal tax rates that NCPs face under these assumptions are much lower—between 23 and 40 percent, as shown in the bottom panel of the table. Although the lag between income increases and child support order increases allows noncustodial parents to have lower implicit marginal tax rates, it does not reflect sound policy. Children should benefit as their parent's income increases.

Like low-income custodial parents, low-income noncustodial parents can face high marginal tax rates. Because NCPs must pay child support, and because they are not eligible for a substantial EITC as custodial parents are, low-income NCPs retain a much smaller proportion of their gross earnings. The disposable income of low-income NCPs is often close to half their gross earnings when they pay their child support order in full and their child support order reflects their current income.

Noncustodial Parents Often Have Less Income than Custodial Parents

The previous section showed that noncustodial parents can often face high marginal tax rates and retain approximately half their gross earnings. The argument for lowering these marginal tax rates or increasing NCP's incomes through earnings subsidies depends somewhat on how the income and marginal tax rates of NCPs compare with those of custodial parents. A direct comparison of incomes would be unfair, because the income of the custodial parent must support herself and the children, while the income of the NCP supports only one person. Thus, incomes are adjusted for family size and are compared as a percentage of the poverty level.

Table 9.4 compares the disposable income as a percentage of the poverty level for a noncustodial parent with that of a custodial parent with two children in California, Maryland, and Texas. The bold numbers indicate where the NCP retains less disposable income as a percentage of FPL than the custodial family. Particularly, in Maryland and California, the custodial parent (CP) almost always maintains a considerable income advantage when the NCP is paying child support. When both parents earn $10,000 in Maryland, the CP has a disposable income equal to 120 percent of FPL, while the NCP's income is only 65 percent of FPL. Similarly, at $10,000 of earnings in Texas, the CP's income is 113 percent of FPL and the NCP's income is

Table 9.4. *Disposable Income of Separated Families in California, Maryland, and Texas, by Earnings, 2003*

		DISPOSABLE INCOME AS PERCENT OF POVERTY LEVEL					
Earnings		California		Maryland		Texas	
CP	NCP	CP	NCP	CP	NCP	CP	NCP
$0	$10,000	**74**	**69**	62	64	50	72
$2,500	$7,500	**92**	**66**	72	63	64	65
$5,000	$5,000	**104**	**58**	83	52	76	54
$5,000	$15,000	**104**	**74**	90	78	84	95
$7,500	$12,500	**115**	**66**	105	67	**98**	**80**
$10,000	$10,000	**127**	**69**	120	65	**113**	**72**
$15,000	$5,000	**139**	**58**	137	53	**132**	**54**
$10,000	$20,000	**134**	**97**	130	107	123	125
$12,500	$17,500	**146**	**94**	140	96	**134**	**110**
$15,000	$15,000	**153**	**75**	147	84	**142**	**95**
$20,000	$10,000	**164**	**69**	162	67	**161**	**72**
$10,000	$30,000	151	142	139	160	132	186
$20,000	$20,000	**191**	**97**	176	111	**174**	**125**
$30,000	$10,000	**209**	**69**	200	70	**205**	**72**

Source: Author's calculations based on child support guidelines for each state.

CP = custodial parent with two children; NCP = noncustodial parent.

Notes: The poverty level in 2003 was $9,573 for a one-person household and $14,824 for a three-person household. Disposable income includes food stamps, TANF, and EITC, and subtracts federal and state income taxes, employee share of payroll taxes, and work expenses (equal to 5 percent of income up to $750). Child support orders are added to the CP's disposable income and subtracted from the NCP's disposable income. Numbers in **bold** show where the NCP has less income than the CP.

72 percent of FPL; in California, the CP's income is 127 percent of FPL, while the NCP's income is 69 percent of FPL. The disparity continues when both parents earn $15,000. In California, the CP's income is 153 percent of FPL, while the NCP's income is only 75 percent of FPL.

One million nonresident fathers are poor and still pay child support, but a quarter of these fathers are paying more than 50 percent of their gross income. Only 2 percent of nonpoor fathers pay this much (Sorensen and Oliver 2002). Many poor fathers face the same barriers to employment as poor mothers do, along with higher rates of incarceration and criminal histories. They are also less likely to participate in employment services offered by TANF and have severely limited access to income support programs and Medicaid, compared with custodial mothers. When these fathers "do the right thing" and pay child support, they sometimes place themselves well below the poverty level.

Alternative Policies That Would Enhance the Well-Being of Fathers and Their Children

The previous sections outline the problematic aspects of child support and demonstrate that in many cases, low-income nonresident fathers face higher marginal tax rates and retain a smaller percentage of their income than custodial parents. This section proposes a new vision of the child support system; highlights the importance of employment supports for noncustodial parents; and suggests three alternative methods for an earnings subsidy for NCPs, conditional on the payment of child support with the goal of increasing employment.

A New Vision for the Child Support System

To address the difficulties with the current system and encourage low-income NCPs to do more to improve their children's well-being, a new vision for the child support system is proposed that better serves children in low-income families (Primus and Daugirdas 2000a). This vision outlines several new policies that could make the child support system more helpful for low-income NCPs. Some changes involve supplementing standard enforcement activities with services for low-income parents that have limited abilities to maintain work and pay child support regularly. All child support initiatives should recognize the heterogeneity of noncustodial parents. Specifically, this vision intends to use the child support system to engage the noncustodial parent in employment services and improve the well-being of children in single-parent families by

- making compliance more reasonable and realistic for low-income NCPs in terms of establishing levels of child support orders, securing modifications to orders when an NCP's income changes, and forgiving large arrearages owed to the state conditional upon the payment of current support;
- providing employment services and stipends to certain low-income NCPs so that through employment they secure the resources to support themselves and pay child support regularly;

- providing case managers to help low-income NCPs negotiate the child support and employment systems and to facilitate enforcement of child support collection;
- incorporating parenting and relationship-building services to help separated low-income parents work together for the health and well-being of their children, regardless of the status of their romantic relationship;
- rewarding low-income NCPs' payment of child support by subsidizing it, similar to how earned income tax credits (and subsidies) reward low-wage work for families with children;
- providing Medicaid coverage to NCPs complying with child support on the same basis as custodial parents; and
- ensuring that children in custodial families are economically better off when child support is paid, regardless of their welfare status.

To work effectively, this vision must be implemented comprehensively; the services provided and changes suggested are designed to be complementary. A program that provides employment services and at the same time addresses NCPs' large arrearages should increase child support payments more than either policy alone. Similarly, assisting unmarried parents in their efforts to work together on behalf of their children should be more effective if the noncustodial parent is paying child support. Economic subsidies are crucial; they reinforce the rewards for working. Thus far, no program that has worked with fathers has provided substantial economic incentives either for employment or for paying child support.

States are beginning to see child support payments as potential income for poor families rather than as reimbursements for the state's welfare expenditures. The elements of this vision reflect this shift away from child support's historic cost-recovery focus, not only by ensuring that all child support payments benefit the children in custodial families, but also by supplementing those payments for low-income NCPs to create an additional economic incentive for paying child support.

A Focus on Employment of Noncustodial Parents

This goal can be accomplished by creating economic incentives for the noncustodial parent to participate in employment services and cooperate with the child support agency and by providing subsidies when the NCP pays child support. Historically, however, employment programs targeted to NCPs have had difficulties recruiting participants. Successful programs would integrate employment services with the child support system, with the latter providing the "carrots," or positive incentives, to encourage low-income NCPs to participate. For NCPs connected to both the CSE system and the criminal justice system, the justice system could be the lead agency, as compliance is mandatory within that system. For incarcerated NCPs, a program within penal institutions should provide employment services and parenting classes six months to a year before release. After release, individual case managers (parole officers plus others) should help these NCPs negotiate the child support system and ensure they receive the necessary employment services.

Work-related services and supports should include services similar to those available to mothers who are or have been TANF recipients; address the range of barriers to employment NCPs face, including transitional employment for those who might benefit (e.g., ex-offenders); and enable low-income fathers to increase child support participation and payment. Program designs should focus on building capacity and support for fathers and their children within the employment, child care, and social service system. The child support enforcement program (or the criminal justice system) would not provide these services but would refer noncustodial parents to employment service providers, closely monitor participation in these activities, and sanction NCPs if they did not participate. Any incentives to participate in employment programs would be removed if the noncustodial parents fail to cooperate.

The employment services offered should intend to increase the earnings and job stability of low-income noncustodial parents and help these NCPs meet their child support obligations more regularly. These employment services could include job search activities, job readiness ("soft skills") training, on-the-job training, publicly funded jobs, and job retention services. The incentives to participate in employment services and cooperate with the child support enforcement system could include access to health care coverage through Medicaid and stipends while NCPs are participating in training or receiving job preparation services and receiving no compensation.

Earnings Subsidies—The Primary Policy Tool

The primary policy tool that could increase the employment of noncustodial parents is an earnings subsidy. To be politically viable, however, this subsidy would have to be contingent on the parent cooperating with the child support enforcement agency and paying child support. Given budget constraints at both the federal and state levels, these subsidies are not likely to be adopted nationwide, or even statewide. However, states could experiment in selected localities with these different approaches and determine whether these policies are feasible and effective.

An earnings subsidy can be structured in three possible ways. The first method provides a supplement—a child support incentive payment (CSIP)—to any collected child support order. The child support agency administers this payment. Each payment to the mother represents the child support payment from the father plus the CSIP. The second method provides a tax credit to the noncustodial parent based on evidence that the NCP met his child support obligations during the previous year. The tax credit is paid to the NCP instead of the custodial parent and appears more like an earnings subsidy than a child support incentive payment. The third method is a general increase in the childless EITC for all low-income adults without dependents.

Lowering Child Support Orders and Matching Funds with Child Support Incentive Payments

This section essentially describes two intertwined proposals: lowering the child support obligations owed by low-income NCPs and matching these reduced orders with a child support incentive payment. While child support orders are sometimes high in terms of a low-income NCP's ability to pay, these orders fall short of the costs of raising a child. On one hand, child support orders for low-income noncustodial parents should take into account their limited ability to pay. On the other hand, child support payments should reflect what it costs to raise a child. Unfortunately, the cost of raising a child is more than what many poor NCPs are able to pay consistently.

An equitable child support system must consider that while many noncustodial fathers are poor, their counterpart custodial families, who have the day-to-day responsibility for their children, also are poor. Child support incentive payments are designed to fill this gap and simultaneously create economic incentives for the payment of child support by increasing the amount of money that actually goes to the child. Incentive payments are also an earnings subsidy for nonresident parents because the wages paid as child support are matched. Whether the NCP would perceive the CSIP as an earnings subsidy and respond in the labor market, as low-income custodial parents have done, remains unclear (Meyer and Rosenbaum 1999).

The CSIPs proposed in this chapter are matching payments made by the government to fill the gap left by lowering orders to a level that low-income NCPs are able to pay. For example, under the current Maryland guidelines, an noncustodial parent with $10,000 in earnings who has two children in a custodial family that also has $10,000 in earnings owes $2,742 in child support. The vision described in this chapter proposes lowering that order to $1,500, and when it is paid by the NCP, matching it with a $1,500 CSIP for a total of $3,000.

Administratively, this system is simpler than it seems. The income of the NCP could be based on last year's income and the matching rate determined annually—probably from tax forms submitted to the child support enforcement agency. Once the matching rate is determined, each child support payment made by the NCP would simply be multiplied by the matching rate, and the order plus the CSIP would be forwarded to the custodial parent.

The reduced child support orders for low-income NCPs are based on the following illustrative formulas: for an NCP with one child, the child support order would be the sum of 5 percent of income between $0 and $5,000, 15 percent of income between $5,000 and $10,000, and 23 percent of income above $10,000. For an NCP with two children, the child support order would be the sum of 5 percent of income between $0 and $5,000, 25 percent of income between $5,000 and $10,000, and 35 percent of income above $10,000. This chapter focuses on low-income NCPs. If applied to NCPs with higher incomes, both these formulas result in orders somewhat higher than current law; this chapter is not necessarily suggesting that these orders be increased.

The CSIP matching rates are based on the income of the noncustodial parent and the number of children in the family. These matching rates decline as NCP income increases and phase out completely for noncustodial parents with incomes above $24,500. Child support incentive payments (the child support paid multiplied by the CSIP matching rate) would be transferred to the custodial family for every dollar of child support paid by low-income noncustodial parents. These matching payments would create an economic incentive for paying child support because each dollar of child support paid by a low-income NCP would make the children of the NCP better off by more than a dollar. The CSIP would not affect eligibility for any other state benefits, including child care subsidies and cash welfare assistance. The CSIP would, however, count in both the gross and net income calculations for food stamp benefits, since food stamp eligibility rules are determined by the federal government rather than by state governments.[6]

Table 9.5 shows how CSIP is calculated using an illustrative formula for a noncustodial parent with two children. As NCP income rises from $0 to $8,000, paid child support would be matched at 150 percent. In this income range, the CSIP matching rate remains constant, but the total amount of the CSIP increases because total child support paid is increasing. Combining this CSIP with the formula for the reduced child support order described above, an NCP with two children and an income of $8,000 would owe $1,000 a year in child support. When this amount was paid, it would be matched with a $1,500 CSIP payment. The children in the custodial family would receive a total of $2,500 in child support.

When a noncustodial parent has income between $8,000 and $12,000, the CSIP subsidy would remain constant at $1,500, while the matching rate decreases to adjust for the increasing amount of child support paid. Thus, an NCP with $12,000 in earnings and two children would owe $2,200 in child support, which would be matched by a $1,500 incentive payment.

Table 9.5. *A Sample Child Support Incentive Payment Plan for a Custodial Family with Two Children*

Gross income of NCP	Child support order	CSIP matching rate	CSIP subsidy	Order + CSIP
$6,000	$500	150.0%	$750	$1,250
$8,000	$1,000	150.0%	$1,500	$2,500
$10,000	$1,500	100.0%	$1,500	$3,000
$12,000	$2,200	68.2%	$1,500	$3,700
$14,000	$2,900	43.3%	$1,255	$4,229
$16,000	$3,600	28.1%	$1,010	$4,684
$18,000	$4,300	17.8%	$765	$5,139
$20,000	$5,000	10.4%	$520	$5,594
$22,000	$5,700	4.8%	$275	$6,049
$24,000	$6,400	0.5%	$30	$6,504
$26,000	$7,100	0.0%	$0	$7,100

Source: Author's calculations.

NCP = noncustodial parent; CSIP = child support incentive payment.

For income above $12, 000, both the matching rate and the total amount of the CSIP subsidy decrease, reaching zero when the noncustodial parent has income of $24,500. The amount of the CSIP benefit for this income range is calculated based on a 35 percent phase-out rate. This means that the CSIP benefit declines by 35 cents for each additional dollar of child support paid.

Conceptually, the benefit level under this alternative is determined in much the same manner as the current federal Earned Income Tax Credit. Figure 9.1 shows both the federal EITC benefit for tax year 2000 and the CSIP benefit for which a family with two children would be eligible under this proposal. The CSIP is based on the noncustodial parent's income, while the EITC is based on the custodial parent's income. In both cases, the amount of the benefit increases over a range of income, plateaus over a range of several thousand dollars, and then phases out. (The federal EITC in this case phases out completely at $33,692.) The kink in the CSIP graph at $5,000 in earnings occurs because the amount of child support owed increases more quickly between $5,000 and $10,000 in earnings than it did between $0 and $5,000 in earnings; as described above, the CSIP matching rate remains constant at 150 percent between $0 and $8,000 of NCP income.

The CSIP would also be similar to the EITC in that it would provide an earnings subsidy for noncustodial parents who are employed and

Figure 9.1. *A Custodial Parent's EITC and CSIP, Assuming Two Children in 2003*

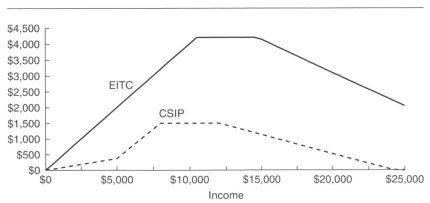

Source: Author's calculations.

EITC = Earned Income Tax Credit; CSIP = child support incentive payment.

complying with the child support system. Although the NCPs themselves would not benefit directly from the CSIP payment, their children would. In essence, their children would receive an "earnings subsidy" from the incentive payment in much the same way that the custodial family receives an earnings subsidy through the EITC.

The CSIP benefit could be structured in several different ways. The parameters described in this section and used throughout the remaining sections of this chapter are primarily illustrative. The key aspect is that the program reward payments are actually made. In establishing this structure, the state must decide the maximum rate at which matching payments will be provided, the range of noncustodial parent income over which this maximum rate will be applied, and the phaseout rate, or how quickly the matching rate will be reduced as the income of the non-custodial parent increases. These parameters determine the income level beyond which noncustodial parents will no longer qualify for matching payments.

To make a significant difference in the lives of children, I would suggest a maximum matching rate for child support payments in the range of 100 to 150 percent, with a maximum matching amount of $750 to $1,100 for one child and $900 to $1,500 for two children. (These numbers could be higher.) The phaseout rate should be between 25 and 35 percent, which would not take effect until NCP annual income reaches $12,000 to $15,000, approximately the same point at which the EITC plateau ends and the phaseout begins for custodial parents. The point at which CSIPs phase out completely would be determined by the above parameters.

The CSIP subsidy also could be implemented without lowering the order. However, since under this proposal the CSIP benefit depends on the size of the order as well as NCP income—and the current Maryland guidelines suggest orders that are high relative to the income of many low-income NCPs—the rates and subsidy amounts could be adjusted accordingly if CSIP is implemented without changing the size of child support orders for low-income NCPs.

A simplified variation of the CSIP subsidy would transfer an incentive payment to the custodial family based on a flat-rate percentage of the non-custodial parent's earnings. If the award percentage were set at 10 percent and the parent was earning $10,000 a year, an additional $1,000 would be paid to the custodial family, regardless of what the NCP had paid during the year. The state would determine the percentage at the beginning of the year. This version of CSIP would act as a kind of child support payment guarantee while also rewarding the NCP for working by providing his children with additional funds.

The practical and theoretical benefits of the CSIP proposal are numerous. First, the child support order is lowered for the noncustodial parent, and child support payments are supplemented—a design that more adequately reflects both the ability of the NCP to pay and the material needs of the child. Second, the CSIP monetary benefit is given directly to the custodial family. Finally, this subsidy is a payment incentive because it is tied directly to the payment of child support.

There are several concerns with a child support incentive payment. One is the implementation challenges and additional strain on the child support system in administering these payments. Another is that subsidizing separated families might create marriage disincentives—a concern addressed below. Also, the noncustodial parent receives no direct incentive for payment, which could perhaps be addressed by combining the CSIP with one of the tax refunds outlined below. The final concern is cost. All these concerns could be addressed by undertaking an experiment in a specific locality.

Noncustodial Parent Tax Credits

This section outlines a tax credit for noncustodial parents conditional on the payment of child support and represents another way to achieve the goals of the CSIP payments: encouraging the payment of child support and simultaneously providing an earnings subsidy to low-income NCPs who pay the child support they owe. This refundable tax credit for NCPs would be similar in structure to the Earned Income Tax Credit (EITC) for families with children. The size of the credit would be roughly half the size of the EITC for families with children. If the NCP pays all the current child support he owes throughout the tax year, he would be eligible for the full credit. If he pays more than half but less than all the child support he owes, he would be eligible for a partial credit.

The credit described in this chapter could be either a new federal credit or a state tax credit—the design issues are essentially the same. The federal credit would be paid out of general revenues, and the refundable portion of the state credit could be paid with TANF or state general revenue monies. This chapter provides one illustrative option for designing this credit. The specifications could be altered, and many other permutations of the general concept would accomplish the same goals. Budgetary costs will undoubtedly dictate the final parameters.

The economic incentive in the CSIP proposal described above does not accrue to the noncustodial parent but to his children. The tax-credit alternative is designed so the noncustodial parent himself receives the earnings subsidy. Eligibility for the NCP tax credit would be based on two criteria: the NCP's income and the proportion of current child support paid in the previous tax year. Noncustodial parents paying child support on behalf of one child would be income-eligible for the credit if their annual earnings were below $29,666 in tax year 2003.[7] Noncustodial parents paying child support on behalf of two or more children (regardless of whether the children live with the same custodial parent) would meet the credit's income eligibility criteria if their annual earnings were below $33,692. To be eligible for the NCP tax credit, a parent must have paid at least 50 percent (or some fraction) of the total current support due in the previous year.[8] I would also suggest that the maximum size for the NCP tax credit at any given income level would be half of the size of the EITC for a family with the same number of children.

There are several reasons NCPs who fail to pay their entire child support orders (but pay more than half) should receive a partial credit. Some NCPs have orders that are high relative to their incomes because they do not secure adjustments to their child support orders when their actual earnings change. If NCPs in these circumstances are paying as much child support as they can consistently, they should be eligible for a partial credit. Other NCPs might pay their child support order in full for most of the year, then lose their jobs and be unable to pay the entire order while unemployed. One option to encourage the payment of all child support is by giving NCPs who pay less than all the child support they owe a smaller credit while creating a bonus for NCPs who pay 100 percent of their child support order. Under this option, NCPs would still be required to pay at least half the child support they owe before qualifying for the credit.

Table 9.6 shows the maximum credit for a noncustodial parent in Maryland who pays his entire child support order. In these examples, the maximum credit (column three) equals 50 percent of the EITC for a custodial parent with the same income. The fourth column shows the total tax liability (federal and state income taxes and employee share of federal payroll tax) for an NCP at that income level. Except for very low earnings (cases in the table where earnings are less than $10,000), the proposed NCP tax credit is less than the NCP's total tax liability at a given

Table 9.6. *Impact of Tax Credit Proposal on the Disposable Income of a Noncustodial Parent with Two Children in Maryland, 2003*

NCP earnings	Child support order	Tax credit if fully paid	Total federal and state tax liability	Disposable income with credit	Disposable income without credit
$6,000	$1,719	$1,200	$77	$6,754	$5,554
$8,000	$2,203	$1,600	$385	$8,281	$6,681
$10,000	$2,742	$2,000	$1,239	$8,720	$6,720
$12,000	$3,194	$2,102	$1,895	$9,137	$7,035
$14,000	$3,605	$2,074	$2,389	$9,380	$7,306
$16,000	$4,047	$1,863	$2,958	$10,108	$8,245
$18,000	$4,420	$1,652	$3,567	$10,915	$9,263
$20,000	$4,784	$1,442	$4,176	$11,732	$10,290
$22,000	$5,214	$1,231	$4,785	$12,482	$11,251
$24,000	$5,565	$1,021	$5,394	$13,312	$12,291
$26,000	$5,928	$810	$6,003	$14,129	$13,319
$28,000	$6,357	$599	$6,612	$14,880	$14,281
$30,000	$6,714	$389	$7,221	$15,704	$15,315
$32,000	$7,067	$178	$7,830	$16,531	$16,353

Source: Author's calculations based on 2003 Maryland child support guidelines.

Note: Disposable income includes food stamps and EITC and subtracts federal and state income taxes, employee share of payroll taxes, child support, and work expenses (equal to 5 percent of income up to a maximum of $750 a year).

income level. The fifth column shows the NCP's disposable income if he fully pays child support and receives the NCP tax credit; the sixth column shows his disposable income if he does not.

As noted above, low-income noncustodial parents who pay child support retain a low proportion of their earnings as disposable income. Without the tax credit, the NCP's disposable income does not reach the poverty level ($9,573) until he earns almost $19,000. With the NCP tax credit, an NCP who pays his child support in full would have disposable income equal to the poverty level when his earnings reach slightly more than $14,000.

This credit does not compensate for the entire cost of the noncustodial parent's child support payment. From a purely financial perspective, NCPs who do not pay child support will continue to be better off than NCPs who pay. NCPs who do not pay child support will, however, be subject to the sanctions and enforcements of the child support agency. This tax credit proposal is designed to encourage NCPs to pay child support, to participate in the formal economy, to pay taxes, and to ensure that the child support agency is aware of their current location so they can receive the 1099-type form that will make them eligible for the credit.

The NCP tax credit creates incentives for both child support payment and employment. The payment goes directly to the NCP, who has paid as much child support as he can and is rewarded for this behavior. But because this credit is tied to work, it would not affect NCPs who are unemployed or working outside the official labor market. These parents may be the hardest group to engage, and they (and their children) have the highest poverty rates. Administratively, while the tax credit would still require considerable effort to implement, using the established tax refund system would be beneficial.

While the previous proposals have been targeted at noncustodial parents, another earnings subsidy proposal would be to simply increase the childless EITC substantially. The childless EITC is a tax credit for poor workers between 25 and 64 years old who do not live with minor children. In 2004, the EITC equals 7.65 percent of poor workers' first $5,100 in earnings, resulting in a maximum credit of $390. The credit begins to phase out at a rate of 7.65 percent once a single worker's income surpasses $6,390 or a couple's income surpasses $7,390. The credit falls to zero when a single worker's income reaches $11,490 or a couple's income reaches $12,490. The proposal could double or triple these amounts and eliminate the age requirement for NCPs who are also paying child support. For example, the childless EITC could be expanded to 15.3 percent of earnings up to $7,000 and phased out starting at $10,000 at a 10 percent rate. The test for paying child support would be extremely simple. The NCP would only have to demonstrate that he paid child support of at least $400, or some other nominal amount.

Here, too, the chapter offers one illustrative option for designing this credit. The specifications could be altered, and many other permutations of the general concept would accomplish the same goals.

This expansion is the simplest of all the proposals but the least targeted. Optimally, this refund would be combined with one of the previous proposals, further increasing ability to pay, providing incentives for both employment and payment of child support, and thus having the greatest benefits for low-income NCPs and, most important, their children.

Arrearages and Earnings Subsidies

Noncustodial parents who have accumulated large arrearages identify these debts as a key deterrent to participating in the child support system (Waller and Plotnick 1999). Anecdotal evidence suggests that large arrearages and the prospect of having significant portions of their earnings consumed by child support expenses may dissuade some NCPs from participating in the formal labor market. Various debt forgiveness or debt compromise policies for low-income NCPs should be considered in certain circumstances. These policies would primarily apply to arrears owed to the state as reimbursement for welfare expenditures.[9]

These incentives must be structured carefully to ensure that compromises on arrearages do not create perverse incentives to accumulate arrearages. Any forgiveness of arrearages owed to the state should be tied to continued payment of the current child support order. This debt forgiveness would apply only to arrearages accumulated before the new policy took effect. In addition, this vision in no way suggests that child support compromises should be permitted for NCPs who are able to pay their child support obligations, have always been able to pay, and have willfully failed to do so.

There are several options for addressing large arrearages:

- The arrearage owed to the state could be reduced by a specified amount or percentage for each month the NCP makes a payment. For example, for every dollar in current child support paid, up to one dollar of the arrears could be forgiven.
- The state could implement a graduated forgiveness policy. For example, if the NCP paid regularly for a year, 30 percent of past due child support owed to the state could be forgiven. If the NCP paid regularly for a second year, 20 percent of the remaining arrears could be forgiven; if he paid regularly for a third year, 15 percent of remaining arrears could be forgiven, and so on.

One-time amnesty is another option, where the debt owed to the state up to a particular point in time is forgiven (with the understanding that this forgiveness will not be offered again). This option may be effective for NCPs who have accumulated very large arrearages and are reluctant to return to the formal child support system.

Child support incentive payments represent another way for non-custodial parents to eliminate arrearages owed to the custodial parent. The noncustodial parent could use his earned incentive payments to eliminate arrearages. Rewarding payment of current child support by reducing child support arrearages should not only enable these noncustodial parents to pay their current orders but also help restore motivation to continue making current payments. CSIPs could be the catalyst that helps the NCP and the custodial parent reach a satisfactory arrearage arrangement.

Marriage Incentives and Earnings Subsidies

One strong argument against implementing earnings subsidies for non-custodial parents is that they may unduly enrich separated low-income families and thus may discourage these families from marrying and raising children together. Although little research establishes a relationship between economic incentives and the living arrangements of families with children, this issue is politically potent. In theory, economic incentives *could* affect living arrangements. Therefore the issue needs to be carefully addressed.

In reality, welfare law does not discriminate against married couples, and two parents are always better off living together. Safety net programs such as TANF, the food stamp program, housing, and Medicaid make no distinction between married parents who live together and unmarried parents who live together with their children. The income of both parents is counted in determining eligibility for and levels of benefits in these programs, regardless of the marital status of parents who live in the same household with their children. In states that impose stricter eligibility requirements on two-parent families, these rules are applied to both co-habiting and married-couple two-parent families. Thus, there is no eligibility "penalty" if a cohabiting couple with a child in common decides to marry. There are clear marriage penalties, however, when a "new" male—a stepparent—is added to the household (Primus and Beeson 2000).

In a state that does not impose additional eligibility restrictions on two-parent families, if the parents decide not to live together, neither parent is likely to be better off financially. Two separate households must now be maintained. The custodial parent and child—who must pay for housing costs with just one income—may be more likely to qualify for means-tested benefits because of the loss of income that occurs when a parent leaves the home. These benefits, however, generally will not leave the family with higher disposable income than when both parents were together. Finally, the noncustodial parent—in addition to paying his or her housing costs—must pay child support to the custodial parent. In short, neither parent has a financial incentive to separate.

The tables on the next two pages compare the disposable incomes of separated families (where the custodial parent and children live apart from the noncustodial parent) with the disposable incomes of married families assuming the same earnings. Disposable income includes federal payroll and income taxes (including the EITC), state income taxes, work expenses (assumed to be 5 percent of earnings up to a maximum of $750 a year), food stamps, TANF, and child support.

According to the analysis (comparing columns four and five to column three in table 9.7), families are better off married under current law than they are if they live separately. The noncustodial parent is always better off living in a married family than living alone. The custodial parent is better off living separated than living in a married family in only three instances. The economies of scale for the two-parent families are a significant factor in this outcome.

Describing income as a percentage of the poverty level standardizes the increased expenses of maintaining separate households. For example, a married-couple family of four living together reached the poverty level with an income of $18,660 in 2003. If the family had split into two households—a single noncustodial parent and a custodial parent with two children—the total income necessary to keep both households at the poverty level is $24,397—31 percent higher.[10] It is more appropriate to assess how different family combinations fare when income is expressed relative to the poverty level for the household unit than by comparing total dollars available to the family members.

Because families have lower incomes relative to expenses when separated than when married, one can provide additional incentives to the noncustodial parent through tax credits or CSIP without creating marriage disincentives. The last three columns of table 9.7 illustrate this for CSIP. In a few instances (bold in the table), the custodial parent is better off separated, but again, there are generally strong incentives for a couple with a child in common to live together. There are no cases using the assumptions employed in this analysis in which both partners face a marriage penalty, or where the weighted average of the separated family is higher than the disposable income of the married family expressed as a percentage of the poverty level. In each case, the NCP is better off living

Table 9.7. *Disposable Income of Married and Separated Families in Maryland, 2003*

			DISPOSABLE INCOME AS PERCENT OF POVERTY LEVEL						
Earnings			If Separated, Current Law			If Separated, with CSIP		
CP	NCP	If married	CP	NCP	Average	CP	NCP	Average
$0	$10,000	93	62	64	63	82	73	80
$2,500	$7,500	93	72	63	68	87	70	83
$5,000	$5,000	93	83	52	67	87	62	81
$0	$15,000	136	62	76	69	91	87	90
$5,000	$10,000	136	85	62	73	102	72	94
$7,500	$7,500	136	99	59	79	103	70	95
$10,000	$5,000	136	**114**	52	83	110	62	98
$5,000	$15,000	124	90	78	84	107	87	102
$7,500	$12,500	124	105	67	86	112	78	104
$10,000	$10,000	124	120	65	93	122	73	109
$15,000	$5,000	124	**137**	53	95	**133**	62	115
$5,000	$25,000	164	98	131	115	105	123	110
$10,000	$20,000	162	130	107	119	134	105	126
$15,000	$15,000	161	147	84	115	**151**	87	135
$20,000	$10,000	162	**162**	67	115	**166**	73	143
$20,000	$20,000	179	176	111	144	**183**	105	164

Source: Author's calculations based on 2003 Maryland child support guidelines.

CP = custodial parent with two children; NCP = noncustodial parent; CSIP = child support incentive payment.

Notes: The poverty level is $18,660 for the married family, $14,824 for the separated custodial family, and $9,573 for the noncustodial parent. Disposable income includes food stamps, TANF, and EITC, and subtracts federal and state income taxes, employee share of payroll taxes, and work expenses (equal to 5 percent of income up to $750 a year). Child support is added to the CP's disposable income and subtracted from the NCP's disposable income. Numbers in **bold** are where the income of the separated custodial parent is higher (as a percent of the poverty level) than income as a married couple. The first $400 of child support and CSIP is disregarded when calculating TANF benefits in the CSIP proposal.

with the mother of his children in a two-parent married or cohabiting family than he is living alone and paying child support.

Table 9.8 compares in detail the disposable income for two parents with two children if the NCP tax credit were enacted. One parent (the custodial parent in the examples where the family is separated) earns

Table 9.8. *The Disposable Income of Married and Separated Families in Maryland, 2003, If the NCP Tax Credit Were Enacted*

| | Married | Separated | | |
		CP	NCP	Total
Earnings	$20,000	$7,500	$12,500	$20,000
Payroll taxes	($1,530)	($574)	($956)	($1,530)
Federal income tax	$4,044	$3,000	($470)	$2,530
State income tax	$276	$540	($589)	($49)
Work expenses	($1,000)	($375)	($625)	($1,000)
TANF	$0	$0	$0	$0
Food stamps	$1,262	$2,046	$0	$2,046
Child support order	NA	$3,428	($3,428)	$0
NCP tax credit	NA	NA	$1,944	$1,944
Disposable income	$23,052	$15,565	$8,376	$23,941
Disposable income as percent of poverty level	124%	105%	87%	101%

Source: Author's calculations.

NA = not applicable

CP = custodial parent with two children; NCP = noncustodial parent.

Notes: Numbers in parentheses are deductions from gross income. Federal and state taxes are positive in some cases because of the Earned Income Tax Credit.

The poverty level is $18,660, for the married family, $14,824 for the separated custodial family, and $9,573 for the noncustodial parent. The poverty level for the "total" separated family is an average weighted by person of the poverty level for the custodial family and noncustodial parent.

$7,500 a year, while the other parent (the NCP in the separated example) earns $12,500, for a total of $20,000. Each row shows a different component of income. The bottom row of the table shows disposable income as a percentage of the poverty level for the married family (124 percent), the separated custodial family (105 percent), the noncustodial parent (87 percent), and an average weighted by person for the entire separated family (101 percent). Even with the NCP tax credit, the NCP is better off living in a married family than he is living alone.

The tax system includes marriage bonuses for some families and marriage penalties for others, depending on the employment status and earning levels of the parents. In contrast, when the added costs of maintaining two separate households and other factors are considered, the social welfare system does not present significant marriage penalties for couples with a biological child in common.[11] Obviously, a program targeted at nonresident parents decreases the gains from marriage. What this analysis shows is that the reduction is not so large that it eliminates the gains from marriage.

Summary

The policies introduced in this chapter offer several options for enhancing the well-being of noncustodial parents and their children. Indirect efforts include reforming the child support system and providing employment support and incentives. Direct efforts include monetary subsidies in the form of payments or tax credits, some of which would be granted directly to the noncustodial parent and others of which would go to the custodial family. The policies can be tied to child support payments, employment, or both, and targeted to NCPs or granted to all low-income adults. It is also important to remember that these policies need not be mutually exclusive but may be combined for more holistic support. Box 9.1 summarizes the proposals and their projected effect on noncustodial parents and children.

Which alternative or combination of alternatives would have the greatest effect on child support paid and employment is unclear. Regardless of final designs, rules, and combinations, these policies overall would enhance NCPs' ability to support themselves and their children.

Implications for the TANF Reauthorization Debate

Cost constraints will inhibit enactment of earnings subsidies as described in this chapter. These ideas should, however, be piloted and enacted on a demonstration basis in one or more localities. Research into whether an earnings subsidy for NCPs would increase their employment is critical to developing a knowledge base on which to build future successful programs. States are unlikely to research this area substantially without federal support and assistance. To support and systemize research in the states, a Family and Child Well-Being Research and Development Fund should be established, using monies previously allocated to the out-of-wedlock bonus to conduct research on programs, including earnings

Box 9.1. Summary of Proposals to Enhance the Well-being of NCPs and Their Children

Proposal	Design	Benefit to NCP	Benefit to child
Child support system reform	Changes orders and arrearage policies to better reflect ability to pay	Case management support and prevention of sanctions and arrears	Increased payment of child support and father involvement
Employment services	Provide case management, barriers to work, and transitional jobs	Increase in income, decrease in or avoidance of arrears	Increased payment of child support and father involvement
CSIP	Lowers orders owed by low-income NCPs and matches these reduced orders with a payment	Lower child support order	Additional child support subsidy goes directly to child
NCP tax credit	Creates a tax credit for NCPs conditional on the payment of child support	Increase in income tied to child support payment	Higher amount of child support paid more frequently
Expansion of childless EITC	Provides a substantial increase for all eligible low-income adults	Increase in income tied to employment	Some additional support to child

subsidies, designed to enhance the well-being of families and children. The Cardin and Carper-Bayh welfare reform bills incorporated such a provision.

In addition, several other items would be beneficial in assisting low-income NCPs.

States should be given some credit toward meeting their TANF work participation rate for low-income fathers of TANF children who are engaged in TANF work activities or pay a sufficient amount of child support. This would provide an incentive for states to extend employment services to more low-income fathers and increase child support collections for low-income children. A state would not be eligible for the credit if the number of mothers receiving employment services declined or other evidence showed resources were being diverted from low-income mothers.

States should be given one-time federal grants to review their child support policies and develop programmatic recommendations to extend employment and parenting services to low-income fathers. As part of the review process, states should develop child support policies that prevent the buildup of unmanageable child support debt and allow for the forgiveness of child support owed to the government when merited. States also should be encouraged to address child support and employment issues in a comprehensive and integrated fashion across a broad array of state programs—child support, employment, criminal justice programs—and to implement programs that match or otherwise subsidize the payment of child support by low-income parents.

Recovery of birthing costs paid by Medicaid from low-income fathers should be prohibited. This practice can saddle low-income fathers with large child support debts even if they consistently keep up with their current support obligations.

States should have the option to extend access to federally funded health care coverage to low-income nonresident parents on the same basis as low-income resident parents.

Finally, states should be given incentives to ensure that more children benefit from the payment of child support.

Families that leave TANF and are owed child support should have first claim on all child support payments made by nonresident parents. While Congress made substantial progress on this front in the 1996 welfare law, child support collected through the interception of federal tax refunds by the IRS—the single largest source of collections of past-due child support—is still retained by the federal government and the states to pay off any unreimbursed costs of providing assistance to the family.

Child support paid by nonresident parents of children receiving TANF should go directly to the child rather than retained by the state. In addition, states should be encouraged to disregard at least a portion of the payment in calculating the family's welfare grant. Where child support is disregarded, states should not have to remit any share of the support to the federal government, as is currently required. As early results from demonstration projects in Vermont and Wisconsin show, child support pass-through and disregard policies can positively affect both the number of fathers who pay child support and the average amount of support paid (Turetsky 2001).

NOTES

1. Since the majority of noncustodial parents are men and the majority of custodial parents are women, this chapter employs gender-specific language and the terms "noncustodial parent" and "noncustodial father" interchangeably. The policies proposed in this chapter would apply to male custodial parents and female noncustodial parents as well.

2. Some 98 percent of overall EITC benefits goes to families with children, with 2 percent going to working individuals and married couples who are not raising minor children. The EITC for childless workers is a tax credit for poor workers between the ages of 25 and 64 who do not live with minor children. In 2004, the maximum EITC for which these workers could qualify was $390.

3. Unpublished tables, Oregon Office of Child Support.

4. An NCP could be part of a cash assistance unit or even receive cash assistance if the state chooses to include him as part of the custodial family that includes his children. Noncustodial parents also are eligible for services funded by TANF, but most NCPs do not receive services, and almost none receive cash assistance.

5. The implicit marginal tax rate is calculated as 100 − [(change in disposable income/change in earnings) × 100].

6. While it would not be possible to change the treatment of food stamps within Maryland law, the federal government should reexamine these policies.

7. This is the point where the EITC for families with one child phased out completely in tax year 2003.

8. If the NCP tax credit were enacted as a federal credit, a provision would be needed to address the disparities in the size of child support orders across states. For example, if an income-eligible NCP were ordered to pay more than 25 percent of his gross income in child support, the minimum child support payment for eligibility for the credit would be half of this smaller amount (12.5 percent of his gross income) rather than half of the actual order. For example, if an NCP with $10,000 in earnings owed $3,000 in child support, the minimum amount of child support he would have to pay to be eligible for the credit would be $1,250—half of $2,500, rather than half of the actual order, or $1,500. This adjustment to

the tax credit would not affect the amount of child support the noncustodial parent owes; it would only affect the size of the tax credit for which an NCP would be eligible.

9. Under federal law, compromises regarding arrearages owed to the custodial family can occur only under specific circumstances and with the voluntary consent and participation of the custodial family. The consent of the custodial parent is not required to forgive arrears owed to the state, because forgiving these arrears would not affect the amount of child support (current or past due) owed to the child.

10. This number is the sum of the poverty threshold for a single individual ($9,573) and the threshold for a family of three ($14,824).

11. For a more complete discussion of these issues, see Primus and Beeson (2000).

REFERENCES

Achatz, Mary, and Crystal A. MacAllum. 1994. "Young Unwed Fathers: Report from the Field." Philadelphia: Public/Private Ventures.

Bell, Stephen H., and L. Jerome Gallagher. 2001. "Prime-Age Adults without Children or Disabilities: The 'Least Deserving of the Poor'—or Are They?" *Assessing the New Federalism* Policy Brief B-26. Washington, DC: The Urban Institute.

Dickert, Stacy, Scott Houser, and John Karl Scholz. 1995. "The Earned Income Tax Credit and Transfer Programs: A Study of Labor Market and Program Participation." In *Tax Policy and the Economy*, vol. 9, edited by James M. Poterba. Cambridge, MA: MIT Press.

Edin, Kathryn. 2000. "Few Good Men: Why Poor Women Don't Remarry." *The American Prospect* 11(4): 26–31.

Eissa, Nada, and Jeffrey B. Liebman. 1996. "Labor Supply Response to the Earned Income Tax Credit." *Quarterly Journal of Economics* 112(2): 605–37.

"The Forgotten Population: Health Disparities and Minority Men: Issue Briefing for Health Reporters." 2003. *Facts of Life* 8(5).

Furstenberg, Frank F., Jr. 1992. "Daddies and Fathers: Men Who Do for Their Children and Men Who Don't." In *Caring and Paying: What Mothers and Fathers Say about Child Support*, edited by Frank Furstenberg, Kay Sherwood, and Mercer Sullivan (36–64). New York: Manpower Demonstration Research Corporation.

Gadsden, Vivian, and R. Karl Rethemeyer. 2001. "Linking Father Involvement and Parental Incarceration: Conceptual Issues in Research and Practice." Philadelphia: National Center on Fathers and Families.

HHS OIG. See U.S. Department of Health and Human Services, Office of Inspector General.

Johnson, Earl S., and Fred Doolittle. 1996. "Low-Income Parents and the Parents' Fair Share Demonstration: An Early Qualitative Look at Low-Income Noncustodial Parents (NCPs) and How One Policy Initiative Has Attempted to Improve Their Ability and Desire to Pay Child Support." New York: Manpower Demonstration Research Corporation.

Meyer, Bruce D., and Dan T. Rosenbaum. 1999. "Welfare, the Earned Income Tax Credit, and the Labor Supply of Single Mothers." Working Paper 7363. Cambridge, MA: National Bureau of Economic Research.

Miller, Cynthia, and Virginia Knox. 2001. *The Challenge of Helping Low-Income Fathers Support Their Children: Final Lessons from Parents' Fair Share.* New York: Manpower Demonstration Research Corporation.

Primus, Wendell, and Jennifer Beeson. 2000. "Safety Net Programs, Marriage and Cohabitation." Paper presented at "Just Living Together: Implications for Children, Families, and Social Policy," University Park, PA, October 30–31.

Primus, Wendell, and Kristina Daugirdas. 2000a. *Improving Child Well-Being by Focusing on Low-Income Noncustodial Parents in Maryland.* Baltimore, MD: The Abell Foundation.

———. 2000b. "Several Suggestions for Improving the Work-Based Safety Net and Reducing Child Poverty." JCPR Working Paper 136. Chicago: Joint Center for Poverty Research, Northwestern University/University of Chicago.

Richer, Elise, Abbey Frank, Mark Greenberg, Steve Savner, and Vicki Turetsky. 2003. *Boom Times a Bust: Declining Employment among Less-Educated Young Men.* Washington, DC: Center for Law and Social Policy.

Roberts, Paula. 2002. *Pursuing Justice: A Strategic Approach to Child Support Arrears in California.* Washington, DC: Center for Law and Social Policy.

Sorensen, Elaine. 2002. "Helping Poor Nonresident Dads Do More." *Short Takes on Welfare Policy* Number 3. Washington, DC: The Urban Institute.

Sorensen, Elaine, and Helen Oliver. 2002. "Policy Reforms Are Needed to Increase Child Support from Poor Fathers." Washington, DC: The Urban Institute.

Sorensen, Elaine, and Chava Zibman. 2000. "Child Support Offers Some Protection against Poverty." *Assessing the New Federalism* Policy Brief B-10. Washington, DC: The Urban Institute.

Turetsky, Vicki. 2001. Written testimony of Vicki Turetsky, Senior Staff Attorney, Center for Law and Social Policy, before the Subcommittee on Social Security and Family Policy, Senate Finance Committee, October 11. Washington, DC: U.S. Government Printing Office.

———. 2002. Testimony presented to the Senate Finance Committee, May 16. Washington, DC: U.S. Government Printing Office.

U.S. Department of Health and Human Services, Office of Inspector General. 2000. *The Establishment of Child Support Orders for Low-Income Non-Custodial Parents.* OEI-05-99-00390. Washington, DC: U.S. Department of Health and Human Services, Office of Inspector General.

U.S. House of Representatives, Committee on Ways and Means. 1998. *1998 Green Book.* Washington, DC: U.S. Government Printing Office.

Waller, Maureen R. 1996. "Redefining Fatherhood: Paternal Involvement, Masculinity, and Responsibility in the 'Other America.' " PhD diss., Princeton University.

Waller, Maureen, and Robert Plotnick. 1999. *Child Support and Low-Income Families: Perceptions, Practices, and Policy.* San Francisco: Public Policy Institute of California.

Zill, Nicholas, and Christine Winquist Nord. 1996. "Causes and Consequences of Involvement by Non-Custodial Parents in Their Children's Lives: Evidence from a National Longitudinal Study." Philadelphia: National Center on Fathers and Families.

10

Poor Fathers and Public Policy
What Is to Be Done?

Ron Haskins

After years of federal government neglect, growing media attention has sparked interest in policies to address the problems of poor and low-income fathers (e.g., DeParle 2004). What are these problems? How are they being addressed? What more should be done? Is Congress prepared to act?

A word is in order about this chapter's focus on disadvantaged fathers, rather than on all disadvantaged men. The two groups, of course, overlap considerably. By the time less-educated young men (those with a high school education or less) are ages 18 to 24, nearly 9 percent are fathers. For black youth, the figure is much higher: by age 24, about one-quarter of young black men are fathers—by age 34, nearly half are (see Nightingale and Sorenson, this volume).

Although much of the evidence reviewed below applies to all less-educated young men, this chapter focuses wherever possible on fathers because they are at the nexus of a host of social problems. As we will see, young disadvantaged fathers are likely to have their children outside marriage. These children begin life with a double problem: they are likely to be poor and to have a weak or nonexistent relationship with their fathers, one of the main engines of growth and development. If young fathers could be helped to improve their own education, find secure employment, pay child support, maintain contact with their children, and even marry the mothers of their children, both the adults and the children would be better off—as would the nation. No social issue on the public agenda is more important than that of disadvantaged fathers and the problems they experience and cause.

The Problem

The disadvantages facing young black fathers are many. Their education levels are low. They have low employment rates and high incarceration rates, with one probably perpetuating the other. They have high levels of divorce and fathering children outside marriage. And many noncustodial fathers are burdened with unreasonably high child support payments and arrearages. This section details each of these problems.

Education

The education deficits of poor men, especially minority men, are well documented. As Nightingale and Sorensen (chapter 8, this volume) demonstrate using data from the National Survey of America's Families, young black men have the lowest educational attainment among black and white men and women. Among 18- to 24-year-olds in this nationally representative data set, 67 percent of black men did not attend college, compared with only 58 percent of white men, 60 percent of black women, and 47 percent of white women.

Although the educational deficits of young black men are undeniable, census data show that, since 1960, the educational levels of black men and women have improved greatly. In 1960, only 18.2 percent of black men had graduated from high school. By 2000, that figure had jumped to 78.7 percent and was still climbing. The figure was lower than the 84.8 percent of white men who had graduated high school, but the gap was closing. Similarly, in 1960, only 2.8 percent of young black men had graduated from college. But by 2000, that figure had jumped to 16.3 percent. As with high school completion, black men were well below white men, but the gap was shrinking (U.S. Census Bureau 2002, 139).

The figures on education for black men establish two patterns that characterize many of the figures reviewed here. One, most black men made progress, but a substantial gap remained between black men and other demographic groups. Two, a group at the bottom either showed no progress or declined.

Employment and Incarceration

Several chapters in this volume testify to the alarming employment status and prospects of disadvantaged black fathers. As Holzer and Offner (chapter 2, this volume) report, many young black men have poor employment records. In 2000, after a decade of nearly steady increases, about 80 percent of young whites and Hispanics with a high school education or less were employed. Similarly, employment by disadvantaged women heading families increased remarkably during the decade. By 2000, the employment rate of never-married mothers was 65.8 percent, up an astounding 52 percent since 1992.[1] By contrast, the percentage of young black men who were employed stood at 56 percent, a decline since the late 1980s.

There are two serious problems here. Not only did the employment of young black men stagnate while a very hot economy contributed to rising employment for other demographic groups, but also the absolute level of employment among young black men was fully 30 percent below the level of other young men. The 1990s was also the first time in recent decades that the wages of low-skilled workers actually increased, which makes the stagnation of black male employment even more serious and less understandable.

Crime and incarceration are major parts of the lives of young black men, and major parts of their employment records. The basic data on their involvement with the justice system is discouraging. As Holzer, Raphael, and Stoll (chapter 4, this volume) show, as many as half of non-institutional black men between the ages of 16 and 34 are either engaged in crime or were in the past. In this age category are about 5.7 million black men. Of these, about 0.7 million (or 12 percent) engage in criminal activity each year, about 0.7 million are in prison, and about 0.5 million are on probation.

Evidence indicates that incarceration affects employment. Freeman (1996) has estimated that ex-offenders have employment rates up to 25 percent lower than nonoffenders, although other researchers have found somewhat smaller effects of incarceration on the probability of being employed. Studies also consistently show that incarceration affects earnings substantially. Holzer, Raphael, and Stoll (chapter 4) estimate that incarceration reduces future earnings by 10 to 20 percent or more.

Although former prisoners may have other characteristics, such as lack of education and unreliable work habits, that reduce their chances of finding employment, most employers simply do not want to hire ex-convicts.

When approximately 3,000 employers in Atlanta, Boston, Detroit, and Los Angeles were asked if they would be willing to hire people from marginal groups (including welfare recipients, the long-term unemployed, and ex-offenders), employers responded that they would rather hire almost anyone other than ex-offenders (Holzer 1996). About 96 percent would hire someone with only a GED, over 90 percent would hire a welfare recipient, and over 80 percent would hire a worker who had been unemployed for more than a year. But less than 40 percent would hire an ex-offender.

Given high and growing rates of incarceration during the 1990s, the number of young men—two-thirds of whom are fathers (Lynch and Sabol 1997)—leaving prison will be very high for the foreseeable future, thereby making the effects of incarceration on employment increasingly salient.

Employment and earnings statistics for young poor and minority men do not paint a pretty picture. But the picture is not entirely bleak, either. Research on poor fathers shows that most of them are working at any given time, that over time nearly all of them work at least occasionally, and that their work records and earnings improve as they get older.

In the Parents' Fair Share research (Martinez and Miller 2000) conducted in seven cities on fathers whose children were or had been on welfare, about 80 percent of the fathers worked in the year after they joined the study. Similarly, in the Fragile Families Study (Center for Research on Child Wellbeing 2002), another large-scale study that involved primarily low-income families, about 80 percent of the fathers of children born outside marriage worked. In fact, they worked nearly 40 hours a week for almost 40 weeks of the year and earned around $16,000, an income that put them well above the poverty level for a single adult. A study of poor and near-poor Wisconsin fathers by Phillips and Garfinkel (1993) found that their earnings more than tripled, from around $5,000 to well over $18,000 (in 1998 dollars) in the seven years after a paternity action.

All these studies found that fathers who married the mothers of their children had much higher earnings. In the Fragile Families study, for example, fathers who lived with the mothers of their children earned only about $16,000, whereas married fathers earned over $33,000. Substantial selection effects are probably evident in these figures—namely that fathers who earn more money are more likely to get married. Nonetheless, even among poor fathers or fathers whose children have received welfare, a high proportion work, and their employment and earnings increase over time. In fact, a considerable portion of poor fathers earn enough to either pay child support or make reasonably attractive partners. Equally important, because the men's work levels and earnings increase as they get older, their ability to support a family increases as well.

But the evidence also shows that a substantial share of young men, especially black young men, has poor work histories and low income. An important consequence of young black men having low earnings is that, as Gibson, Edin, and McLanahan's (2002) recent interviews with poor and low-income mothers show, they are less attractive to women as marital partners.

Family Composition

Another serious problem faced by poor young men—especially black men—is fulfilling their family role as fathers. Observing that the United States has a serious problem with family composition is now commonplace (Lerman 2002). Evidence is strong that both children (McLanahan and Sandefur 1994) and adults (Waite and Gallagher 2000) do better in married families. In the case of children, the benefits seem to accrue only when the marriage consists of the biological parents of the children. Married adults and their children show advantages on a broad range of measures: more wealth, better health, and more and better sex for the former; greatly reduced odds of living in poverty, higher school achievement, and reduced rates of teen pregnancy for the latter.

Even so, since roughly the 1950s, every measure of family composition has deteriorated. Marriage rates have declined, illegitimacy rates have soared, the divorce rate has leaped to nearly 50 percent and has remained near that high level for two decades, and the percentage of children living with their married biological parents has fallen steadily (Ellwood and Jencks 2001). Thankfully, most of these measures stabilized in the mid-1990s, and some have even shown a little improvement for some groups (Acs and Nelson 2001; O'Hare 2003; Primus 2002). But all remain very high.

The levels are higher still for blacks. By 1995, around 70 percent of black children were born outside marriage (Ventura and Bachrach 2000). Of the 30 percent born to married parents, over half would experience a divorce. About 85 percent of black children spend some or all of their childhoods in a female-headed family. Because married parents provide the best rearing environment for children, it follows that 85 percent of black children are deprived of the optimum environment in which most children, including their cohorts in school and in the workplace, are reared. These statistics are simply astounding. The single greatest factor eroding black progress in America is—and has been for several decades—the overwhelming percentage of black children reared in single-parent families (Moynihan 1965a, 1965b).

The repercussions of family dissolution on the development of black boys are legion, although they are not necessarily in accord with the presumptions of middle-class America. Many Americans think of young black men as wild men who reject major parts of civilized life. The black male criminal, sex machine, misogynist, and street tough portrayed in rap music is not an unfamiliar character. After all, the Willie Horton gambit worked (Patterson 1998). Daniel Patrick Moynihan captured this view of black men as early as 1965:

> From the wild Irish slums of the 19th century Eastern seaboard, to the riot-torn suburbs of Los Angeles, there is one unmistakable lesson in American history: a community that allows a large number of young men to grow up in broken families, dominated by women, never acquiring any stable relationship to male authority, never acquiring any set of rational expectations about the future—that community asks for and gets chaos. Crime, violence, unrest, disorder—most particularly the furious, unrestrained lashing out at the whole social structure—that is not only to be expected; it is very near to inevitable. And it is richly deserved. (Moynihan 1965a, 280)

While stipulating that Moynihan is on to something important, this description is overly dramatic and somewhat one-sided. As shown by research reviewed in this volume, especially the Parents' Fair Share study (Martinez and Miller 2000), poor young black men who are only sporadically employed and have criminal records actually want to have a good job and want to be good fathers—even if they rarely see their children. The discrepancy between values and behavior is a pattern seen frequently among low-income families (and even, it is rumored, among wealthier families). Mothers on welfare tell interviewers they want to work; mothers and fathers who have had children outside marriage say they want to be married; poor fathers say they want to work and support their families.

Good news, especially about black men, is to be savored. That even absent fathers want to work and support their children is encouraging.

Helping them would be much more difficult if poor fathers were as uncaring as they are often portrayed. They want to be helped; policymakers want to help them; professionals and volunteers want to help them. Under these circumstances, progress is possible.

Since Moynihan's provocative and somewhat speculative conclusions about the effects of absent fathers on the development of boys, developmental psychologists have created a substantial empirical literature documenting the impact of fathers on child development (Lamb 1997). In short, this research shows that fathers play an important positive role in children's development—and that their absence often has negative effects on children's development and behavior. Hence, the consequences of the decline in marriage on the development of black boys is especially sobering.

The percentage of all adult men who are married has been declining steadily, from 68.4 percent in 1980 to 61.5 percent in 2000. But the absolute level and rate of decline is much worse for blacks than for either whites or Hispanics. Specifically, in 2000, the proportion of adult black men who were married was only 46.7 percent, compared with 63.5 percent for whites and 59.6 percent for Hispanics. Between 1980 and 2000, the percentage of married black men declined by nearly 15 percent, compared with about 9 percent for whites and 11 percent for Hispanics (U.S. Census Bureau 2002, 47).

Thus, black men's marriage rate declined more than that of whites and Hispanics over the two decades following 1980. Clearly, young men who impregnate their girlfriends but do not marry them are a major part of the problem. As a result, many children grow up without fathers, frequently with bad consequences. Family formation among poor and minority families in the United States is a mega-issue.

Child Support Enforcement

No government program (except taxes) affects noncustodial fathers more than the Child Support Enforcement program. Created in 1975, Child Support Enforcement is a joint federal–state program that locates fathers who do not live with their children, establishes paternity, obtains support orders, and collects payments. The program, which now employs more than 60,000 people nationwide and costs more than $5 billion yearly to operate, is divided into two parts—one focused on child support for mothers and children on welfare and the other focused on families not on welfare. The nonwelfare program is financed by federal and state governments, and almost all collections of child support payments are given to the custodial parent. States collect a small fee of $25 or less per case, part of which they can retain to recover costs, although most states do not. Thus, the nonwelfare program is paid for by taxpayers. Of course, many advocates, child support administrators, and researchers argue that the program produces hidden savings: without the child support program, fewer fathers would pay child support and, as a result, more of their children would need public benefits. Child support payments also help some mothers stay off welfare, thereby saving public dollars.

By contrast, the welfare part of the child support program is partially self-financing because the government retains some of the child support payments made by noncustodial parents. At the beginning of the program in 1975, the government could keep all collections above $50 per month while the family was on welfare and a significant fraction of collections once the family left welfare. The 1996 welfare reform legislation, however, eliminated the $50 payment to families on welfare but also required states to pay an increasing portion of collections to custodial parents and children who had left welfare. Even so, nearly $2.5 billion a year in collections is retained by the government (and split between the federal and state governments) to offset welfare costs (Office of Child Support Enforcement 2000).

For this and other reasons, the child support program has retained a very high level of popularity and support among policymakers in Washington. Not surprisingly, women's groups have been very strong supporters, as have most child advocates and scholars. Conservatives support the program because it helps or forces parents to meet their financial responsibilities to their children and supplements the income of working mothers so they can avoid welfare.

Apart from the political strength of the program in Washington, the underlying rationale for having a government program to collect child support enjoys huge public support. Thus, it is no surprise that Congress has revamped and strengthened the child support program on several occasions, most recently in the 1996 welfare reform bill. All the reforms have enjoyed extensive bipartisan support.

A faint criticism is sometimes whispered about the program—that it tends to regard fathers as a means to an end; namely, to provide money for children and their mothers. A slowly increasing number of state child support programs are more understanding of the needs and rights of fathers, but the overall program is, to put it mildly, not conducted to help fathers except to help—or compel—them to meet their financial obligations to their children.

When fathers and children live apart, agreement seems to be nearly universal that children will be better off, and their development best supported, if they maintain a relationship with both parents. In the real world of nonmarital births and divorce, maintaining a relationship with both parents is difficult. Once parents end their romantic relationship, their subsequent relationship is often characterized by distrust, hostility, and conflict, the opposite of the stable, warm environment most conducive to normal child development. For these and other reasons, nonmarital birth fathers have difficulty even maintaining contact with their children.

An important study of these fathers, conducted by Rangarajan and Gleason (1998), found that only half of fathers who had babies outside marriage with teenage mothers had any contact with the mother by the time the children were 2½ years old. Only 30 percent had contact at least weekly. It takes a disciplined and devoted father, with the support of an understanding mother, to overcome the formidable obstacles separating parents and children who do not live together.

In the case of poor fathers, added to and perhaps intensifying the problem of maintaining contact with their children is the accumulation of child support debt. A typical low-income man who fathers a child outside marriage is about 20 years old. At the time of the birth and for some months thereafter, most fathers have a close relationship with the mother and child. But the vagaries of life are such that the mother and father usually separate. Soon thereafter, many young mothers apply for welfare, and child support officials begin looking for the father. By the time they find him, many months or years later, he has accumulated child support debt. A poor father may owe $5,000 or more in child support before he realizes the severity of his situation. A father earning less than $10,000 a year looking at a debt of $5,000 may decide to go underground. In this case, everybody loses—not least the child.

Summary

Admittedly, this overview of poor fathers borders on alarming. When they are under, say, age 25, poor (and especially black) fathers have inferior records of educational attainment, employment, and earnings. In addition, they are likely to have been involved in crime, and many have been incarcerated. Many have children that they do not live with and do not support. Even so, the majority work most of the time and have earned income. Equally important, their rates of criminal behavior decline and their earnings improve with age. Another plus is that young fathers who do not live with or support their children consistently tell interviewers that they want to do the right thing for their children. Love and feelings of responsibility for their children provide a hook that programs can exploit to help them improve themselves. In short, though bleak, the picture is not entirely dark.

What to Do: A Few Good Ideas

One reason for maintaining optimism is that so few serious attempts to help poor fathers have been made. Most American children are socialized through a combination of married-parent families, churches and other community organizations, good schools, and worthy peers. But as a nation, we seem to have embarked on a gruesome experiment to determine whether some young men can be properly socialized without any of these determining factors. The resulting problems are momentous. Solutions will have to be substantial and long-term, with prevention playing an important role.

Yet the interventions attempted to date have been mostly puny. The Parents' Fair Share program (Martinez and Miller 2000) is one of the few large-scale attempts to help disadvantaged fathers. A major lesson from this study is that initiating help many years after fathers have children outside marriage is probably too late. Similarly, research on how to help the shockingly high number of black fathers leaving prison is more or less primitive, and large-scale demonstrations are virtually unknown. Nor have prevention efforts been implemented on a large-enough scale. But one is entitled to pessimism only when a broad range of serious interventions have failed to produce results. Meanwhile, opportunities to help these fathers abound.

Education

Since at least President Johnson's War on Poverty, beginning in 1964, policymakers have been aware that children from poor and minority families are already behind children from middle-class and white families by the time they enter public schools. Whether these differences are accounted for by genetic or environmental factors has been the subject of hot debate, much of it colorful (Herrnstein and Murray 1994; Jensen 1969). Yet even those who believe genetic factors are important agree that environment affects the development of skills important to schooling (Rowe and Rodgers 1997; Scarr and Weinberg 1978; Turkheimer et al. 2003). Thus, not surprisingly, one of the most lasting and popular of the War on Poverty programs has been Head Start, which helps children prepare for school, bringing them to educational parity with more affluent children (Moynihan 1968).

The years since the creation of Head Start in 1965 have seen an outpouring of early childhood programs. Empirical studies, some based on random assignment, have shown that high-quality preschool programs can reduce special education assignments and grade repetition, reduce juvenile delinquency, promote college attendance, and reduce welfare use (Campbell and Ramey 1995; Lamb 1998; Schweinhart, Barnes, and Weikart 1993). These findings are by no means universal, and there is much less evidence that large-scale preschool programs can replicate these remarkable results (Duncan and Magnuson 2001; Haskins forthcoming; Karoly 2002; Karoly et al. 1998).

If Head Start approximates what happens when a model program expands dramatically, effects will likely be more modest. Nonetheless, some evidence shows Head Start can produce lasting effects on children's school performance (Currie and Thomas 1995; Garces, Thomas, and Currie 2000; Oden, Schweinhart, and Weikart 2000). Garces and her colleagues even conclude, based on longitudinal but nonexperimental data, that "African-American men who attended Head Start are more likely than their siblings to have completed high school" (2000, 1).

Whatever the precise effects of preschool education, two broad conclusions are supported by research. First, the evidence that high-quality preschool programs produce lasting effects on school performance and perhaps delinquency and other outcomes is stronger than evidence for almost any other type of intervention program. Second, the effects of large-scale programs are modest but real. Thus, ensuring that poor youngsters receive high-quality preschool education to prepare them for public schools may well be a worthwhile investment. Better yet would be improving the quality of Head Start, which would have pervasive effects.

The world of preschool education and child care has changed in the past decade or so. Not only have federal and state expenditures on preschool education and child care doubled to around $25 billion since the mid-1990s, but 40 or more states now invest their own money in preschool education programs that attempt to prepare poor children for public schooling (Barnett et al. 2004; Gallagher, Clayton, and Heinemeier 2000; Schumacher, Greenberg, and Lombardi 2001; U.S. General Accounting Office 2000). The typical state now has a crowded field of preschool education and child care programs—some federal, some state—that includes Head Start, Early Head Start, various state preschool initiatives, the huge (nearly $5 billion) Child Care and Development Block Grant, Title I preschool, several programs for disabled preschoolers, and more. With better coordination, many states could offer one year of high-quality preschool education to all or most 4-year-olds from poor families using just the resources currently available.

For this to happen, two reforms are necessary. First, states need the authority to control spending and activities in all preschool education and child care programs (Haskins and Sawhill 2003). Second, states need to develop a curriculum for all 4-year-olds that is tailored specifically to the academic skills needed to succeed in kindergarten and after.

The major program outside state control is Head Start. With a spending level of nearly $7 billion and serving nearly a million children in 2003, Head Start is also the single largest source of funding for preschool programs. Because funds flow directly from the federal Department of Health and Human Services to local Head Start grantees, however, states are completely cut out of the action. Thus, in trying to organize the current glut of preschool programs, states have little or no leverage to induce Head Start programs to cooperate.

In 2003, the Bush administration proposed to give states the option of taking over Head Start if they agree to a series of conditions, such as maintaining state funding levels for preschool programs, developing preschool curricula to promote school readiness, testing to determine if school readiness among poor children is improving, and maintaining comprehensive services. This proposal was strongly opposed by the National Head Start Association, child advocates, and most Democrats. Thus, Republicans in the House of Representatives modified the Bush proposal to allow up to eight states to conduct demonstration programs that would determine whether state control of Head Start would facilitate coordination of preschool programs, increase efficiency, and improve school readiness. Even if this proposal does not pass, allowing a few states to coordinate their preschool funds to create something like a universal program for poor and low-income children, combined with careful evaluations of school readiness, seems a reasonable approach. Head Start should not, however, be largely turned over to states until evidence shows that states can better prepare children for school than Head Start does.

In contrast to evidence on preschool programs, the evidence that public schools can offset family and neighborhood influences on young men is downright discouraging (Armor 2003). The major concentrations of poor people and risky neighborhoods are in the inner cities of America. Virtually every big city in the nation has a "dark ghetto" (Clark 1965) populated by poor minorities and characterized by female-headed families, high crime, and drug selling and addiction. Yet it is precisely big cities that have the worst educational systems (Howell and Peterson 2002).

As with preschool programs, the presidency of Lyndon Johnson was the cradle of federal support for public education. And as with preschool programs, the federal government was primarily concerned with ways to reduce poverty. Thus, Title I of the Elementary and Secondary Act of 1965 directed its resources primarily to poor districts and to programs that would help the poor. Unfortunately, after more than 35 years and many billions of dollars, Title I programs have had little detectable impact on the achievement of poor children (Farkas and Hall 2000; Finn 2000; Kosters and Mast 2003). Released in 1983, the widely discussed blue-ribbon panel report *A Nation at Risk* (National Commission on Excellence in Education 1983) found that the entire system of public education in the United States was failing. If a foreign nation had perpetrated the public school system on the United States, the report asserted with vigor, we would declare war.

Evidence clearly shows that public schools do a bad job of preparing poor children for college or the world of work (Ravitch 2000). Perhaps Americans have grown so used to public schools' poor-to-mediocre performance that the low educational attainment of poor children is overlooked.

However, public schools continue to successfully educate children from middle-class families. Indeed, the middle class has expanded rapidly since roughly the mid-1960s and is now a substantial fraction of most minority populations (Thernstrom and Thernstrom 1997). As reviewed previously, this achievement is reflected in the hugely improved percentages of various minority groups that complete high school and attend college.

But many poor children, especially those in the inner city, have been left behind. The conclusion that public schools, Title I, and Head Start have failed black students—along with other poor children and families—is unavoidable. An obvious, but still controversial, policy initiative would allow students in failing schools to exercise choice and transfer to other schools, public or private. The major goal of this approach, of course, is to unleash the potential of market competition to improve education.

Recent research suggests that competition may improve schools. Howell and Peterson review evidence on 16 voucher programs in seven states and the District of Columbia as well as one national program (2002; see table 2.1, 28). They find solid evidence, some from random-assignment experiments, that vouchers can improve test performance. In addition, some programs modestly influence such social measures as self-confidence, religious observance, and political tolerance. Equally important, Howell and Peterson review evidence that public schools improved, as measured by test scores, in some cities where voucher programs were mounted. Competition may boost the entire school market's performance. However, many more demonstrations must be implemented before making major claims about the potency of school choice. Intervention programs for the poor often don't work as well in one area as they do in another.

The recently enacted No Child Left Behind Act disappointed voucher advocates because it did not contain funds for voucher programs (Fordham Foundation 2002). However, the act did include a modest voucher-like provision that requires local school districts to allow students in failing schools to transfer to other schools. A vital part of this provision is extensive testing for children in grades 3 through 8. These tests will yield scores every year by school, thereby constituting a first and essential step toward increased public accountability for education. This accountability testing, coupled with the provision allowing students to transfer out of failing schools, is probably the most hopeful development for poor children in the nation's public schools in several decades. Because the schools most likely to fail are those in the inner city, the mechanism of competition and its potential to improve educational achievement may be greatest precisely where it is most needed.

But implementation of the No Child Left Behind Act, and expansion of any market-based mechanisms growing out of it, will take many years. In the meantime, the Department of Education, in cooperation with foundations and other funding sources, should encourage school systems to adopt policies and programs that increase competition. Wherever possible, the programs should include both public and private schools to maximize choice and competition.

Although teachers' unions are rabid opponents of these competitive approaches and have blocked their widespread implementation, many cities have nonetheless shown interest in vouchers and have allowed limited programs to be conducted in their school systems. The Department of Education should play an aggressive role in expanding this movement. Until inner-city schools feel more pressure to perform or lose their funding, it seems doubtful that they will fulfill their responsibility of helping poor children achieve basic competence. So far, despite massive resources, the schools have failed in this vital mission.

Employment and Prisoner Reentry

The federal government has long worked to help disadvantaged youth and adults prepare for, find, and hold jobs. The modern era of federal employment assistance for the disadvantaged began with the Area Redevelopment Act of 1958. Since that time, the federal government has sponsored a series of comprehensive programs that offered employment services to the poor. These include the Manpower Development and Training Act of 1962, the Economic Opportunity Act of 1964, the Comprehensive Employment and Training Act of 1973, the Job Training Partnership Act of 1982, and the Workforce Investment Act of 1998.

Although these comprehensive acts differ, especially in their levels of funding, they have typically offered four types of services to the poor (LaLonde 1995). The first service is classroom training, usually GED programs or skills training for particular jobs. The second is on-the-job training (OJT), in which participants learn job skills as part of their employment. A third service, which has been used extensively in employment programs for both the poor and the unemployed, is the job search program. Job search programs, which are the least expensive employment programs, help potential workers find jobs, usually by providing lists of openings, résumé preparation services, and phone banks. Fourth, work experience programs provide inexperienced workers with the opportunity to hold a job, usually with a government agency or nonprofit organization. Their major goal is to help those with poor work histories develop what are now widely referred to as "soft skills"—the ability to come to work every day, be on time, take directions, be courteous and responsive to customers, and get along with coworkers. These programs can also provide experience and references (Holzer 2002).

A large body of literature, a considerable portion of it based on random-assignment studies, has been established on the effectiveness of these four types of employment programs. LaLonde, in a concise overview, concludes that "the best summary of the evidence about the impact of past programs is that we got what we paid for" (1995, 149; see also Karoly 2002). In other words, most programs have been pretty cheap, thereby producing modest, if any, outcomes.

But within this generalization, several more specific conclusions are possible. First, job search programs have been shown repeatedly to increase employment, raise earnings, and save public dollars by helping workers previously on welfare and those covered by unemployment insurance (Corson et al. 1989; Gueron and Pauly 1991; Hamilton et al. 2002). Second, the other three types of programs have produced mixed, not notably positive, results. Third, most programs are less successful with men. Fourth, the expensive Job Corps program, which costs about $17,000 per participant, consistently shows substantial effects on educational attainment, employment, earnings, and criminal activity (Job Corps 2001; McConnell and Glazerman 2001).

Job Corps may achieve its consistent results because it differs in two major differences from most other programs. One difference is that Job Corps training takes place in government facilities, requiring participants to leave their neighborhoods and reside in the Job Corps facility. Although research is not abundant, it stands to reason that getting poor young adults out of the inner city and away from their low-achieving peer group is a plus. The second difference is that the typical Job Corps program lasts about seven months, although a few young people stay in the program for two years or more (Job Corps 2001). Reflecting LaLonde's observation that substantial results require substantial investments, Job Corps shows that high-intensity programs lasting many months can produce significant outcomes—even for men.

Unfortunately, evidence does not show that other current intervention programs substantially improve fathers' and other young men's employment records. Even the Parents' Fair Share program, which concentrated specifically on poor fathers by offering them employment services and counseling, was not very successful. Data hinted that Parents' Fair Share affected the duration and quality of employment for the least job-ready fathers, but even these effects were modest (Martinez and Miller 2000). On the whole, the Parents' Fair Share results, like the rest of the literature, show that improving the employment prospects of poor fathers without enrolling them in long, high-intensity programs is difficult.

Although the history of employment programs for men does not support exuberant predictions of success, boosting employment and earnings nonetheless must be central to any strategy of helping poor fathers. For most adults, work is the main source of income. And in American culture work signifies independence, self-sufficiency, and the sense of full membership in society (Kaus 1992). Employment is also central to becoming an attractive marital partner. For all these reasons, any comprehensive policy to help poor men simply must include proposals to improve their employment and earnings. If the literature shows little success, old approaches must be refined and new ones tried.

Two policies are promising. First, Job Corps has been repeatedly shown to increase employment and earnings and to reduce crime. Because of its great expense, the current level of participation (around 70,000 enter the program each year) could not be boosted to include all who are eligible, especially since both men and women should and do participate in the program. A more moderate and achievable step would be for Congress to increase Job Corps slots gradually over a period of years, beginning with an increase of 50,000. At current enrollment proportions, about 30,000 of these slots would go to young men. If these new participants are like current participants, their average length of enrollment will be about seven months and the additional cost will be around $850 million a year ($17,000 per participant × 50,000 slots = $850 million). This cost could be covered in part by shifting funds from less-successful programs within the Workforce Investment Act (of which Job Corps is a constituent program), but new funds would be necessary. In addition, as will be discussed in more detail following, all Jobs Corps participants should take systematic courses on the advantages of marriage, avoiding aggression, and building and sustaining healthy marriages (Stanley and Markman 1992). To ensure quality is maintained as the program is expanded, program effects should be continuously monitored by the type of random-assignment study that has assessed Job Corps outcomes in the past (McConnell and Glazerman 2001).

Second, a demonstration program to promote employment, marriage, and parenting among poor fathers, supported by federal and state funding of around $20 million per year for the next seven or eight years, should be authorized by Congress. Programs would recruit married and unmarried couples whose incomes are below 150 percent of the poverty level (or some other income criterion) at or before the birth of their first child. (The Fragile Families research project has demonstrated the feasibility of contacting young fathers and mothers through hospitals and clinics—see McLanahan et al. 2003.) Although the Parents' Fair Share demonstration programs failed to produce major impacts on fathers' employment, all the participating fathers were already behind in child support payments and many had more than one child, some of whom came from different mothers. These multiple-child, multiple-parent situations are perhaps the most difficult to mend. These problems would be avoided by directing the intervention at first-time parents, most of whom, as shown by McLanahan and her colleagues, are in an exclusive and loving relationship during the pregnancy and birth and shortly thereafter (Carlson, McLanahan, and England 2003).

The programs, which must include random-assignment evaluation, should follow clear protocols that include the type of immediate job search programs now used with many mothers on welfare. Programs should include activities and curricula designed to promote marriage. Some fathers should also be selected for additional education or training, perhaps through community colleges, once they are employed, to determine whether immediate employment combined with training is effective. State and local government, private nonprofit organizations, for-profit organizations, and faith-based entities should be encouraged to compete for funding. All proposals must involve the state child support enforcement program and must include guidelines for handling arrearages owed by participating fathers.

The advantages of these two proposals are that they combine immediate impact with a research and demonstration proposal that could produce more economical long-term results. Their combined cost is reasonable, and much of it could be covered by shifting funds from current programs. They also send a clear signal that policymakers are aware of the problems with employment and marriage among poor fathers, and that they intend to devote public resources to solving these problems.

Another important goal of employment programs for poor fathers should be to design and evaluate interventions for fathers with criminal records. These programs are more important than in the past because so many young men are in prison. In 1999, more than 1.3 million people were in state and federal prisons, an explosion by more than a factor of four since 1973. More people in prison means more people leaving prison. By 2000, nearly 600,000 people were leaving prison each year (Travis, Solomon, and Waul 2001).

Policy to help former inmates must balance two worthy goals—maintaining public safety and helping former inmates adapt to life outside prison. The largest study ever conducted of released prisoners showed maintaining public safety is a serious issue (Beck and Shipley 1989). The study tracked inmates released from prisons in 11 states in 1983. During the three-year tracking period, 63 percent of the former prisoners were rearrested, 47 percent were convicted, and 41 percent were reincarcerated. Many arrests were for violent crimes.

Despite political infeasibility, programs to help prisoners successfully reenter society are a must if the nation is to reduce poverty and family dissolution, especially among blacks. That nearly half of young black men have some involvement with crime or the criminal justice system, and that two-thirds of them are fathers, is justification enough for policies to help them make the transition from prison to society. The Beck and Shipley data in the previous paragraph reflect that little is being done to help prisoners adapt to life outside prison.

Recidivism data also raise the issue of whether programs to help prisoners successfully adapt to life outside prison might save money. Every rearrest means that residents or businesses in the community are experiencing property loss or, in some cases, bodily injury requiring health care. Police work, court time, and the expense of maintaining rearrested criminals in jail add to the cost. Investments in programs that even modestly reduce recidivism are likely to be cost-effective.

Even a cursory review of the characteristics of prisoners shows the depth of the problem. More than half of those leaving prison do not have a high school diploma; most have only modest job experience; nearly 75 percent have a history of substance abuse; 16 percent suffer from mental illness; and up to 25 percent have serious health problems such as AIDS, hepatitis C, or tuberculosis (Lawrence et al. 2002; Travis et al. 2001). And all have an additional strike against them—they have prison records.

Nor do criminals have a very good public image. Politicians have been elected to office at least partly because they promised to be tough on criminals. And as a society, we have been increasingly tough on criminals for the past two decades or so. But this trend has produced a large number of men, especially minority men, who must overcome the residue of imprisonment if they are to establish themselves as law-abiding citizens who meet their personal responsibilities, including to their children.

The recent explosion in the number of young men sent to prison and the long sentences many receive, often under mandatory sentencing laws, bear critical scrutiny. In 1998, nearly 120,000 people were given state felony convictions for drug possession; 65 percent of those convicted received active jail sentences. An additional 1,500 federal convictions were handed down for drug possession, almost 90 percent of which resulted in active jail time (Durose, Levin, and Langan 2001). Some of these convicted drug users, as well as society, would undoubtedly be better off if treatments other than prison were used more often. The shocking number of young men with prison records and all their attendant problems could perhaps be reduced by granting first-time drug offenders suspended sentences contingent on periodic drug tests, employment, and community service.

A more basic approach to crime would be to prevent it in the first place, although evidence that prevention is effective is weak (Bushway and Reuter 1997). Reducing nonmarital births and divorce, improving preschool and school-age education, and improving and expanding programs such as Job Corps that boost the employment of the poor may have some impact on the number of young men going to prison in the first place. Improving programs for juveniles who commit crimes may also prove helpful, but programs in place today that involve detention are at least as likely to turn delinquents into criminals as they are to rehabilitate them (National Research Council 2001).

At best, the evidence indicates that prevention programs will be only modestly successful. Thus, programs to help young men while they are incarcerated are essential. In recent years, spending on these programs has actually declined; per capita spending, given the large increase in the prison population, has declined even more (Travis et al. 2001). A recent survey of seven midwestern states showed that well under half of prisoners participated in education, vocational, or work programs while in prison (Lawrence et al. 2002). Of equal concern, less than 30 percent of prisoners received job search training before leaving prison. Another prison tradition that seems to be fading is prison industry, in which prisoners learn skills by working at actual jobs such as laundry, license plate manufacturing, or agriculture.

An additional policy that could help young men return to productive and responsible life outside prison is funding programs that help former prisoners make a successful transition to the community. These programs should begin with careful attention to the needs of former prisoners at the moment of release from prison. Do they have identification? A place to live and a way to get there from the prison? A job? Money to tide them over until they are employed? Treatment for medical or health problems, including addictions, that they have at the time of release? Has any planning occurred with their families? Adaptation to post-prison life can also be facilitated by work-release programs in which prisoners begin work outside the prison while serving the final months or years of their prison term. Because of expense and perhaps other reasons, only about one-third of prisons operate work-release programs today, and fewer than 3 percent of prisoners participate in them (Travis et al. 2001, 19).

Nearly 80 percent of prisoners have some sort of supervision when they leave prison, consisting of two distinctly different types of activities—parole and rehabilitation. Virtually all prisoners released into supervisory status have some type of mandatory reporting to the legal system, usually through a parole officer. Most paroled prisoners meet with their parole officer once or twice a month for perhaps 15 minutes. Experts such as Jeremy Travis of John Jay College of Criminal Justice believe that these brief sessions do not substantially help men trying to adapt to life outside prison. This is especially the case since the number of parolees has jumped well over threefold to more than 700,000 in the last 20 years without a corresponding increase in resources (U.S. Bureau of Justice 2001).

The second type of post-prison program includes some type of treatment. Research suggests that prisoners will adapt to life in the community only if their post-prison supervision has a rehabilitative component (Sherman et al. 1997). Drug treatment programs appear to be especially important because so many men leaving prison have addictions. RAND's review of the research found that spending on drug treatment programs is 15 times more effective than spending on incarcerating drug offenders (Caulkins et al. 1997).

Some doubt that rehabilitation programs work. Indeed, the United States' approach to crime has always cycled between treatment and punishment. Rehabilitation was one of the foundational principles of the American corrections system—as is suggested by the very term "corrections." However, Robert Martinson's masterful 1974 review of empirical studies on rehabilitation programs found little evidence that rehabilitation actually works. When Martinson's review emerged in a society increasingly concerned with crime, a "nothing works" school of thought developed. Then, as now, conservatives argued for long mandatory sentences, while liberals insisted on addressing "root causes," such as bad neighborhoods and poverty, and providing treatment.

As in nearly every field of intervention research, most studies of prison programs are deeply flawed. The major problem is that comparison groups are not comparable. Attrition and poor measurement are also culprits. Even so, several balanced reviews of evidence have been published in recent years that generally show some programs aimed at rehabilitation have increased employment and reduced recidivism.[2] Again, as is typical for evaluations of social programs, the effects are not massive. But they are real and constitute the first step in an analysis that, like the RAND study on drug treatment, may show that investments in intervention programs save money and mayhem. Moreover, given that around two-thirds of the men leaving prison are fathers (Lynch and Sabol 1997), spending money on interventions to prevent crime and rehabilitate offenders is an essential part of an overall strategy to help poor fathers become better fathers, better employees, and better citizens.

Child Support Enforcement

It is a matter of settled policy that the federal–state Child Support Enforcement program will aggressively locate and extract money from fathers who do not live with their children and do not voluntarily pay child support. But the question arises, can the program can collect money while doing as little damage as possible to the father's relationship with his children and their mother (Primus and Beeson 2002)? Examining current law and practice through this lens suggests some changes are desirable.

Let us begin with who gets the money collected by the child support program. For families that have never been on welfare, the issue is straightforward—the mother and children get the money. As we have seen, the states charge a small one-time fee and try to recover some of their costs, but in practice nearly all the money goes to the mother and children. Of course, this practice means that nonwelfare cases are financed almost entirely by tax dollars, mostly supplied by the federal government.

By contrast, in current and former welfare cases, the rules governing who gets the money are complex and vary from state to state. The basic rules (to which exceptions occur) are that, while the family is on welfare, all collections are retained by the state and split with the federal government to offset welfare costs. Once the family leaves welfare, payments on current support are given to the family. Collections on past-due support (arrearages), however, are split between the family on the one hand, and federal and state governments on the other.

Consider an example. If a mother on welfare has a child support order for $300 a month and the state child support program collects $300 from the father, the state retains the entire payment and splits it with the federal government. Once the mother leaves welfare, if the state collects exactly the current amount of $300, the entire payment goes to the family. But if the state collects $400, the current support amount of $300 goes to the family, and the remaining $100 is split between the state and the family, with roughly $50 going to each. The state's $50 is then split with the federal government.

Some child support payments are retained by government because the program's original goal was to recover welfare payments. Leaders in guiding the legislation through Congress, especially Senator Russell Long of Louisiana, were interested primarily in welfare cases. They believed it was wrong for fathers to desert their children and, in effect, send the childrearing bill to taxpayers. So they created the child support program to make fathers reimburse taxpayers.

Since 1975, a second rationale for the program has gradually emerged. The central goal of federal welfare reform, especially after the 1996 legislation, is to reduce welfare dependency by promoting self-sufficiency through work and marriage. Federal and state policies are now increasingly focused on helping mothers avoid welfare if possible, leave welfare quickly if it cannot be avoided, and prevent falling back on welfare after leaving.

To further these objectives, 1996 legislation changed the rules on distribution of child support payments. Collections on arrearages for mothers who leave welfare must now be split between government and the family, with mothers and children receiving about half the money. This reform puts an additional $200 million or so per year in the hands of mothers who have left welfare (Congressional Budget Office 1996). It both improves mothers' and children's standard of living and increases the odds that they will remain off welfare. Equally important, giving more of the father's child support payments to his children and their mother could improve family relations by providing children with additional evidence of their father's commitment to them.

Many policymakers now believe still more child support payments on arrearages should be returned to mothers and children (Primus, this volume). The policy to pay more child support to families, which has been passed twice by the House of Representatives in recent years, could result in as many as one million mothers and their children receiving as much as several hundred million dollars per year—in addition to the child support they now receive. Despite widespread support, this policy does have some downsides. A major issue, as always, is cost. Further movement toward sending higher proportions of child support collections to families is movement away from reimbursing taxpayers. A related concern is that the child support program has often been justified to Congress as one of the few federal programs that pays for itself. This claim is incorrect, but the program does generate revenues that offset a major part of its costs. As more money is given to families, the claim that the program is cost-beneficial, which is especially useful when the time comes to reform or expand the program, will be even less correct than it is now.

Another important issue is whether giving more money to families is a mandate or an option for states. The 1996 policy changing the distribution rules for families leaving welfare was a mandate on states and imposed costs on every state. Congress takes seriously imposing mandatory costs on states. In fact, the Congressional Budget Office is required to examine every piece of legislation that comes to the House or Senate floor and determine whether the legislation imposes what is called an "unfunded mandate" on states.

Requiring states to give families child support collections that states can now retain is just such a mandate. Not only would the mandatory approach violate budget rules, but it would also guarantee opposition from powerful state organizations such as the National Governors Association, the American Public Human Services Association, and the National Conference of State Legislatures. Legislation can be passed despite the opposition, but Congress does not like to. The solution is to make the policy a state option.

This solution could be made attractive to states by dropping the requirement that states pay the federal share of collections on arrearages. The Congressional Budget Office has estimated that, if the federal government forgave its share of the collections, the policy of sending more money to families would result in states with around 40 percent of the child support caseload adopting the policy. Although, under the state option, only about 40 percent of funds that could be returned to families would be, the option would have a much better chance of getting through Congress. As an added bonus, because many states would keep the current policy of retaining the collections and splitting them with the federal government, the option would reduce costs to the federal government.

Whether the child support program should try to extract payments from fathers who cohabit with the mother of their children is another issue that is gaining more attention. Primus and Beeson (2002) argue forcefully that these fathers should not be required to pay child support.

According to Primus, the goal of policy should be for fathers to live with their children so they can effectively fulfill their parenting role. In addition, although evidence may be skimpy, it stands to reason that fathers living with their children are contributing to the mothers' household expenses.

Facilitating financial and emotional support of children are two major goals of the child support system. If fathers are fulfilling these goals without government interference, the child support program should leave them alone. Further, if the government pursues these fathers, they might desert the mother and child and go underground to avoid paying child support. This unfortunate outcome would be especially likely if the father owes substantial arrearage payments, as many of them do.

The Primus–Beeson proposal is reasonable, although suspending child support payments when the father simply resides with the mother invites gameplaying. Moreover, there is something to be said for a child support policy that encourages marriage rather than cohabitation, if for no other reason than cohabiting is notoriously unstable (Manning 2002; Smock and Gupta 2002). Still, if cohabitation is a step toward marriage and permanency for children, which it sometimes is, there may be good reason to make special provisions for cohabitation.

A two-provision compromise might win support from policymakers. First, as Primus and Beeson (2002) propose, establishing paternity and child support orders would continue to be required in all cases in which the parents are not married, even if the parents cohabit. Second, states would be given the option of suspending child support payments—both payments due on arrearages and payments on current support—as long as the father lives with or marries the mother and provides financial support to the family. Establishing the facts in these cases and keeping track of changes would, of course, be difficult. But these details would be left up to any state that decided to adopt the policy.

Because this policy would result in the loss of some child support collections in welfare child support cases, it would impose a revenue loss on both the federal government and the states. According to the Congressional Budget Office, however, the loss would probably be modest. And to the extent that this policy helped poor parents stay together, and perhaps even encouraged marriage, the cost would be justified—and might lead to savings in welfare spending.

These reasonable changes in child support could be expected to improve single mothers' and children's lives while potentially strengthening the bonds between fathers and their children—and even between fathers and mothers. They also have an excellent chance of being enacted by Congress in the near future. Indeed, most of them have already been enacted by the House of Representatives and were stopped in the Senate by unusual circumstances.

Welfare Programs

A major goal of public policy at both the federal and state levels is to provide assistance to the poor and disadvantaged. Beginning roughly with the Social Security Act of 1935, which contained both the Aid to Dependent Children program (later the Aid to Families with Dependent Children, or AFDC, program) and the Maternal and Child Health program, the federal government has played the leading role in crafting policies and spending money to aid poor Americans. This tradition of special federal responsibility for the poor and those at risk of falling into poverty is now almost universally accepted, even by those on the political right. To be sure, whether programs should be created or expanded and how much money should be spent are controversial, but few conservatives—especially in even-numbered years—question that the federal government should have programs to fight the causes and effects of poverty.

For historical and cultural reasons, antipoverty programs have almost always concentrated on mothers and children. Consider the Maternal and Child Health program just mentioned. To understand how often fathers are forgotten by policymakers, try to imagine a federal program called "Paternal and Child Health." Thus, for poor or near-poor mothers and children, the nation has programs to pay cash welfare, provide health insurance, and provide food to all or nearly all who are qualified. Other usually less elaborate and expensive programs subsidize housing, maternity care, food supplements, home heating, work preparation, and similar needs. Of this vast panoply of programs, only the work preparation programs, the food stamps program, and the child support enforcement program have substantial enrollment by adult men—and the benefits of the last accrue to mothers and children at the expense of fathers. Clearly, the welfare state was constructed with only scant regard for adult men or fathers.

Despite the emphasis on mothers and children in these programs, the principle that federal policy should help the poor should extend to men. Indeed, it could be argued that one of the greatest failings of federal poverty policy is that it has largely ignored adult men and the important role fathers play in children's development. The goals and particulars of programs should be different for able-bodied adults than for children, and given the mothers' usual role as the custodial parent, focusing more programs and more funds on them—especially to meet basic needs—makes great sense. But we should not ignore fathers. For work programs, the goal for both mothers and fathers should emphasize employment so that, either separately or together, they can achieve self-sufficiency for themselves and their children, especially since families dependent on welfare are by definition in poverty.

Research shows clearly that, at least before the welfare reform law of 1996, a few million mother-headed families in any given year were in the midst of long spells of welfare dependency (Bane and Ellwood 1983; Pavetti 1994). The only practical way to help these families rise above poverty was—and still is—through employment and marriage (Sawhill and Haskins 2003). Thus, fathers can play a valuable role in the nation's strategy for fighting poverty and inequality in current and subsequent generations. Promoting work and marriage should be the central goals of both the nation's programs for fathers and the nation's strategy for fighting poverty. Working fathers are more likely to support their children and to maintain a stable relationship—including marriage—with their children's mother. In this regard, the reformed welfare system, in combination with the workforce system of programs that provide job search, job training, and job development for all Americans who need these services, is potentially much friendlier to fathers than the previous system based primarily on cash and in-kind gifts to the poor.

State and federal welfare programs and other programs for low-income families should be carefully reviewed to remove bias against fathers and against married couples. Penalties in the Earned Income Tax Credit (EITC) are especially unfortunate because they sometimes provide an incentive for cohabitation and a disincentive for marriage. The most straightforward way to reduce the EITC bias against marriage is to lower the rate at which the credit phases out for married couples compared with singles. But this policy would be very expensive. Congress slightly reduced the phaseout rate for married couples in the 2001 tax reform legislation, but seems unlikely to take additional steps in the foreseeable future (Carasso and Steuerle 2002).

Two actions could be taken by states to reduce marriage penalties. First, nine states still discriminate against married parents in their TANF (Temporary Assistance for Needy Families) programs by imposing something called the 100-hour rule—if the father works 100 or more hours per month, the family cannot qualify for welfare. This policy has the intended effect of moving married parents capable of work off the welfare rolls. But it does so at the cost of creating a disincentive for marriage, especially when mothers and fathers cohabit and the father works. States should eliminate the 100-hour rule and other TANF policies that constitute a disincentive for marriage. Similarly, the TANF statute should require the same number of work hours for single-mother and married-couple families.

The second action states should take is to include fathers in TANF welfare-to-work programs. Most states have redesigned their TANF programs so that promoting work through job search and job training is central. But mostly, these work supports are given to single mothers, thereby—once again—leaving fathers out of the picture. Nearly every child of a single mother on welfare has a living absent father. Any program based on the principle of replacing welfare with work should, in the name of equity, serve both mothers and fathers so income from both can help the family avoid or leave welfare.

The TANF and Child Support Enforcement programs at the state and local levels should strive to change how fathers perceive child support. Consider the recent sweeping changes in how mothers understand TANF. The new state TANF programs have been so successful in large part because participants know, even before they apply, that the program's basic expectation is work and work preparation. This widely shared understanding, which contrasts sharply with the welfare entitlement message given by the old AFDC program, was achieved by changing policies and practices.

A host of reforms have conspired to change this basic understanding of the purpose of TANF. These include changing the name of state welfare offices to something like "work opportunity" offices, making sure that applicants are clearly informed of work expectations beginning the day they apply for benefits, and implementing sanctions against recipients who do not meet program requirements. Word of mouth has taken care of the rest. The "on the street" understanding of the purposes of TANF has changed.

Through close coordination between the TANF and child support programs at the state and local levels, creating similar changes in fathers' perception of the child support program should be possible. When mothers apply for TANF, they are already required to provide extensive information about the father. Workers in either the TANF program or the child support program can use this information to contact fathers and offer them job services. Overdue child support cases can be handled more aggressively. Fathers who refuse to participate in work programs can be given the choice between participation and incarceration. Although this approach produced limited success in the Parents' Fair Share study (Martinez and Miller 2000), if an entire state adopted this policy and followed it for several years, the response by fathers might be more impressive. In addition, if the reform includes indefinite suspension of arrearages as long as fathers remain current on child support, fathers would have good reason to find and retain employment. The key to success in this type of program will be close cooperation between the child support and TANF programs.

To facilitate the implementation of programs of this type, Congress should increase the TANF research budget by around $10 million a year for five years to fund large-scale demonstrations of this approach.

Family Formation

In addition to programs that promote work, fathers should be an integral part of what is rapidly becoming a powerful new weapon in federal antipoverty strategy. The unfortunate tendency of low-income adults to have children outside marriage and to divorce at high rates is causally related to the high levels of poverty and other domestic social problems in the United States (Sawhill and Haskins 2003). If something could be done to increase the number of children being raised in married-couple families, a broad range of positive developments for children and society would follow (Ellwood and Jencks 2001; McLanahan and Sandefur 1994; Thomas and Sawhill 2002).

The Bush administration seized on this idea and made marriage promotion a major part of its proposal for reauthorizing the 1996 welfare reform law. But even before the Bush initiative, marriage and fatherhood were very much on the congressional agenda. In the sweeping 1996 welfare reform law, Congress made family formation an explicit goal of the nation's antipoverty policy and included more than a dozen provisions intended to reduce births outside marriage. Since that time, several states have started designing and implementing first-generation programs to promote and strengthen marriage.

In addition, since roughly 1998, a host of bills establishing programs for fathers have been introduced in Congress. Indeed, the House of Representatives enacted legislation by overwhelming bipartisan votes in both

1999 and 2000 to promote fatherhood programs. The House vote in August 2000 was 212 to 18, showing the huge support that fatherhood programs can muster in Congress. The goals of the legislation that drew such impressive bipartisan support were to promote marriage, employment, and better parenting, including payment of child support. Nearly $2 billion was to be spent over five years, primarily on community-based, including faith-based, programs that would have been carefully evaluated. Unfortunately, the House bill, which enjoyed bipartisan support in the Senate, was killed by a very small group of senators who were worried about increasing the national deficit and opposed the child support provisions of the bill because they imposed mandates on states. Doubtless, considerable support exists in the nation's capital for programs that help poor fathers help themselves and their children and that promote two-parent married families.

A slight problem with formulating policies to reduce nonmarital births and promote marriage is that research on programs that could achieve these goals is thin. Even so, a three-part strategy holds some promise.

Promoting marriage, and its precondition of doing no harm to marriage, should become even more central to federal policy. The underlying purpose of this goal is to restore marriage to its former exalted place in American culture. The politicians, scholars, and advocates trying to restore marriage aim to overcome the nation's three-decade-long movement away from confining sex primarily and childbearing exclusively to married couples. Given the goal statement of the 1996 TANF program to "prevent and reduce the incidence of out-of-wedlock pregnancies," to promote "job preparation, work, and marriage," and to "encourage the formation and maintenance of two-parent families," the nation's social policy has taken an important initial step toward achieving the first goal.

As the debate about the Bush administration's marriage initiative demonstrates, not all participants in the national debate on poverty agree with marriage as a goal of federal programs. But as Sara McLanahan and her colleagues (2003) have shown, marriage continues to be a goal of between 70 and 80 percent of poor mothers and fathers who are unmarried. Federal policy on promoting marriage would help poor parents do what they already want to do (and even expect to do); it would not be trying to convince anyone to get married.

When the *Washington Post*—not a reliable friend of conservative social policy initiatives—editorializes that a federal marriage initiative makes good sense because marriage is central to children's development,[3] acceptance for marriage as a goal of national policy has been achieved. The more often and more prominently marriage promotion is discussed by politicians and other public figures at the national, state, and local levels, the higher the odds that the central place of marriage in social policy will become widely known, thereby increasing its impact on people's behavior.

The second plank in a pro-marriage policy should be to reduce nonmarital births. Couples who have babies outside marriage, even when they live together at the time of birth, usually do not marry (Manning 2002). Once the father leaves, the mother has much lower odds of marrying than if she had not had a baby (Lichter and Graefe 2001). This chain of events leads inevitably to the conclusion that illegitimacy not only greatly increases the risk for all sorts of malign conditions, such as poverty, school failure, crime, and second-generation nonmarital births, but also reduces the odds of subsequent marriage for the mother. Fortunately, for the last decade or more, both federal and state policy has focused intently on reducing nonmarital births.

If there is still disagreement that marriage should be a goal of national policy, there is no disagreement that everything possible should be done to reduce teen births and very little disagreement that action should be taken to reduce nonmarital births among women of all ages. Again, the welfare reform law of 1996 marked a watershed. That legislation was packed with provisions intended to reduce nonmarital births, both among teens and older women, including a new national program called "abstinence education," strong requirements for paternity establishment, strengthened child support enforcement provisions, new requirements for states to show progress reducing nonmarital births, and cash bonus payments to states that reduce their nonmarital birth rates.

At least in part as a result of these and similar interventions by the public and private sector, many predating the 1996 welfare reforms, the teen birth rate has declined every year since 1991 (Ventura and Bachrach 2000). Although the U.S. teen birth rate is still higher than that of other industrialized countries, the reduction is an important achievement.

Well over two-thirds of nonmarital births, however, are to women beyond their teen years (Martin et al. 2002). Here, progress has been less striking. Even so, after several generations of relentless increases, almost every measure of nonmarital births among women of all ages has leveled off since 1994. In the case of black women, the rate has actually declined slightly. The flattening out of the nonmarital birth rate may be in part attributable to welfare reform and to the measures written into the 1996 welfare reform law, but whatever its cause, it is welcome.

Amid the moderately good news on the overall nonmarital birth rate and the even better news on teen births, a substantial conflict has been playing out over the best policy for reducing nonmarital births. Until recently, family planning—including birth control pills, injections, and condoms—was the preferred strategy for reducing illegitimacy. But since roughly the early- to- mid-1990s, a growing movement in Washington and around the country has been emphasizing the importance of abstinence, especially among adolescents.

Sound and fury have erupted as doctrinaire views have often prevailed on both sides of the debate. The "abstinence only" side claims that condoms are ineffective because most people—especially teenagers—fail to use them consistently and correctly. Moreover, condoms offer poor protection against some types of venereal disease, a claim supported by recent reports from the National Institute of Allergy and Infectious Diseases (2001) and from the Medical Institute for Sexual Health (2002). The supporters of abstinence-only programs are opposed to systematically teaching young people to use condoms and other forms of birth control because this approach presents young people with a dual message—"don't have sex, but if you do, use a condom." According to the abstinence-only view, this dual message inevitably weakens young people's resolve to achieve the self-control necessary to remain abstinent. The main premise of abstinence-only supporters is captured by the popular line used by many conservatives: "Only abstinence works every time."

By contrast, those who support sex education and family planning respond that little solid empirical evidence indicates that abstinence programs reduce teen pregnancy. Moreover, evidence indicates that family planning programs do reduce teen pregnancy (Kirby 1997, 2001); and since most adolescents and young adults cannot always rely on self-control, abstinence education will not work for many of them. Yet sex education and family planning forces have seemingly revised their message in response to the growing influence of abstinence-only forces. Whereas many sex education and family planning advocates used to dismiss abstinence out of hand as unsuited to modern attitudes and practices regarding sex outside marriage, they now recognize the importance of the abstinence message and its popularity among the American public, especially parents of teenagers and teenagers themselves. Indeed, more than 90 percent of both parents and teens say that "teens should be given a strong message from society that they should abstain from sex until they are at least out of high school" (National Campaign to Prevent Teen Pregnancy 2002, 1).

Thus, many sex education and family planning advocates now call their approach "abstinence first." They argue that programs should emphasize abstinence but also ensure that teens are exposed to accurate information about birth control and how to use it. They also hold that teens should have easy access to birth control pills, injections, and condoms. Both sides favor youth development programs that include public service, supervised social activities, and mentoring.

The Bush administration has brought something of a compromise solution to this increasingly loud debate. As part of its welfare reform reauthorization package released in February 2002 (Executive Office of the President 2002), the administration proposed to increase funding of abstinence programs for youth to $135 million a year—the amount the administration estimates is spent on sex education and family planning programs. This approach would leave intact all current funding of sex education and family planning (or abstinence first) programs through Title X and other federal sources. By implication, the Bush policy would make money available for both abstinence-only and abstinence-first programs and would let local communities and such institutions as schools and places of worship decide which approach they prefer. This solution will probably not calm the abstinence-only versus abstinence-first debate, but would acknowledge that neither side is likely to prevail in the near future. Meanwhile, from the perspective of those interested in reducing teen sex and parenthood as part of a broader strategy to help poor fathers, the debate is healthy and cannot help but call more attention to the importance of reducing births outside marriage.

The third part of a national strategy to increase the number of children in two-parent families is to fund programs that promote marriage. The Bush administration approach is to provide a substantial sum of money each year for five years (about $1.5 billion in all) to encourage states and other organizations to plan, conduct, and carefully evaluate large-scale demonstration programs that promote marriage. This approach is based on two assumptions. First, because so little research exists on the efficacy of marriage-promotion programs with low-income fathers and mothers, the first step should be to provide financial incentives for states and community organizations to conduct marriage-promotion demonstrations.

This is a cost-efficient, rational way to develop policy that may identify promising programs. Second, because government involvement in marriage promotion is still controversial, funds for program development would be distributed only to state and local governments and other organizations that volunteer to participate. Similarly, only individuals who join programs voluntarily should participate.

Although marriage promotion is at a rudimentary stage, a surprising array of programs have been implemented; some have produced useful data. Several programs have been developed, for example, that promote marriage education and relationship skill building. These include the Prevention and Relationship Enhancement program (PREP), the Relationship Enhancement program (RE), the Art and Science of Love, and the Practical Application of Relationship Skills (PAIRS) program (Dion et al. 2002, 32–33). Reasonably strong evidence is that PREP can improve the quality of a married couple's relationship, reduce negative communications, and reduce family violence for up to five years after the end of the program (Markman et al. 1993). Unfortunately, PREP and the other programs have been developed and used with predominately middle-class couples. Thus, these programs will need to be adapted if they are to be used successfully with poor couples.

In addition to marriage education and relationship skill building, a second type of program attempts to improve the marriageability of potential spouses. This type of program is especially important for poor men because they have above-average rates of characteristics that are barriers to marriage, including low job skills, addictions, criminal records, sexual infidelity, and a tendency toward violence. Although little research has shown that any programs have made poor fathers better marriage material, some programs have successfully reduced each characteristic. Thus, programs for helping poor fathers improve their prospects for marriage should be able to reduce these barriers, either through direct treatment or through referrals to other services.

As we have seen, some researchers believe that a program to help poor fathers and mothers by promoting marriage should be implemented at or just before a birth. The marriage policy now being pursued by the Bush administration would provide money to launch and evaluate several of these programs around the nation. The Department of Health and Human Services has funded Mathematica Policy Research to work with experts to develop a comprehensive review of how such an intervention program might be designed, conducted, and evaluated (Dion et al. 2002;

Dion, Strong, and Hershey 2004). It is hoped that several such demon-stration studies will be conducted in the next several years.

Faith-Based Programs

Faith-based initiatives are now a major topic of discussion and policy-making in Washington. John DiIulio (2002), the first head of the Office of Faith-Based and Community Initiatives in the Bush administration, has recently proposed that religion can affect behavior in three distinct ways. "Organic religion" is the set of beliefs and practices that constitute the substance of religious affiliation. People who participate in organic religion believe in God, attend services, give money to their religious institutions, and often participate in other activities sponsored by the institution. Literally hundreds of studies have established that people who participate in organic religion are healthier, have less mental illness, commit fewer crimes, and live longer than people who do not participate in organic religion (Johnson 2002; Johnson and Larson 1998).

The second way religion can affect behavior is through what DiIulio calls "programmatic" religion. In this case, religious groups conduct pro-grams that deliver social services such as child care, mentoring, prison ministries, treatment for addicts, and food kitchens. The 1996 welfare reform law included a provision called "charitable choice" that explicitly allowed religious groups to receive funds under the TANF block grant. Since 1996, the charitable choice provision has been applied to several other programs that provide federal funds for social interventions. Thus, religious groups can compete with other organizations for federal dollars to deliver several types of social services to needy groups. The 1996 provi-sion allows religious groups that receive federal dollars to retain their reli-gious identity, to deliver their services in church (or synagogue or mosque) facilities, and to show preference in hiring to people who subscribe to their religious beliefs. Government dollars cannot be used to proselytize or pay for religious indoctrination or worship, but religious groups can retain their religious characteristics while using federal dollars to provide social services. Thus, the groundwork has been laid for expanded involvement in programmatic religion by groups attempting to help poor fathers.

The third type of religious influence identified by DiIulio is "ecologi-cal" religion. To be influenced by ecological religion, people do not need to believe in God, pray, attend services, or participate in any other reli-gious activities or programs sponsored by religious groups. Rather, the ecological religious factor conditions the environment in which people live. Some poor neighborhoods have lots of churches, residents who bring religion into their day-to-day activities, and self-improvement projects conducted by people of faith. The very presence of churches, people of faith, and faith-based activities affects the entire ecology of neighborhoods. On a simple level, the presence of religious institutions and of religious citizens who engage in positive social activities and conduct themselves in accord with religious principles may have some impact on other citizens, even if those citizens do not believe in God or participate in any religious activities. On a more profound level, over a period of time, living in the presence of these ecological influences can have an impact on the character and behavior of nonbelievers and even convert some of them to religious beliefs and practices.

Unlike the abundance of research on organic religion, research on programmatic and ecological religion is sparse. As often happens in these situations, people involved in religious programs and people who believe in the programs make extravagant claims for their power to shape human behavior and change souls. But research on these claims will not bear their weight. It is not that many studies have been conducted but have failed to find positive effects; rather, few studies have been conducted, and almost no random-assignment studies are available on programmatic or organic religion.

This lack of research is unfortunate because the claim that programmatic religion can change souls and positively influence behavior is compelling. Indeed, the very types of behavioral change most needed by young men are rooted in their willingness to violate society's laws and values. Secular programs are usually incapable of reaching these men. What they most need is better character. And, of course, it is precisely character change that lies at the heart of all religious doctrine and practice. Because millions of Americans have directly experienced the growth of their own and their children's character under the influence of religious beliefs and practices, many believe that religious social programs will work. Religion, but not social science, is based on faith. To prove these programs work, and to establish and expand their access to public dollars, programmatic religion must agree to abide by the rules of social science and willingly submit to evaluation.

The policy recommendation here is simple enough. The federal Office of Faith-Based and Community Initiatives and the corresponding offices in each of the five federal cabinet-level agencies that administer social programs should place a priority on recruiting religious-based programs to compete for federal grants and then should carefully evaluate these programs—using random assignment whenever possible—to determine whether they live up to their potential. At a minimum, these programs should include prison ministries, school mentoring, employment and training, drug rehabilitation, illegitimacy reduction, and marriage promotion.

Conclusion

The picture of young minority men portrayed by much of the data reviewed in this volume is somewhat grim. But there are good reasons to believe that, despite the difficulties, progress over the next decade and beyond is possible. First, minority adolescents and adults have made dramatic progress in recent decades, and a higher and higher portion of minority young adults should continue to improve their educational and economic status. Second, poor and minority men are not content with their lot in life. Surveys show that they want to work, would like to have happy marriages, and above all want to provide for the financial and emotional needs of their children. Third, as several votes in Congress since the late 1990s have shown, policymakers are aware of the problems faced by young minority men and have been willing to take action on their behalf. These factors alone lead to optimism that progress in reducing delinquency and crime and increasing education, work, income, and marriage among minority men is possible, even likely.

Large-scale demonstrations that are evaluated by random-assignment designs are a proven means of testing whether policy interventions work. Yet this method has been used only sparingly to develop effective programs for young men. More aggressive and widespread use of this method will lead to the more rapid accumulation of knowledge about effective and ineffective interventions. Social science has a significant role to play in the formulation of effective public policy to improve the well-being of these young men. They, their wives and girlfriends, their children, and the nation need it.

NOTES

1. Tabulations of unpublished U.S. Bureau of the Census data by Gary Burtless, taken from personal communication with the author, 2005.

2. See, for example, Cullen and Gendreau (2000); Travis et al. (2001); and Wilson, Gallagher, and MacKenzie (2000).

3. "The Left's Marriage Problem," *Washington Post*, 5 April 2002, A 22.

REFERENCES

Acs, Gregory, and Sandi Nelson. 2001. " 'Honey, I'm Home': Changes in Living Arrangements in the Late 1990s." *Assessing the New Federalism* Policy Brief B-28. Washington, DC: The Urban Institute.

Armor, David J. 2003. "Family Policy and Academic Achievement." In *One Percent for the Kids: New Policies, Brighter Futures for America's Children,* edited by Isabel Sawhill (93–112). Washington, DC: Brookings Institution Press.

Bane, Mary Jo, and David T. Ellwood. 1983. "Slipping Into and Out of Poverty: The Dynamics of Spells." Working Paper 1199. Cambridge, MA: National Bureau of Economic Research.

Barnett, W. Steven, Jason Hustedt, Kenneth Robin and Karen Schulman. 2004. *The State of Preschool: 2004 State Preschool Yearbook.* New Brunswick, NJ: National Institute for Early Education Research, Rutgers University.

Beck, Allen J., and Bernard E. Shipley. 1989. "Recidivism of Prisoners Released in 1983." NCJ 116261. Washington, DC: U.S. Department of Justice, Bureau of Justice Statistics.

Bushway, Shawn, and Peter Reuter. 1997. "Labor Markets and Crime Risk Factors." In *Preventing Crime: What Works, What Doesn't, What's Promising,* by Lawrence W. Sherman, Denise C. Gottfredson, Doris L. MacKenzie, John Eck, Peter Reuter, and Shawn D. Bushway (233–80). Washington, DC: U.S. Department of Justice, National Institute of Justice.

Campbell, Frances A., and Craig T. Ramey. 1995. "Cognitive and School Outcomes for High-Risk African-American Students at Middle Adolescence: Positive Effects of Early Intervention." *American Educational Research Journal* 32(4): 743–72.

Carasso, Adam, and C. Eugene Steuerle. 2002. "How Marriage Penalties Change under the 2001 Tax Bill." Tax Policy Center Discussion Paper No. 2. Washington, DC: The Urban Institute.

Carlson, Marcia, Sara McLanahan, and Paula England. 2003. "Union Formation in Fragile Families." Working Paper 01-06-FF. Princeton, NJ: Center for Research on Child Wellbeing, Princeton University.

Caulkins, J. P., C. P. Rydell, W. Schwabe, and J. R. Chiesa. 1997. "Throwing Away the Key or the Taxpayers' Money?" Publication MR–827-DPRC. Santa Monica, CA: RAND Corporation.

Center for Research on Child Wellbeing. 2002. "Diversity among Unmarried Parents." *Fragile Families* Research Brief 10. Princeton, NJ: Center for Research on Child Wellbeing, Princeton University.

Clark, Kenneth. 1965. *Dark Ghetto: Dilemmas of Social Power.* Hanover, NH: Wesleyan University Press.

Congressional Budget Office. 1996. *Federal Budgetary Implications of the Personal Responsibility and Work Opportunity Reconciliation Act of 1996.* Washington, DC: Congressional Budget Office.

Corson, Walter, Paul T. Decker, Shari Dunstan, and Anne R. Gordon. 1989. "The New Jersey Unemployment Insurance Reemployment Demonstration Project Final Evaluation Report." Princeton, NJ: Mathematica Policy Research.

Cullen, Francis T., and Paul Gendreau. 2000. "Assessing Correctional Rehabilitation: Policy, Practice, and Prospects." In *Policies, Processes, and Decisions of the Criminal Justice System,* vol. 3 of *Criminal Justice 2000,* edited by Julie Horney (109–76). Washington, DC: U.S. Department of Justice.

Currie, Janet, and Duncan Thomas. 1995. "Does Head Start Make a Difference?" *American Economic Review* 85(3): 341–64.

DeParle, Jason. 2004. *American Dream: Three Women, Ten Kids, and a Nation's Drive to End Welfare.* New York: Viking.

DiIulio, John J. 2002. "The Three Faith Factors." *Public Interest* 149: 50–64.

Dion, M. Robin, Barbara Devaney, Sheena McConnell, Melissa Ford, Heather Hill, and Pamela Winston. 2002. *Helping Low-Income Unwed Parents Build Strong and Healthy Marriages: A Conceptual Framework for Interventions.* Princeton, NJ: Mathematica Policy Research.

Dion, M. Robin, Debra A. Strong, and Alan M. Hershey. 2004. "Implementing Healthy Marriage Programs for Unwed Parents." Document No. PP04-48. Princeton, NJ: Mathematica Policy Research.

Duncan, Greg J., and Katherine Magnuson. 2001. "Individual and Parent-Based Intervention Strategies for Promoting Human Capital and Positive Behavior." Unpublished manuscript, Institute for Poverty Research, Northwestern University.

Durose, Matthew R., David J. Levin, and Patrick A. Langan. 2001. "Felony Sentences in State Courts, 1998." Bureau of Justice Statistics Bulletin. NCJ 190103. Washington, DC: U.S. Department of Justice.

Ellwood, David T., and Christopher Jencks. 2001. "The Growing Difference in Family Structure: What Do We Know? Where Do We Look for Answers?" Unpublished manuscript, John F. Kennedy School of Government, Harvard University.

Executive Office of the President. 2002. *Working toward Independence.* Washington, DC: Executive Office of the President.

Farkas, George, and Shane Hall. 2000. "Can Title I Attain Its Goal?" In *Brookings Papers on Education Policy: 2000,* edited by Diane Ravitch (59–103). Washington, DC: Brookings Institution Press.

Finn, Chester E., Jr. 2000. "Comment." In *Brookings Papers on Education Policy: 2000,* edited by Diane Ravitch (104–108). Washington, DC: Brookings Institution Press.

Fordham Foundation. 2002. *No Child Left Behind: What Will It Take?* Washington, DC: Fordham Foundation.

Freeman, Richard. 1996. "Why Do So Many Young American Men Commit Crimes and What Might We Do about It?" *Journal of Economic Perspectives* 10(1): 25–42.

Gallagher, James J., Jenna R. Clayton, and Sarah E. Heinemeier. 2000. "Education for Four-Year-Olds: State Initiatives." Technical Report 2. Chapel Hill: National Center for Early Development and Learning, University of North Carolina.

Garces, Eliana, Duncan Thomas, and Janet Currie. 2000. "Longer-Term Effects of Head Start." Working Paper 8054. Cambridge, MA: National Bureau of Economic Research.

Gibson, Christina, Kathryn Edin, and Sara McLanahan. 2002. "High Hopes but Even Higher Expectations: The Retreat from Marriage among Low-Income Couples."

Working Paper 2003-06-FF. Princeton, NJ: Center for Research on Child Well-being, Princeton University.

Gueron, Judith M., and Edward Pauly. 1991. *From Welfare to Work*. New York: Russell Sage Foundation.

Hamilton, Gayle, Stephen Freedman, Lisa Gennetian, Charles Michalopoulos, Johanna Walter, Diana Adams-Ciardullo, and Anna Gassman-Pines. 2002. "How Effective Are Different Welfare-to-Work Approaches? Five-Year Adult and Child Impacts for Eleven Programs." New York: Manpower Demonstration Research Corporation.

Haskins, Ron. Forthcoming. "Preschool Programs and the Achievement Gap: The Little Train that Could." In *In One Generation: The Elimination of Race Differences in Educational Achievement*, edited by Paul E. Peterson. Lanham, MD: Rowman & Littlefield Publishers, Inc.

Haskins, Ron, and Isabel Sawhill. 2003. "The Future of Head Start." *Welfare Reform and Beyond* Policy Brief 27. Washington, DC: The Brookings Institution.

Herrnstein, Richard J., and Charles Murray. 1994. *The Bell Curve: Intelligence and Class Structure in American Life*. New York: Free Press.

Holzer, Harry J. 1996. *What Employers Want: Job Prospects for Less-Educated Workers*. New York: Russell Sage Foundation.

———. 2002. "Can Work Experience Programs Work for Welfare Recipients?" *Welfare Reform and Beyond* Policy Brief 24. Washington, DC: The Brookings Institution.

Howell, William G., and Paul E. Peterson. 2002. *The Education Gap: Vouchers and Urban Schools*. Washington, DC: Brookings Institution Press.

Jensen, Arthur R. 1969. "How Much Can We Boost IQ and Scholastic Achievement?" *Harvard Educational Review* 39: 1–123.

Job Corps. 2001. *Job Corps Annual Report: PY 2000*. Washington, DC: U.S. Department of Labor.

Johnson, Byron R. 2002. "Objective Hope: Assessing the Effectiveness of Faith-Based Organizations: A Review of the Literature." Philadelphia: Center for Research on Religion and Urban Civil Society, University of Pennsylvania.

Johnson, Byron R., and David B. Larson. 1998. *Religion: The Forgotten Faith Factor in Cutting Youth Crime and Saving At-Risk Urban Youth*. New York: Manhattan Institute.

Karoly, Lynn A. 2002. "Investing in the Future: Reducing Poverty through Human Capital Investments." In *Understanding Poverty*, edited by Sheldon H. Danziger and Robert H. Haveman (314–56). Cambridge, MA: Harvard University Press.

Karoly, Lynn A., Peter W. Greenwood, Susan S. Everingham, Jill Houbé, M. Rebecca Kilburn, C. Peter Rydell, Matthew Sanders, and James Chiesa. 1998. *Investing in Our Children: What We Know and Don't Know about the Costs and Benefits of Early Childhood Interventions*. Santa Monica, CA: RAND Corporation.

Kaus, Mickey. 1992. *The End of Equality*. New York: Basic Books.

Kirby, Douglas. 1997. *No Easy Answers: Research Findings on Programs to Reduce Teen Pregnancy*. Washington, DC: National Campaign to Prevent Teen Pregnancy.

———. 2001. *Emerging Answers: Research Findings on Programs to Reduce Teen Pregnancy*. Washington, DC: National Campaign to Prevent Teen Pregnancy.

Kosters, Marvin H., and Brent D. Mast. 2003. *Closing the Education Achievement Gap: Is Title I Working?* Washington, DC: American Enterprise Institute.

LaLonde, Robert J. 1995. "The Promise of Public Sector-Sponsored Training Programs." *Journal of Economic Perspectives* 9(2): 149–68.

Lamb, Michael E. 1997. *The Role of the Father in Child Development.* 3rd ed. New York: John Wiley & Sons.

———. 1998. "Nonparental Child Care: Context, Quality, Correlates, and Consequences." In *Child Psychology in Practice,* vol. 4 of *Handbook of Child Psychology,* edited by William Damon, Irving E. Sigel, and K. Ann Renninger (73–133). 5th ed. New York: John Wiley & Sons.

Lawrence, Sarah, Daniel P. Mears, Glenn Dubin, and Jeremy Travis. 2002. *The Practice and Promise of Prison Programming.* Washington, DC: The Urban Institute.

Lerman, Robert I. 2002. "Marriage and the Economic Well-Being of Families with Children: A Review of the Literature." Washington, DC: The Urban Institute.

Lichter, Daniel T., and Deborah Roempke Graefe. 2001. "Finding a Mate? The Marital and Cohabitation Histories of Unwed Mothers." In *Out of Wedlock: Causes and Consequences of Nonmarital Fertility,* edited by Lawrence L. Wu and Barbara Wolfe (317–43). New York: Russell Sage Foundation.

Lynch, James P., and William J. Sabol. 1997. "Prison Use and Social Control." In *Policies, Processes, and Decisions of the Criminal Justice System,* vol. 3 of *Criminal Justice 2000,* edited by Julie Horney (7–44). Washington, DC: U.S. Department of Justice.

Manning, Wendy D. 2002. "The Implications of Cohabitation for Children's Well-Being." In *Just Living Together: Implications of Cohabitation on Families, Children, and Social Policy,* edited by Alan Booth and Ann C. Crouter (121–52). Mahwah, NJ: Lawrence Erlbaum Associates.

Markman, H. J., M. J. Renick, F. J. Floyd, Scott M. Stanley, and M. Clemens. 1993. "Preventing Marital Distress through Communication and Conflict Management Training: A 4- and 5-Year Follow-Up." *Journal of Consulting and Clinical Psychology* 61: 70–77.

Martin, Joyce A., Brady E. Hamilton, Stephanie Ventura, Fay Menacker, and Melissa M. Park. 2002. "Births: Final Data for 2000." *National Vital Statistics Report* 50(5). Hyattsville, MD: National Center for Health Statistics.

Martinez, John M., and Cynthia Miller. 2000. *Working and Earning: The Impact of Parents' Fair Share on Low-Income Fathers' Employment.* New York: Manpower Demonstration Research Corporation.

Martinson, Robert. 1974. "What Works? Questions and Answers about Prison Reform." *Public Interest* 35(Spring): 22–54.

McConnell, Sheena, and Steven Glazerman. 2001. "National Job Corps Study: The Benefits and Costs of Job Corps." PR01–51. Washington, DC: Mathematica Policy Research.

McLanahan, Sara, and Gary Sandefur. 1994. *Growing Up with a Single Parent: What Hurts, What Helps.* Cambridge, MA: Harvard University Press.

McLanahan, Sara, Irwin Garfinkel, Nancy E. Reichman, Julien Teitler, Marcia Carlson, and Christina Norland Audigier. 2003. *The Fragile Families and Child Wellbeing Study: Baseline National Report.* Revised March 2003. Princeton, NJ: Center for Research on Child Wellbeing, Princeton University.

Medical Institute for Sexual Health. 2002. *Sex, Condoms and STDs: What We Now Know.* Austin, TX: Medicaid Institute for Sexual Health.

Moynihan, Daniel P. 1965a. "A Family Policy for the Nation." *America* (September 18): 280–83.

————. 1965b. *The Negro Family: The Case for National Action.* Washington, DC: U.S. Department of Labor.

————. 1968. "The President and the Negro: The Moment Lost." In *The Triple Revolution: Social Problems in Depth,* edited by Robert Perrucci and Marc Pilisuk (431–60). Boston: Little, Brown and Company.

National Campaign to Prevent Teen Pregnancy. 2002. *With One Voice, 2002: America's Adults and Teens Sound Off about Teen Pregnancy.* Washington, DC: National Campaign to Prevent Teen Pregnancy.

National Commission on Excellence in Education. 1983. *A Nation at Risk: The Imperative for Educational Reform.* Washington, DC: U.S. Government Printing Office.

National Institute of Allergy and Infectious Diseases. 2001. *Scientific Evidence on Condom Effectiveness for Sexually Transmitted Disease Prevention.* Bethesda, MD: National Institutes of Health.

National Research Council. 2001. *Juvenile Crime, Juvenile Justice.* Washington, DC: National Academy Press.

Oden, Sherri, Lawrence J. Schweinhart, and David Weikart. 2000. *Into Adulthood: A Study of the Effects of Head Start.* Ypsilanti, MI: High/Scope Educational Research Foundation.

Office of Child Support Enforcement. 2000. *Child Support Enforcement: Twenty-Third Annual Report.* Washington, DC: U.S. Department of Health and Human Services.

O'Hare, William. 2003. "Recent Changes in the Percent of Children Living in Single-Mother Families." *Kids Count* Working Paper. Baltimore: Annie E. Casey Foundation.

Patterson, Orlando. 1998. *Rituals of Blood: Consequences of Slavery in Two American Centuries.* New York: Basic Books.

Pavetti, LaDonna. 1994. "Policies to Time-Limit AFDC Benefits: What Can We Learn from Welfare Dynamics?" Paper presented at the annual research conference of the Association for Public Policy Management, Chicago, Oct. 29.

Phillips, Elizabeth, and Irwin Garfinkel. 1993. "Income Growth among Nonresident Fathers: Evidence from Wisconsin." *Demography* 30(2): 227–41.

Primus, Wendell. 2002. "Child Living Arrangements by Race and Income: A Supplementary Analysis." Washington, DC: Center on Budget and Policy Priorities.

Primus, Wendell, and Jennifer Beeson. 2002. "Safety Net Programs, Marriage, and Cohabitation." In *Just Living Together: Implications of Cohabitation on Families, Children, and Social Policy,* edited by Alan Booth and Ann C. Crouter (191–228). Mahwah, NJ: Lawrence Erlbaum and Associates.

Rangarajan, Anu, and Philip Gleason. 1998. "Young Unwed Fathers of AFDC Children: Do They Provide Support?" *Demography* 35(2): 175–86.

Ravitch, Diane, ed. 2000. *Brookings Papers on Education Policy: 2000.* Washington, DC: Brookings Institution Press.

Rowe, David C., and Joseph L. Rodgers. 1997. "Poverty and Behavior: Are Environmental Measures Nature and Nurture?" *Developmental Review* 17: 358–75.

Sawhill, Isabel, and Ron Haskins. 2003. "Work and Marriage: The Way to End Poverty and Welfare." *Welfare Reform and Beyond* Policy Brief 28. Washington, DC: The Brookings Institution.

Scarr, Sandra, and Richard A. Weinberg. 1978. "The Influence of 'Family Background' on Intellectual Attainment." *American Sociological Review* 43: 674–92.

Schumacher, Rachel, Mark Greenberg, and Joan Lombardi. 2001. *State Initiatives to Promote Early Learning: Next Steps in Coordinating Subsidized Child Care, Head Start, and State Prekindergarten.* Washington, DC: Center for Law and Social Policy.

Schweinhart, Lawrence J., Helen Barnes, and David Weikart. 1993. *Significant Benefits: The High/Scope Perry Preschool Study through Age 27.* Ypsilanti, MI: High/Scope Educational Research Foundation.

Sherman, Lawrence W., Denise Gottfredson, Doris Layton MacKenzie, John Eck, Peter Reuter, and Shawn D. Bushway, eds. 1997. *Preventing Crime: What Works, What Doesn't, What's Promising?* College Park, MD: Department of Criminology and Criminal Justice, University of Maryland.

Smock, Pamela J., and Sanjiv Gupta. 2002. "Cohabitation in Contemporary North America." In *Just Living Together: Implications of Cohabitation on Families, Children, and Social Policy,* edited by Alan Booth and Ann C. Crouter (53–84). Mahwah, NJ: Lawrence Erlbaum and Associates.

Stanley, Scott, and Howard Markman. 1992. "Commitment: The Role of Dedication and Constraint in Personal Relationships." *Journal of Marriage and the Family* 54(3): 595–608.

Thernstrom, Stephan, and Abigail Thernstrom. 1997. *America in Black and White: One Nation, Indivisible.* New York: Simon and Schuster.

Thomas, Adam, and Isabel Sawhill. 2002. "For Richer or Poorer: Marriage as an Antipoverty Strategy." *Journal of Policy Analysis and Management* 21(4): 587–99.

Travis, Jeremy, Amy L. Solomon, and Michelle Waul. 2001. *From Prison to Home: The Dimensions and Consequences of Prisoner Reentry.* Washington, DC: The Urban Institute.

Turkheimer, Eric, Andreana Haley, Mary Waldron, Brian D'Onofrio, and Irving I. Gottesman. 2003. "Socioeconomic Status Modifies Heritability of IQ in Young Children." *Psychological Science* 14(6): 623–28.

U.S. Bureau of Justice. 2001. *Correctional Populations in the United States, 1980–1999.* Washington, DC: Bureau of Justice Statistics.

U.S. Census Bureau. 2002. *Statistical Abstract of the United States: 2001.* 121st ed. Washington, DC: U.S. Government Printing Office.

U.S. General Accounting Office. 2000. "Title I Preschool Education: More Children Served, but Gauging Effect on School Readiness Difficult." GAO/HEHS-00-171. Washington, DC: U.S. General Accounting Office.

Ventura, Stephanie J., and Christine A. Bachrach. 2000. "Nonmarital Childbearing in the United States, 1940–99." *National Vital Statistics Reports* 48(16; revised). Hyattsville, MD: National Center for Health Statistics.

Waite, Linda J., and Maggie Gallagher. 2000. *The Case for Marriage.* New York: Doubleday.

Wilson, David B., Catherine A. Gallagher, and Doris L. MacKenzie. 2000. "A Meta-Analysis of Corrections-Based Education, Vocation, and Work Programs for Adult Offenders." *Journal of Research in Crime and Delinquency* 37(4): 347–68.

11

Toward a Fruitful Policy Discourse about Less-Educated Young Men

Hillard Pouncy

The employment and incarceration problems of young, less-educated black men are both chronic and acute—and not completely race-based. All things held equal, if less-educated young men could change their skin color or their ethnicity, their employment and incarceration woes would be reduced but not eliminated. If they could change their educational status to include an education beyond high school, their employment and incarceration problems would essentially vanish. This means the employment problem most visible among less-educated young black men represents a much more serious problem potentially affecting most men with a high school education or less.

The 1990s featured increased employment rates—the policy measure labor economists most associate with ending poverty—with one exception. The employment rate for young, less-educated young black men in 1979 was over 60 percent; by 1999 that rate had fallen to just above 50 percent (Holzer and Offner, this volume). The employment rates for this group's white and Hispanic peers were 80 percent or higher in 1979. Rates declined 8 percent for whites and 14 percent for Hispanics in the 1980s, but by the end of the 1990s they were almost back to their 1979 levels. If this were the only point Holzer and Offner make, we would have a straightforward and unfortunate story about young black men falling behind. Holzer and Offner also find, however, that less-educated young black men responded better than their peers to cyclical employment trends. For every 1 percentage point decrease in national unemployment rates, the unemployment rate of less-educated young black men decreased by nearly 3 percentage points.

Holzer and Offner (this volume) suggests that the short-term employment sensitivity of less-educated young black men is attributable to their involvement in lower-paid, less-desired (secondary) sectors of the labor market, where they are picked up quickly when the economy improves and discarded quickly when the economy declines. Young black men may also be heavily involved in secondary labor markets as a consequence of their reputation for being involved with crime (Holzer, Raphael, and Stoll, this volume). Crutchfield and Pitchford (1997) confirm that those in secondary markets are more likely to dabble in other activities, including crime.

This possibility is illustrated in figure 11.1, a cross-sectional look at youth by race from the 1979 National Longitudinal Survey of Youth, which asked who obtained money from illegal activity. Seemingly, black youth are more likely than their white and Hispanic peers to report that they obtain money from illegal activity even when they are employed (Bushway 1998; Reuter, MacCoun, and Murphy 1990). Given that employers fear hiring criminals, and that employers either cannot afford to or are unwilling to screen accurately for criminal involvement, Holzer,

Figure 11.1. *Young Men Earning Money from Illegal Activity, by Race/Ethnicity and Employment Status, 1979 (percent)*

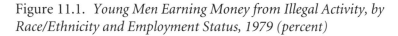

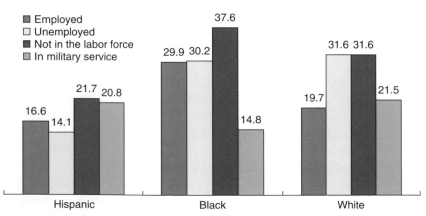

Source: Author's calculations based on data from the 1979 National Longitudinal Study of Youth.

Notes: Self-reported data. Young men are age 14 to 21.

Raphael, and Stoll find that employers take the easy way out and simply refuse to hire blacks as a proxy for keeping crime out of their shops.[1]

More important, this is not just a problem affecting less-educated young black men. To be sure, over the past two decades black men were seven to eight times more likely to be incarcerated than white men (figure 11.2).[2] However, incarceration rates for all less-educated men increased fivefold over the past two decades (Western, Kleykamp, and Rosenfeld 2003). Across all racial groups, incarceration rates for less-educated young men were higher than for their better-educated counterparts. For all groups, incarceration rates among young men who did not finish high school were five times as high as their counterparts who had attended college (figure 11.3).

There are also variable costs to incarceration by race (Bushway 1998). Incarcerated white men suffer individual consequences as ex-offenders (Western, Kling, and Weiman 2001). Blacks suffer a group consequence. Less-educated black men who commit no crime still suffer employment harms as a consequence of high incarceration levels experienced by blacks

Figure 11.2. *Incarceration Rates of Men Age 18 to 65 by Race and Ethnicity, 1980–2000*

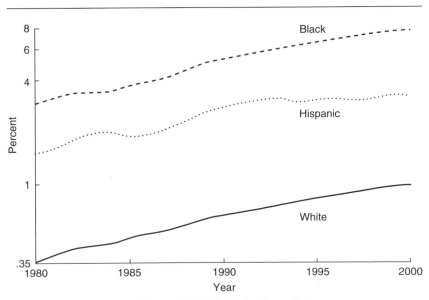

Source: Western, Kleykamp, and Rosenfeld (2003). Used with permission.

Figure 11.3. *Incarceration Rates of Young Men by Race/Ethnicity and Education Level, 1980–2000*

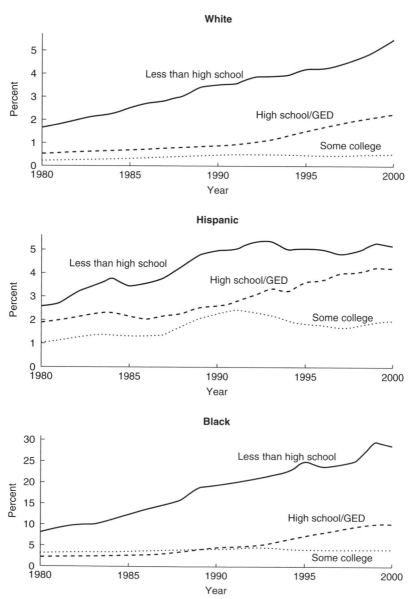

Source: Western, Kleykamp, and Rosenfeld (2003). Used with permission.

Note: Young men are age 20 to 40.

(Holzer, Raphael, and Stoll, this volume). Similarly, black women who cannot or do not marry the father of their child because of the father's unemployment record are affected (Mincy, Lewis, and Han, this volume).

What makes this an extremely important social problem, perhaps as serious as the problems leading up to the civil rights movement, is the possibility of the following dynamic. Not only did declines in crime have little effect on incarceration rates, but incarceration rates increased steeply as crime declined rapidly (figure 11.4). Western and others suggest "crime rates fall most rapidly where employment rises . . . but incarceration increases as inequality rises" (Western et al. 2003). If these dynamics hold up under the scrutiny of further research, high incarceration rates may be identified as a permanent fixture of the new inequality, especially for less-educated men.

What compounds the problem are present-day politics and programs that stymie efforts to assist these men. New research on the aspirations and job opportunities for these men may stimulate new politics and policies that help them. Specifically, we would like to know the answers to three research questions:

One, do less-educated young black men have the values and preferences that Young (2000, 2004) ascribes to them—do they have a strong work ethic and a preference for "masculine jobs"?

Figure 11.4. *Violent Crime and Incarceration Rates, 1970–2000*

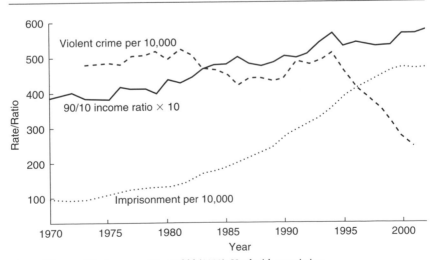

Source: Western, Kleykamp, and Rosenfeld (2003). Used with permission.

Two, do these men lack information about the "good jobs" in traditionally male occupations that Nightingale and Sorensen argue are available (chapter 8, this volume)? The jobs Nightingale and Sorensen discuss do not pay as much as the manufacturing jobs of previous decades, but they are also not as dirty or dangerous. Plus, these new jobs pay more than most less-educated, non-enrolled young men currently earn, and they require little postsecondary schooling or training. What barriers currently prevent young men who want those jobs from finding them?

Three, are employers who offer these "good jobs" in traditionally male occupations willing to hire young men that most employers perceive as likely criminals (chapter 4, this volume)? If so, why aren't they currently hiring less-educated young black men?

Having answers from research demonstrations at the size and scale of the Parent's Fair Share effort of the early 1990s is useful for its own sake, but, as we note below, demonstrations and new facts may help policymakers and politicians determine how and why investments in young, less-educated men are good for their own constituents.

This chapter briefly reviews current political and policy barriers to helping young men. It then outlines a theory of how and why new research may help alleviate those barriers and details the likely policy outcomes.

Background

The federal government has launched two major efforts in the past 10 years to help less-educated young men, indirectly and directly. Since 1999, Congress has signaled some interest in providing training and other services to the fathers of children on welfare, men who are disproportionately likely to be young and less educated. More recently, the Bush administration included $100 million for fatherhood programs in its proposed Healthy Marriage Initiative. The legislation encouraged fathers to secure marriage counseling, but it also allowed practitioners to provide job training and other employment-related skills in their programs. This legislative action was primarily symbolic; the funds were authorized but not allocated. Because support for fathers is a non-allocated budget item that requires its supporters to track down new monies, possibly from non-welfare funding sources, the bill still has to attract greater legislative support and gain a permanent footprint in welfare reauthorization packages.

Two major groups oppose providing that support to young men. Welfare rights advocates regard efforts to redirect welfare funds to help young, never-married fathers as "raids" on already tight welfare budgets. They believe that investments in men will not pay off for their clients, welfare mothers.

Making less-educated young men into a problem group also threatens the status of less-educated mothers in a second respect. In a society without a universal safety net, one way to motivate help for one group is to build a case that some other group has not or cannot live up to its responsibilities. Help for widows and orphans after the Civil War implied a dead husband, father, and/or mother (Gordon 1994; Moynihan 1973; Skocpol 1992). Help for deserted mothers in the early 1920s implied "home slacker" husbands (Gordon 1994; Willrich 2000). Help for dependent children in the 1930s implied mothers too busy with work to care for them properly (Gordon 1994). Help for temporarily poor divorced or separated wives implied "deadbeat" husbands in the 1970s (Garfinkel 1992, Johnson, Levine, and Doolittle 1999). Currently, help for young, less-educated, never-married mothers implies "dead-broke" fathers too poor to meet their responsibilities (Mincy and Pouncy 1997). If the problems of dead-broke men were to be seriously addressed, dependent women and children would no longer have a "bogeyman" with empty pockets from whom they require rescue.

Conservatives also oppose providing support to less-educated young men. Although some conservatives in the House and Senate have supported the fatherhood initiative, an important group opposes it. Opponents argue that government programs have had only modest effects on employment outcomes among men and that improvements in the employment and earnings of men would have only modest effects on marriage rates among unmarried parents (Rector and Johnson 2004).

Although Democrats and Republicans are both prepared to fund job training for less-educated young men, if they cannot show a return on their investments, it is difficult to imagine how they will persuade those two veto groups. Hence a Catch-22 policy situation emerges, in which the investments necessary to produce evidence about useful programs and policies are stymied—by lack of evidence.

Outside Congress, direct support for less-educated young men has come from the Bush administration's Office of Faith-Based and Community Initiatives and its $300 million prisoner reentry initiative, which provides ex-offenders with job training and placement services, transitional housing, and mentoring. While useful, this program may create perverse incentives: less-educated men first have to become criminals or never-married fathers to secure benefits otherwise unavailable to them.

The Importance of New Facts, New Findings

In the welfare debates of the 1980s and 1990s, members of the public held positive views toward the program when exposed to positive views about welfare policy and recipients. When exposed to negative views and debates about welfare, they held negative views about it. Similarly, when the public is asked about helping low-income fathers, 90 percent report that it is important "to help low-income fathers who are not living with their children to find jobs, pay child support, and become better parents" (Lake Snell and Associates 2002). Three-quarters of the public considers helping low-income fathers a very important policy goal. However, when asked about crime and people identified as criminals, the public places crime as a continuing policy priority even when crime rates decline significantly, identifies less-educated young black men as likely criminals, and values penal sanctions as a policy response.

In the absence of evidence about what increases employment among less-educated men, political figures and policymakers are equally free to focus on policies to harm young men (incarceration policies) as they are to provide job-training policies that help them. Interestingly, the possibility of research and debate is already in place in seven dimensions, but it lacks a trigger. Before discussing how new research might trigger such a transformation, we review the policy terrain for a positive discussion on young men.

One set of proposals emulates the universalistic themes of welfare reform. In chapter 2 of this volume, Holzer and Offner note that at the tail end of a strong economy, employment among black men increased. In chapter 3, Rodgers suggests maintaining a strong economy that keeps unemployment rates low is a necessary but probably insufficient condition for raising employment among young black men. He forecasts that a continuously tight economy is likely and that, while such an economy would increase the labor force participation of less-skilled black men, this increase would probably not close the labor-force participation gap between young black and white men. In sum, he suggests macroeconomic policy is a vital condition for any attempt to expand opportunities for young black men, although targeting would be necessary.

The second analogue to devolution is the self-empowerment strategy illustrated by the Million Man March. The march itself was a textbook example of an empowerment effort (Morris 1996; Pouncy 2002). It raised public consciousness about a group's common problem at the same time it raised the group's consciousness about its plight and options. It identified a strategy by which the group could claim power—self-help and responsibility—and received significant attention both within and outside the black community (as an empowerment strategy should).

The approach also demonstrated the weaknesses of an empowerment approach, generally and specifically. The general problem was that it could not be sustained. It was a one-time effort. It was a broadcast message (several problems bundled together), not a narrow-cast one (focused on, say, employment problems or crime). The specific problem was that, even if young black men become more empowered, they face unemployment in the job market. The march could not address employer perceptions of young black men as criminals (or potential criminals). In general, it is difficult to calibrate weapons of the weak (protest, social movements, civil disturbance, and disobedience) to job market problems.

Between the universal and the self-empowerment proposals lie a range of ideas that, like their welfare equivalents, feature incentives and punishments in various combinations. Normally, the job training proposal offered by Nightingale and Sorensen (chapter 8) would be an example of a prevention and rehabilitation strategy, because most clients do not regard access to job training as an incentive to change their behavior. The Nightingale and Sorensen strategy adapts an idea from Young (2004), creating a "work identity" approach to job training.[3] A generic job training effort simply matches job candidate to generic jobs for which they qualify. It ignores the "masculinity" barrier that Young hypothesizes may be a factor in employment stability of young black men. Specifically, Young observes that young, low-skilled black men prefer blue-collar jobs to other opportunities at their skill levels, as if they conflate their male identity with the jobs to which they aspire.

Nightingale and Sorensen (chapter 8, this volume) respond with data that suggest the prospects for blue-collar jobs that pay well (200 percent of the poverty level for a family of three) are good. Young black men are likely to perceive these jobs as "male"—machinists, technicians, and the like. Nightingale and Sorensen further suggest their policy ideas could be implemented by reconfiguring already existing policy opportunities. Specifically, they suggest that relevant employment programs take the following steps: monitor local occupational projections carefully, flag high-growth/high-wage blue-collar occupational opportunities, and increase investment in occupation-specific training tagged to these opportunities in ways that also improve the educational ability and occupational skills of young black men (see box 11.1 for further comment).

The prisoner reentry initiative better illustrates the prevention and rehabilitation theme. This faith-based effort is based on the idea that for roughly a third of prisoners who reenter society, policymakers have only a few days to provide effective services. In that time frame, policymakers must provide housing, employment leads, and other services, or these vulnerable ex-offenders will turn to their old associates to solve problems and start down a path to recidivism.

The child support policies are the male analogue to the New Paternalism policies of welfare reform. Primus's proposals for increasing compliance among less-skilled fathers (chapter 10, this volume) match in many respects what welfare-to-work policy did with low-skilled mothers. To have Earned Income Tax Credits extended to them, non-custodial fathers would have to engage in behavior leading to responsible fatherhood—acknowledging paternity, becoming a good team parent, and meeting their child support obligations. When they do not have jobs, their participation in both job training and responsible fatherhood training efforts "stands in" for their child support payments. When they begin earning, their child support payments increase accordingly.

Finally, welfare reform included disincentives for behaviors policymakers wanted to deter. For example, almost all mothers who did not help establish paternity of their children were to be excluded from welfare benefits. At this end of the policy spectrum, policymakers would simply increase the consequences of crime until they achieved a deterrent against more crime. These measures would include more incarceration and tougher crime enforcement strategies.

Three Policy Triggers

From this account of the welfare reform endgame, three triggers emerge that might generate a new, positive discourse on policies and programs serving young less-educated men. Democratic and Republican politicians enmeshed in the Catch-22 dilemma outlined above can talk back

Box 11.1. The Bridges to Work Initiative

The lessons from a national demonstration to determine whether transportation was a barrier to securing blue-collar jobs reinforce some of what Nightingale and Sorensen suggest. The Bridges to Work Initiative, a random assignment demonstration, operated from 1996 to 2000 in four sites—Baltimore, Denver, Milwaukee, and St. Louis—and served up to 3,100 people (Elliot, Palubinsky, and Tiernay 1999). Most participants were black and 51 percent were men. The evaluation results are incomplete, but interim reports with the usual caveats offer initial impressions. In a tight economy, once ready-to-work blue-collar people and needy employers were made known to each other, connections occurred. Outcomes by gender are not available, but program managers did not perceive any obvious differences by gender.

As the economy gained strength in the second phase of the program, blue-collar jobs for easy-to-place people opened up in the central city, making transportation a less critical barrier. As a result, fewer ready-to-work participants needed the program. Because the program partnered with firms offering blue-collar jobs for the ready-to-work, these firms were less willing to accept program participants who were now less ready to work. The role of services to make people ready to work therefore became more critical.

The results of this program suggest that transportation and information barriers are relatively easy to circumvent in a tight market. Making people ready to work remains a significant problem. Compared with other factors—readiness to work, nature of the job, a tight market, and access to information—transportation is relatively less important.

In the words of the program evaluators, "Yes, lack of transportation prevents many poor people from reaching job-rich locations. But most low-income job seekers will need a variety of supports in order to get and stay employed" (Elliot et al. 1999, 19).

to influential gatekeepers on their political flanks as researchers unearth new facts about when, how, and why investments in young, less-educated men pay off.

Trigger One: Sector development employment pilot programs and demonstrations provide one trigger for talking back to gatekeepers. Over the past four decades, the nation's job training efforts successfully helped low-skilled women enter the job market. But the programs were less successful in helping low-skilled men with some job experience achieve wage growth or job stability. However, a generation of sector development employment strategies targeted services to specific high-wage or high-growth jobs that employers had not already identified for themselves. Several approaches successfully increased wages and job stability for less-educated men. These programs worked best with clients whose job entry and job retention problems had already been resolved. Democratic and Republican lawmakers can use new facts about these programs to support further demonstrations, pilot projects, and programs for less-educated young men.

Trigger Two: Covering gaps between fathers' child support payments to welfare families and the costs of raising children will become a more serious component of future welfare reauthorization debates. Depending on the performance of the Healthy Marriage Initiative, more attention to family formation among never-married parents is also likely. Both child support payment and marriage rates would be higher among families on welfare if employment rates and earnings were higher among the fathers of children receiving welfare. Therefore, new facts about what increases employment and earnings among less-educated young men will be highly pertinent to welfare reauthorization. Politicians and policymakers will be in a stronger position to bring along gatekeepers, who currently resist investments in less-educated men, with arguments that such investments s are part of a larger strategy to alleviate poverty and stabilize families. Recognizing the relationship between the employment and earnings of less-educated men and child support and marriage among families on welfare, Congress has authorized welfare reform funds for initiatives benefiting noncustodial fathers (Turetsky 2005). Unfortunately, Congress has not appropriated such funds.

Trigger Three: The ex-offender reentry initiative is a faith-based response to crime and incarceration trends of the 1990s discussed throughout this book (Holzer, Raphael, and Stoll, this volume; Pager 2003). It features a mentoring approach to reducing recidivism, and its target population overlaps with the young, less-educated men who are the policy target of this volume. Although the initiative emphasizes mentoring, most funded programs include a conventional employment component (Good and Sherrid 2005). White House efforts to re-fund this initiative are an opportunity for policymakers and grantees to innovate and incorporate the blue-collar, wage growth job-training approaches outlined by Nightingale and Sorensen (this volume).

These targeted strategies (sectoral employment, increasing child support and marriage by increasing male employment and earnings, and reentry programs) are more politically feasible than the full employment strategy, which could achieve the same goal. Holzer and Offner (chapter 2, this volume) and Rodgers (chapter 3, this volume) both note that sooner or later extended spells of employment growth would soak up less-educated young men. However, several factors cast doubt on the political feasibility of this approach. First, the political costs of such a policy are high. Second, running an economy at such high rates of employment would create contentious debates over whether tax cuts or various trade policies were the best routes to sustained growth. Finally, operating an economy at such high levels of employment inevitably raises the risk of inflation.

Going into welfare reform, conventional wisdom held that incentive-based reforms encouraging people to leave the rolls, such as universal health care, were fiscally expensive but politically popular. In line with that view, Wilson (1996) argued that popular coalitions built around efforts benefiting the majority of Americans would secure widespread political support and link the fortunes of the poor with those of the non-poor. The lesson from the Clinton administration's abortive health care policy is that universal proposals cost a lot in political capital as well as money.

As Congress and policymakers friendly to these policy initiatives engineer a new discourse about less-educated young men, their efforts will inevitably confront the connection some Americans and some American politicians make between black men and crime. According to Western (forthcoming) the crime/race connection has been central to American politics since the beginning of the prison boom in the 1970s. White working-class resentments and concerns about the riots and social disorder that had followed the early successes of the civil rights movement found a home in a Republican Party prepared to connect civil rights activism and violent crime. In this sense, the American civil rights revolution begat the prison boom and reduced opportunities for less-educated men as a result.

The good news is that similar political resentments lay behind welfare policy before welfare reform helped erode the stigma attached to welfare mothers. Welfare mothers are now less likely to be seen as dependent and unwilling or unable to work. For young black men, the new policy discourse addressed in this volume will help eradicate the criminal image attached to them (Loury 2002; Wolfe 1996).

What would a fruitful policy discourse about less-educated young men look like, and why is it important to achieve? Notice this volume asked what might expand opportunities for less-educated young black men. Each author's response was useful, but the more important contribution was the discussion itself. To enter the discussion, each participant was required to contribute a fruitful suggestion to the question of what expands or contracts opportunities for a group left behind. That discussion is very different from one in which Congress and state legislatures try to determine how much of their budget to allocate to prison expansion or how much stricter prison sentencing policies should be.

And why does the shape and quality of a policy discourse matter? Holzer, Stoll, and Raphael suggest that a discourse about black males as criminals is directly responsible for employer discrimination against them. Eradicating that image should decrease that discrimination.

So just as welfare reform was the tip of iceberg in terms of women succeeding in the workforce, prisoner reentry policies and child support enforcement reforms could play a similar role for men.

If policymakers could reduce the Catch-22 dilemma for less-educated young men, would there be a political will or motive for politicians to challenge the objections of veto groups? The survey that shows most Americans favor efforts to support fathers suggests that support for less-educated men may be available in the general population.

Would it lead to policies favoring such men? The lessons of welfare reform suggest it is possible to erode ill will toward highly stigmatized groups, like welfare mothers. While a lack of ill will is not the same as good will, it is a start.

Summary

Less-educated black men are currently in a position analogous to welfare parents in the last century. Before the 1970s, when most boats really did rise and fall with the business cycle, able-bodied mothers on welfare were the most noticeable group not carried along by rising economic tides. Cash assistance and social service programs regulated them, so in good economic times, public opinion turned against them and regulations for entry tightened. In bad times, public opinion turned more favorable and regulations were relaxed (Heclo 2001; Piven and Cloward 1972). In effect, the poor were regulated into and out of the labor market by these ebbs and flows in public support, which in turn responded to ebbs and flows in the business cycle.

Young, less-educated black men differ from welfare mothers in that they are not uniquely linked to politically sensitive means-tested social service programs. Nor does their economic fate ebb and flow with changing levels of public opinion. But they do share one key attribute associated with pre-1970s welfare mothers—economic and political isolation.

If current trends continue, young black men will also share an attribute of welfare populations that developed after the 1970s. Increasingly after 1980, the working poor joined the welfare poor as a group left out of improvements in the business cycle. Even among those whose fortunes responded to the business cycle, some boats rose higher during surges and fell farther during declines.

This new inequality meant two things. Policymakers could more easily blur distinctions between the working and nonworking poor on grounds that they shared fates during economic change. They could build support for programs affecting the poor by including low-income working people in their target groups. Yet, policymakers could also heighten animosity toward programs serving the poor on the grounds that the working poor (and others) faced the same problems as the nonworking poor, but the former secured more help than the latter.

The new inequality supported a politics of inclusion and universalism (Ellwood 1996) as easily as it supported a politics of envy, recrimination, and incarceration (Wolfe 1998). Policymaking for young black men could feature either dynamic. Deciding between inclusion or envy has been the political project of welfare policy for the past quarter-century. For less-educated young black men and their less-educated male peers, these choices now affect them as well.

There is resistance to programs directed at less-educated young black men from both the right and the left. The right opposes such assistance because of the limited success of previous job training programs and other services targeting this population. The left opposes these programs to protect funding for programs serving low-income women and children.

The ambivalence of the general public acts as an additional barrier. While efforts to assist disadvantaged fathers received support during the 1990s, opponents note the disproportionate share of these fathers who are black. Once the race card is in play, disadvantaged fathers are viewed as the undeserving poor, diluting support for efforts to assist them.

The race card, if played, should not be an absolute trump card, because white and Hispanic men experience the same problems as black men, though to a far lesser degree. Young white men saw only minor improvements in their labor market during the 1990s boom, and the gap between their incomes and their child-support obligations is also growing. Incarceration rates rose among less-educated non-enrolled white and Hispanic young men.

Finally, Blank and Gelbach (chapter 5, this volume) have shown that strong local economies benefit less-educated young men as well as young women. Clearly children do better if both their mothers and fathers are able to support them, although Rodgers (chapter 3, this volume) suggests that a return to the 1990s boom economy is unlikely in the short term. This establishes a urgent need to identify policies and programs that can help less-educated young men to take better advantage of the more modest economic growth that lies ahead.

NOTES

1. Although labor economists remain skeptical of the experimental design of employment audit studies (Heckman and Siegelman 1993), such studies consistently confirm Holzer's and Stoll's supposition (Pager 2003).

2. On an average day in 2000, 30 percent of black men age 20 to 40 with less than a high school education were in prison or jail, compared with less than 10 percent of white men and 10 percent of Hispanic men. For a younger cohort, black men in their 20s (the group under study in this book), incarceration rates exceeded 40 percent for those who dropped out of high school, "making time in prison or jail more common than employment for this very low-skill group" (Pettit and Western 2003).

3. When asked "why do we work?" the usual answers range from fulfillment to security, custom, and pragmatic reasons. In most cases, work is also an important component of identity. Young suggests that young black men perceive an engendered workplace, in which "masculine" jobs strengthen their fragile masculinity and non-masculine jobs threaten that fragile identity (Young 2004).

REFERENCES

Bushway, Shawn. 1998. "The Impact of an Arrest on the Job Stability of Young White American Men." *Journal of Research in Crime and Delinquency* 35(4): 454–79.

Crutchfield, Robert D., and Susan R. Pitchford. 1997. "Work and Crime: The Effects of Labor Stratification." *Social Forces* 76:93–118.

Elliot, Mark, Beth Palubinsky, and Joseph Tierney. 1999. *Overcoming Roadblocks on the Way to Work.* Field Report Series. Philadelphia, PA: Public/Private Ventures.

Ellwood, David. 1996. "Welfare Reform as I Knew It." *The American Prospect* 7(26).

Garfinkel, Irwin. 1992. *Assuring Child Support.* New York: Russell Sage Foundation.

Good, Joshua, and Pamela Sherrid. 2005. *When the Gates Open: Ready4Work—A National Response to the Prisoner Reentry Crisis.* Philadelphia, PA: Public/Private Ventures.

Gordon, Linda. 1994. *Pitied but Not Entitled: Single Mothers and the History of Welfare, 1890–1935.* New York: Free Press.

Heclo, Hugh. 2001. "The Politics of Welfare Reform." In *The New World of Welfare,* edited by Rebecca Blank and Ron Haskins (169–200). Washington, DC: Brookings Institution Press.

Heckman, James J., and Peter Siegelman. 1993. "The Urban Institute Audit Studies: Their Methods and Findings." In *Clear and Convincing Evidence: Measurement of Discrimination in America,* edited by Michael Fix and Raymond J. Struyk (187–258). Washington, DC: Urban Institute Press.

Johnson, Earl S., Ann Levine, and Fred Doolittle. 1999. *Father's Fair Share: Helping Poor Men Manage Child Support and Fatherhood.* New York: Russell Sage Foundation.

Lake Snell and Associates. 2002. "Public Views on Welfare Reform and Children in the Current Economy." Prepared for *The Future of Children.* Princeton, NJ: The Woodrow Wilson School of Public Affairs at Princeton University and the Brookings Institution.

Loury, Glenn. 2002. *The Anatomy of Inequality.* Cambridge, MA: Harvard University Press.

Mincy, Ronald B., and Hillard Pouncy. 1997. "Paternalism, Child Support Enforcement, and Fragile Families." In *The New Paternalism,* edited by Lawrence M. Mead (130–60). Washington, DC: Brookings Institution Press.

Morris, Lorenzo, 1996. "The Million Man March and Presidential Politics." Unpublished paper, Howard University.

Moynihan, Daniel. 1973. *The Politics of a Guaranteed Income: The Nixon Administration and the Family Assistance Plan.* New York: Random House.

Pager, Devah. 2003. "The Mark of a Criminal Record." *American Journal of Sociology* 108(5): 937–75.

Pettit, Rebecca, and Bruce Western. 2003. "Inequality in Lifetime Risks of Imprisonment." Unpublished paper, Princeton University.

Piven, Frances Fox, and Richard Cloward. 1972. *Regulating the Poor: The Functions of Public Welfare.* New York: Vintage Books.

Pouncy, Hillard. 2002. "Between and Among: A Report on African-American Male Involvement in Urban Communities." Washington, DC: Spectrum Consulting Associates.

Rector, Robert E., and Kirk A. Johnson 2004. *Roles of Couples' Relationship Skills and Fathers' Employment in Encouraging Marriage.* Center for Data Analysis Report 04-14. Washington, DC: The Heritage Foundation.

Reuter, Peter, Robert MacCoun, and Patrick Murphy. 1990. *Money from Crime: A Study of the Economics of Drug Dealing in Washington, D.C.* R-3894-RF. Santa Monica, CA: RAND Corporation.

Skocpol, Theda. 1992. *Protecting Soldiers and Mothers: The Political Origins of Social Policy in the United States.* Cambridge, MA: Harvard University Press.

Turetsky, Vicki. 2005. Written statement of Vicki Turetsky, Senior Staff Attorney, Center for Law and Social Policy, before the Subcommittee on Human Resources, House Committee on Ways and Means, February 24. Washington, DC: U.S. Government Printing Office.

Western, Bruce. Forthcoming. *Punishment and Inequality in America.* New York: Russell Sage Foundation.

Western, Bruce, Jeffrey R. Kling, and David F. Weiman. 2001. "The Labor Market Consequences of Incarceration." *Crime & Delinquency* 47(3): 410–27.

Western, Bruce, Meredith Kleykamp, and Jake Rosenfeld. 2003. "Crime, Punishment, and American Inequality." Princeton, NJ: Princeton University.

Michael Willrich. 2000. "Home Slackers: Men, the State, and Welfare in Modern America." *Journal of American History* 87(2): 460–89.

Wilson, William J. 1996. *When Work Disappears: The World of the New Urban Poor.* New York: Knopf.

Wolfe, Alan. 1996. "Guess Who Likes Affirmative Action?" *The New Yorker,* November 25.

———. 1998. *One Nation After All: What Middle-Class Americans Really Think about God, Country, Family, Racism, Welfare, Immigration, Homosexuality, Work, the Right, the Left, and Each Other.* New York: Penguin.

Young, Alford A., Jr. 2000. "On the Outside Looking In: Low-Income Black Men's Conceptions of Work Opportunity and the 'Good Job.' " In *Coping with Poverty: The Social Contexts of Neighborhood, Work, and Family in the African American Community,* edited. by Sheldon Danziger and Ann Chin Lin (141–71). Ann Arbor: University of Michigan Press.

———. 2004. *The Minds of Marginalized Black Men: Making Sense of Mobility, Opportunity, and Future Life Chances.* Princeton, NJ: Princeton University Press.

About the Editor

Ronald B. Mincy is the Maurice V. Russell Professor of Social Policy and Social Work Practice at the School of Social Work, Columbia University, where he teaches graduate courses on social welfare policy, program evaluation, and microeconomics. Dr. Mincy is a co-principal investigator for the Fragile Families and Child Well-being Survey, a birth cohort study of children born to unmarried parents that is nationally representative of births in large cities. He has published widely about the effects of income security policy on child and family poverty, family formation, and child well-being; responsible fatherhood; the urban underclass; and urban poverty.

Before joining the Columbia faculty, Dr. Mincy was the senior program officer for the Ford Foundation's Program in Human Development and Reproductive Health, where he developed the Strengthening Fragile Families Initiative (SFFI). SFFI was a Ford Foundation grant-making initiative that worked with federal, state, and local human services agencies on reforming income security policies to enable low-income mothers and fathers to provide emotional, financial, and developmental support to their children receiving welfare.

Dr. Mincy is a member of the National Advisory Child Health and Human Development Council, an advisory group for the National Institute of Child Health and Human Development Policy. He serves on the board of trustees for Children's Futures; the national advisory board for the National Poverty Center, University of Michigan; the technical work groups for the Building Strong Families and Community Healthy Marriage Initiatives; and on the advisory board for the African American Healthy Marriage Initiative. Dr. Mincy is a member of MacArthur Network on Family and the Economy and a former member of the research task force for the Association for Public Policy Analysis and Management. He has been a speaker and consultant for donors, researchers, policymakers, and social workers contemplating fatherhood initiatives in South Africa, the United Kingdom, Jamaica, and throughout the United States.

About the Contributors

Rebecca M. Blank is dean of the Gerald R. Ford School of Public Policy at the University of Michigan, Henry Carter Adams Collegiate Professor of Public Policy, and a professor of economics. She is also the codirector of the Ford School's National Poverty Center. Before coming to Michigan, she was a member of the President's Council of Economic Advisers, a professor of economics at Northwestern University, and the first director of the Northwestern University/University of Chicago Joint Center for Poverty Research. Professor Blank's 1997 book, *It Takes a Nation: A New Agenda for Fighting Poverty*, won the Richard A. Lester Prize for the Outstanding Book in Labor Economics and Industrial Relations. Her recent work includes *Finding Jobs: Is the Market Moral?* (written with William McGurn, Brookings Institution Press, 2003). She has served in numerous advisory and professional roles and is a faculty affiliate of the National Bureau of Economic Research and a member of the American Academy of Arts and Sciences.

John A. Foster-Bey Jr. is the senior advisor to the director for research and policy development at the Corporation for National and Community Services in Washington, D.C., where he is responsible for managing and producing various research products related to volunteerism and community service. Before coming to the Corporation, Foster-Bey was a senior associate and director of the Program for Regional Economic

Opportunity at the Urban Institute's Metropolitan Housing and Communities Policy Center. The Program examined the factors that improve low-skilled, low-income individuals' and communities' access to employment and economic opportunity within local regional economies. Mr. Foster-Bey has written several studies on employment access and workforce training opportunities for low-skilled, low-income individuals. He has also completed studies on the role of targeting industries as a welfare-to-work strategy, spatial mismatch and access to employment for low-skilled workers, barriers to accessing living wage employment, and factors related to career mobility for low-wage workers.

Jonah B. Gelbach has been on the faculty in the department of economics at the University of Maryland since 1998. His research interests include incentive effects of and program design issues in welfare policy, as well as other issues in labor and public economics and applied econometrics. While in graduate school, Professor Gelbach spent a year as a staff economist at the President's Council of Economic Advisers. As an assistant professor, he spent two years on leave as a Robert Wood Johnson Foundation Scholar in Health Policy at the University of California at Berkeley. Professor Gelbach's papers have been published in several academic journals, including the *American Economic Review*, the *Journal of Political Economy*, *Demography*, and the *Journal of Human Resources*.

Harry J. Holzer is a professor and associate dean of public policy at Georgetown University and a visiting fellow at the Urban Institute in Washington, D.C. He is a former chief economist for the U.S. Department of Labor. He is a senior affiliate of the National Poverty Center at the University of Michigan and is also a research affiliate of the Institute for Research on Poverty at the University of Wisconsin-Madison. His recent books include *Moving Up or Moving On: Who Advances in the Low-Wage Labor Market?* (with Fredrik Andersson and J. Lane, Russell Sage Foundation, 2005) and *Reconnecting Disadvantaged Young Men: Improving Schooling and Employment Outcomes* (with Paul Edelman and Paul Offner, Urban Institute Press, forthcoming).

Wen-Jui Han is an assistant professor of social work at the School of Social Work, Columbia University. Her teaching and research interests focus on social policy with particular attention to children and families, poverty and inequality, immigrant and immigration policy, and statistics and research methodology. She has published articles on maternal employment, child care, family leave policy, nonstandard work schedules, children's cognitive and behavioral outcomes, and immigrant children's well-being.

Ron Haskins is a senior fellow in the Economic Studies Program and codirector of the Center on Children and Families at the Brookings Institution and a senior consultant for the Annie E. Casey Foundation. In 2002 he was the senior advisor to the president for welfare policy. Before joining Brookings and Casey, Dr. Haskins spent 14 years on the staff of the House Ways and Means Human Resources Subcommittee, first as welfare counsel to the Republican staff, then as the subcommittee's staff director. He edited the 1996, 1998, and 2000 editions of the *Green Book*, a 1,600-page compendium that analyzes domestic policy issues. His other edited books include *Welfare Reform and Beyond: The Future of the Safety Net* (with Andrea Kane, Isabel Sawhill, and Kent Weaver, Brookings Institution Press, 2002) and *The New World of Welfare* (with Rebecca Blank, Brookings Institution Press, 2001). In 2005, Dr. Haskins received the President's Award for Outstanding Contributions to the Field of Human Services from the American Public Human Services Association.

Charles E. Lewis Jr. has been on the faculty of the Howard University School of Social Work since 2002. He teaches courses in social policy, research methods, and data analysis. Dr. Lewis's current research focuses on mental health issues among adolescents. In his doctoral dissertation, "Incarceration and Fathers in Fragile Families," he examined the effects of incarceration on the employment and earnings of fathers with newborn children in a nationally representative sample. He also examined the impact of incarceration on marriage and cohabitation rates. Dr. Lewis is the president of the Mental Health Association of the District of Columbia.

Demetra Smith Nightingale is principal research scientist at Johns Hopkins University's Institute for Policy Studies, where she teaches social policy and program evaluation methods. Before joining JHU, Dr. Nightingale was at the Urban Institute for nearly 30 years, most recently as a program director in the Labor and Social Policy Center.

Paul Offner (1942–2004) enjoyed a distinguished career spanning government, research, and education. After earning his Ph.D. in economics from Princeton University, he was elected to the Wisconsin State Assembly, then to the Wisconsin State Senate. He served as deputy director of the Ohio Department of Human Services before moving to the federal government, first as a legislative assistant to Senator Daniel Patrick Moynihan, then as chief health and welfare counselor for the Senate Finance Committee. His accomplishments include terms as commissioner of Health Care Finance for the District of Columbia, as a research professor for Georgetown University's Institute for Health Care Research and Policy, and as a consultant for the Urban Institute. A prolific researcher and writer, he counted among his many publications *Medicaid and the States* (Century Foundation Press, 1999) and the *Journal of Human Resources* article "Labor Force Participation in the Ghetto" (1972).

Hillard Pouncy is a visiting lecturer of public and international affairs at the Woodrow Wilson School of Public Policy at Princeton University. He is currently working on a book, *Strengthening Fragile Families: Reforming Income Security Policy for Modern American Childhood Poverty*, with Ronald Mincy. Dr. Pouncy was the principal investigator on a three-year project for the Office of Child Support Enforcement examining differences in how minority and non-minority noncustodial fathers perceive the child support enforcement system.

Wendell Primus is the senior policy advisor on budget and health issues to House Democratic Leader Nancy Pelosi. Before his appointment to this position in March 2005, Dr. Primus was the minority staff director at the Joint Economic Committee. Before coming to Capitol Hill, Dr. Primus was the director of income security for the Center on Budget and Policy Priorities in Washington, D.C. He served in the Clinton administration as the deputy assistant secretary for human services policy in the Office of the Assistant Secretary for Planning and Evaluation at the Department of Health and Human Services, where he developed policy and conducted research and evaluation on income assistance, employment, and related human services programs. Dr. Primus has also served as chief economist for the House Ways and Means Committee and staff director for the Committee's Human Resources Subcommittee. During his 15-year tenure at Ways and Means, he edited 13 editions of the Committee's *Green Book*.

Steven Raphael is an associate professor at the Goldman School of Public Policy of the University of California, Berkeley.

William M. Rodgers III is professor of public policy at the Edward J. Bloustein School of Planning and Public Policy, Rutgers University. He is also chief economist at the Heldrich Center for Workforce, also at Rutgers. Rodgers is a senior research affiliate of the National Poverty Center, University of Michigan. Before coming to Rutgers, he served as chief economist at the U.S. Department of Labor from 2000 to 2001, appointed to that position by Alexis Herman, U.S. Secretary of Labor. His research examines issues in labor economics and the economics of social problems.

Elaine Sorensen is a labor economist and principal research associate at the Urban Institute. Dr. Sorensen is nationally recognized as a leading expert on child support policy and research. Before joining the Urban Institute, Dr. Sorensen was an assistant professor of economics at the University of Massachusetts, Amherst. She has been at the Urban Institute since 1987.

Michael A. Stoll is an associate professor of public policy in the School of Public Affairs and associate director of the Center for the Study of Urban Poverty at the University of California, Los Angeles. He also served as a visiting scholar at the Russell Sage Foundation in New York City. Dr. Stoll main research interests include the study of urban poverty and inequality, specifically the interplay of labor markets, race/ethnicity, geography, and workforce development. He recently completed a major monograph, *African Americans and the Color Line*, which documents the degree of African American social and economic progress over the past two decades. This study was featured on NPR's *Tavis Smiley* show and appears in *The American People: Census 2000*, published by the Russell Sage Foundation. Currently, Dr. Stoll is examining the labor market consequences of mass incarceration in the United States and the social and economic consequences of urban sprawl.

Alford A. Young Jr. is the Arthur F. Thurnau Professor and an associate professor of sociology at both the University of Michigan and the University's Center for Afroamerican and African Studies. In the past decade he has conducted research on low-income, urban-based African

Americans, blue-collar employees at an automobile manufacturing plant, African American scholars and intellectuals, and the classroom-based experiences of faculty as they pertain to diversity and multiculturalism. Although primarily an ethnographic interviewer, Professor Young has made use of formal ethnography as well as document analysis in his research. He has published *The Minds of Marginalized Black Men: Making Sense of Mobility, Opportunity, and Future Life Chances* (Princeton University Press, 2004) as well as articles in *Sociological Theory*, *The Annual Review of Sociology*, and other journals.

Index